Revised!

Spirito

Laura Zisette
Charlene Zundel
Kathleen Lloyd

Three Cranky Women

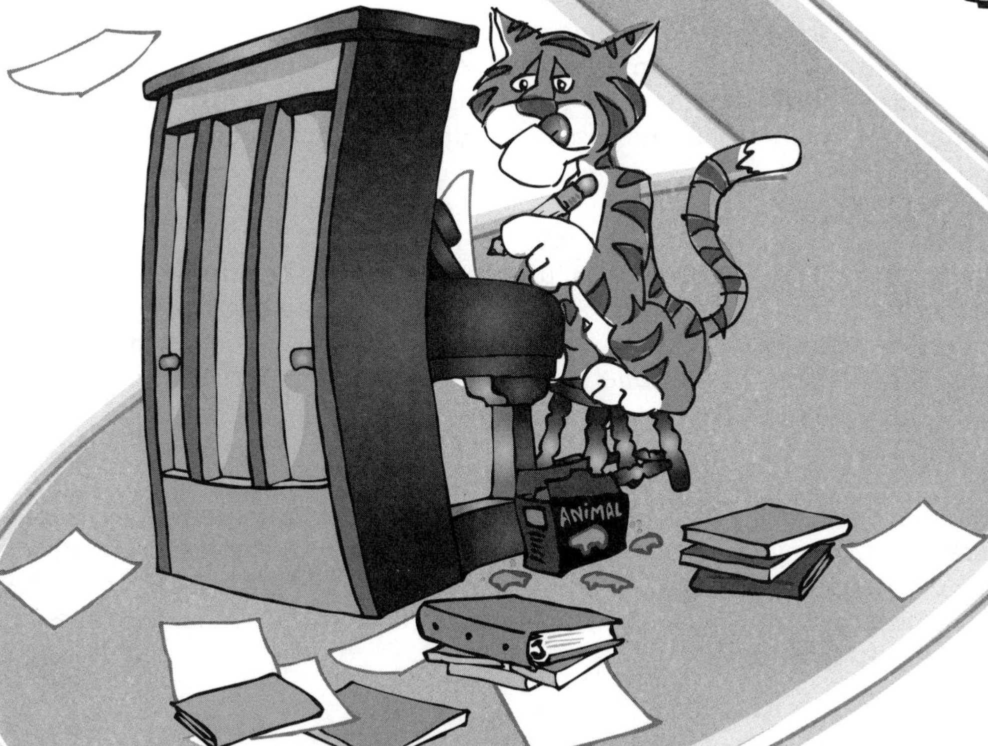

Kjos
Neil A. Kjos
Music Company

ISBN-10: 0-8497-6378-9
ISBN-13: 978-0-8497-6378-6

Foreword

This Teacher Guide was created as a teacher timesaver. It contains the following:

Cranky Hints from the Three Cranky Women (TCW)
- Suggested group activities for each unit
- A list of TCW games that apply the concepts the students are learning
- Suggested list of listening pages to go along with each unit

Listening List
- List of suggested music for student listening by the featured composer

Theory Gymnastics Answer Key and Listening Resources
- Standard answers for the theory and listening pages
- Ear-training examples for the listening pages

Testing Resources
- Reproducible theory tests (forms A and B) and answer keys
- Reproducible ear-training tests (forms A and B) and answer keys
- Ear-training examples to administer the ear-training tests

The Theory Gymnastics Series
We hope you find the Theory Gymnastics Series to be a fun and motivational vehicle for engaging and challenging your students. We have found this approach to be effective in both individual and group study.

Standard answers are offered for the theory pages in the theory gymnastics answer key. However, due to the emphasis on creative thinking, some pages/exercises have more than one possible answer. These pages are noted throughout the guide. To encourage critical thinking, the authors feel that if the student can convincingly defend their answers as an appropriate response, these answers should be considered correct.

Individual Instruction
The units in the theory books are laid out in a progressive order, but may be prescribed in any order to fill an individual student's needs. Teachers may choose to assign pages from units which correspond to the repertoire being studied. The *Practice* pages are worksheets which give students an opportunity to explore the concept. The *Challenge* and *Thinker* pages further reinforce the concept, but are more difficult—and lots of fun!

Listening Pages
Listening pages reinforce concepts studied in the theory section and may reflect concepts studied in a corresponding theory unit. Many students enjoy a short break from the lesson routine to work on listening skills. Younger students like being on the floor with a box of crayons to color their listening pages. Recordings for these listening pages are available online in the Kjos Multimedia Library at www.kjos.com. See page 44 for details.

Group Instruction
The theory books also provide a well-planned curriculum for group theory study. The varying degrees of difficulty found in the *Practice*, *Challenge*, and *Thinker* pages give the group instructor many teaching options. Because abilities vary among students who are in the same level, the teacher may choose to send early finishers on to the *Challenge* and *Thinker* pages while others in the group are completing the *Practice* pages.

The *Challenge* and *Thinker* pages may also be used as take home or bonus activities. Many students find the *Challenge* and *Thinker* pages to be so enjoyable that the teacher may choose to use these pages as a special incentive. One of the benefits of using theory books in a group situation is the fact that the teacher can easily evaluate each student's level of comprehension.

We do not advocate using only the theory books in group lessons. They are meant to be a resource for teaching music concepts in an organized manner. We do advocate the use of supplementary activities (games, hands-on activities, etc.) for further exploration of the concepts offered in the theory books.

Group classes offer a superb setting for ear training. The teacher has the opportunity to present listening examples to more than one student at a time. The group environment provides students with the opportunity to learn from one another as methods of identifying and reinforcing concepts are discussed.

Reproducible Tests
There are two forms (A and B) of the theory and ear-training tests for each level. Teachers may choose to use one form of the theory test to prepare the students for the final test or as a placement test for new students. The other theory test is useful for testing students at the completion of their theory book to assess their readiness to continue on to the next level. On all tests each question has a point value that is shown in small type to the right of its question. Determine how many points the student has earned for each correct answer (100 possible) and score the tests by adding up these numbers (x/100). The authors use the following guideline for student assessment on the theory test: If students can complete the test with a score of 70% or higher they can successfully continue on to the next book–with the help of their teacher to strengthen their weak areas. If they receive less than a 70% it may be useful for them to repeat the level, the advantage being that they will become more fluent in the theory they know, and they will be able to fill in the "holes" of the concepts they missed or didn't completely understand, including ear training. (These test scores can be used for the Keyboard Gymnastics® Achievement Program.)

NOTE: Because the theory and ear-training tests are reproducible and can potentially be administered to many students over a period of years, it will be important to take steps to preserve their integrity. For example, do not send tests home with students. Administer tests in an environment where proper precautions can be taken in the distribution and gathering of the test. **The theory and ear-training test answer keys and ear-training test examples may not be duplicated.**

Our Objective
Our objective is to always put the students' needs first as we nurture them along in their musical experience. However, as teachers we know what a boon it is to have resources and materials that work for us and for our students! Enjoy!

The Three Cranky Women,
Laura, Kathleen and Charlene

Laura, Kathleen and Charlene

Supporting Materials for

SPIRITO

Teacher Aids

◇ **Student Flashcards** (TW430) ★

◇ **Teacher Flashcards** (TW530)

◇ **Music Money** (TW540) ★

◇ **Kreative Keyboard®** (TW605)
Cloth keyboard and grand staff

◇ **Kreative Keyboard® Collection** (TW604)
Book of 24 games

◇ **Kreative Keyboard® Game Materials** (TW607)
Reproducible game props

Games

◇ **Crazy Eighths** (TW615) ★

◇ **Slap Me Silly** (TW611)

◇ **Note Nabber** (TW620) ★

◇ **Tapping Telephones®** (TW601) ★
Levels A and B

◇ **Flashy Fingers** (TW616)

◇ **Rockin' Rhythms** (TW617A)
Beginning and Elementary levels

◇ **Wacky Words** (TW614A) ★
Starring Wanda

◇ **Musical Spoons® —Notes** (TW602A) ★

◇ **Musical Spoons® —Triads** (TW602C) ★

◇ **Screamin' Match** (TW610A)
Beginning level

◇ **Scale Scramble®** (TW603) ★

◇ **Nifty Notes** (TW550)

◇ **Perfect One** (TW613)

◇ **Music Blitz** (TW612)

★ *Available in revised version.*

All above materials available from Neil A. Kjos Music Company
www.kjos.com

Contents

Tests Form A:

Tests Form B:

Cranky Hints for Teaching Group Classes

1. Teach the students to say the name of their theory book. (You can find this information on the Foreword page in the theory book.)
2. Group class can be structured in as many different ways as there are teachers. We have found the following "formula" to be very flexible, yet effective:
   - Review last week's assignment (this could include correcting pages)
   - Play a game to review the concept introduced last week (or any concept that needs reinforcement)
   - Practice ear training—perhaps on the concept(s) covered last week
   - Discuss the new concept
   - Conduct an activity using the new concept
   - Play a game to reinforce the new concept
   - Assign the *Practice* pages and let the students begin during class time so their questions can be answered.
   - Look ahead to the *Challenge* and *Thinker* pages with your students for anything that may need clarification. (This also gets the students excited to go on to these pages).
3. Read the *Discovery* pages together with your students so you can "discover" what they do and do not understand before they go home to work on the *Practice, Challenge,* and *Thinker* pages.
4. Give out Music Money (TW540) freely to reinforce good behaviors such as correct answers, being on time, good teamwork, winning games, etc. Give short quizzes for those who are on time to earn music money. Money can be spent periodically in a prize closet for candy, toys, movie tickets, or anything that motivates the students. Have fun!
5. Discuss class rules at the first group class such as:
   - Bring all your materials each time (including a pencil)
   - Have your homework done each time you come to class
   - No chewing gum
   - No talking while the teacher explains something
   - No noisy or distracting electronic devices are allowed in class

We have found from experience that if students participate in setting the rules for the class, they tend to keep those rules. Keep the rules short and few so everyone can remember them. You might consider having the students set a consequence for breaking each rule and a class reward for keeping the rules. For example, a consequence for not having your homework done each time may be that during game time, the offending student(s) have to work on their theory homework.

Another fun way to encourage positive classroom behavior and participation is to work toward a "popcorn party". A large jar or clear container is placed in the front of the class. Each class period, the students may earn handfuls of un-popped popcorn which are placed into the jar. They could earn these handfuls of popcorn by being on time, bringing all their materials, being kind to one another, etc. You may even wish to let certain students put in the popcorn as a reward for personal behavior. When the jar is full, the students have earned their popcorn party.

Cranky Hints for each Unit in Spirito

Unit 1: The Grand Staff

Activity 1: Seat the students in a circle. Each student, in turn, draws one part of the staff on a piece of paper or the board. Give students Music Money for each part of the staff they draw correctly.

Activity 2: Have students decorate a cupcake with a treble clef and a bass clef sign after practicing with frosting on waxed paper.

Specific Page Suggestion: Spirito p. 8–Before they begin this page, remind students how many lines are in each staff.

Suggested Games: ***Screamin' Match***, ***Slap Me Silly***

Listening Unit 19: page 128 "Pitch"; page 130 "High or Low"; page 130 "Loud or Soft"

Unit 2: Notes on the Staff and Keyboard

Activity 1: Use the ***Nifty Notes***–Mousee game and ***Teacher Flashcards*** to review the guidepost C's, F's, and G's. Have students find these guidepost notes first, then play more rounds where they find any A, B, D, E, F and G.

Activity 2: Place one color of the letter cards A-G from the different colored ***Music Blitz*** decks in front of each student. Show a ***Teacher Flashcard***. Have the students race to grab the correct letter name and gently toss it toward the teacher. The student's card with the correct answer that is nearest to, but not on or past the teacher wins a point.

Specific Page Suggestion: Spirito p.17–Use the ***Kreative Keyboard***, the ledger line transparencies, and cookies or candy for notes. Discuss the placement of notes on ledger lines by reminding them 1) to draw (or place) the ledger lines before they place the notes and 2) to count from the staff outward when placing the ledger lines. Name a ledger line note and have the students place the cookie or candy on the ledger line. After they have placed three "notes" correctly, they get to eat the cookie or candy.

Suggested Games: ***Musical Spoons®–Notes***, ***Note Nabber***, ***Nifty Notes***—Around the World, Don't Eat Pete, Quarter Note Football, ***Kreative Keyboard®***—Legendary Ledgers

Listening Unit 19: page 128 "Melody"; page 131 "High or Low and Loud or Soft"

Unit 3: Note Values and Time Signatures

Activity 1: Sort the quarter note, half note, dotted half note and whole note cards from the other ***Screamin' Match*** cards. Play *memory* using these cards. The student must give the correct name of each of the notes in order to keep the matches.

Activity 2: Use the rhythm cards and wizard cards from ***Crazy Eighths*** that have quarter, half, dotted half and whole notes. Clap and count the rhythms in different fun ways according to the instructions on the wizard cards.

Specific Page Suggestion: Spirito p. 22–Use the rhythms on this page to play rhythm basketball with a small NERF® basketball and three trash cans labeled with the $\frac{2}{4}$, $\frac{3}{4}$, and $\frac{4}{4}$ time signatures (use the time signature cards from the ***Crazy Eighths*** card deck). Divide the class into two teams. The first student from each team is assigned one of the rhythms from the basketballs on page 22 to clap together. Set a timer for one minute. Time begins when the two players begin to clap and count the rhythm. When they are successful the two players take turns trying to throw the Nerf® basketball into the appropriate time signature trash can. If one of the team members is successful before the time runs out he/she gets two points for their team. Continue playing with the next two team members. Play until one team earns ten points.

Suggested Games: ***Rockin' Rhythms*** (Beginning), ***Tapping Telephones®*** (Levels A and B) ***Crazy Eighths*** using only the cards with whole, dotted half, half and quarter notes and rests.

Listening Unit 19: page 137 "Same or Different Rhythm"

Unit 4: Two Eighths

Activity: Use Hershey's® chocolate bars to visually reinforce the concept of eighth notes. Break each bar to create sections with 8 pieces and give each student a small paper plate with one 8-piece section on it. (Note: Hershey's "giant size" bars have 16 pieces, other sizes have 12 pieces.)

Demonstrate the dividing of beats by placing one 8-piece block of candy into a "measure" to equal a whole note. Break that piece into two 4-piece blocks to demonstrate two half notes in a whole note. Break one of the 4-piece blocks into two 2-piece blocks to demonstrate two quarter notes in a half note. Finally, break one of the 2-piece blocks into two 1-piece blocks to demonstrate two eighth notes in a quarter note.

Direct the students to break their "whole note" bars into two half notes, then break one of the "half note" bars into two "quarter notes", then break one of the "quarter note" bars into two "eighth notes".

Ask the students how many single pieces (eighth notes) would be in a dotted half note and demonstrate with your 4-piece "half note" plus one 2-piece "quarter note".

Don't eat the candy yet! Have the students make two measures in $\frac{2}{4}$ time represented by their chocolate bar pieces. (Draw a barline with a pencil, or use licorice.) When they can clap and count their chocolate rhythm correctly, they can eat their chocolate bar.

Specific Page Suggestion: Spirito p. 29–This page can be tricky! If students are unable to figure it out going from the top to the bottom, have them try it backward, going from the castle to the carriage.

Suggested Games: ***Crazy Eighths***, ***Rockin' Rhythms*** (Elementary), ***Tapping Telephones®*** (Level B)

Listening Unit 19: page 138 "Rhythmic Dictation"

Unit 5: Accidentals – Sharps, Flats, and Naturals

Activity: Have the students practice placing sharps, flats, and naturals before notes on the ***Kreative Keyboard®*** staff and after the letter name cards (from the **Scale Scramble®** deck).

Suggested Game: ***Kreative Keyboard®***—Easy Enharmonics

Listening Unit 19: page 139 "Rhythmic Dictation"; *Unit 20:* page 152 "Solfeggio"

Unit 6: Steps and Skips, Half Steps and Whole Steps

Activity: After discussing steps and skips on the white keys, have the students sit in a circle. Tell the first student the name of a note for which he/she names the note a step up. The students continue around the circle-naming the note a step up as quickly as they can. When a student makes a mistake or you've gone completely around the circle, continue by naming notes a step down. Play in a similar manner with a skip up and a skip down. Discuss half steps and whole steps, then play around the circle as before naming the note a half step up, a half step down, a whole step up, and a whole step down.

Specific Page Suggestion: Spirito p. 38–Be sure students work out each shape with a pencil before committing their answer in color.

Specific Page Suggestion: Spirito p. 39–Remind students that when they are stepping and skipping on this page, don't begin by counting the key they are already on.

Specific Page Suggestion: Spirito p. 42–Have students number their answers on the keyboard as they go.

Specific Page Suggestion: Spirito p. 43 – Have students eliminate examples that are not steps before circling their final answers.

Suggested Games: ***Slap Me Silly, Kreative Keyboard®***—Smart Snakes, Sticky Steps and Stretchy Skips

Listening Unit 19: page 135 "Ascending or Descending"

Unit 7: Review #1 – Note Races

Activity: Flash card drills – Have students drill each other on their flashcards. Students should keep track of missed notes by placing them in a stack as they go. Put all the missed notes together for a final class note drill.

Suggested Games: ***Musical Spoons®–Notes, Note Nabber, Slap Me Silly, Wacky Words (Wanda), Nifty Notes***—Quarter Note Football

Listening Unit 19: page 132 "Slow or Fast"; page 133 "Steady or Unsteady"

Unit 8: Major Five-Finger Patterns and I Chords

Activity 1: Purchase "sandwich" cookies (like Oreos®) which are white-white-white (snowman group), black-white-black (ice cream sandwich group), white-black-white (hamburger group). Discuss the keys that belong to these I chord groups. If the students can spell the I chords that belong to a group, they get to eat a cookie from that group. To illustrate the "oddball" group let the students disassemble and reassemble cookies to show the B♭, B and F♯ I chords.

Activity 2: Give each student a deck of ***Music Blitz*** cards. Race to spell the five-finger patterns one group at a time. Give Music Money for each correct answer.

Specific Page Suggestions: Spirito pp. 58-61, 63–These pages are much easier for the students if they have been learning to play their five-finger patterns with the ***Keyboard Gymnastics® Technic Charts.***

Teacher Note: Dedicate sufficient time for this unit to be sure the students feel secure in their major five-finger patterns.

Suggested Games: ***Flashy Fingers, Scale Scramble, Music Blitz, Kreative Keyboard®***—Fabulous Five, Five-Finger Frenzy

Listening Unit 19: page 143A "Major Five-Finger Patterns"; p. 144A "Major I Chords"

Unit 9: Unisons, 2nds, 3rds, 4ths, and 5ths

Teacher Note: Students should have a good grasp of their major five-finger patterns before beginning this unit.

Activity: Question students: What is the 4th note of the A five-finger pattern? (They should answer "D.") Then say, "from A to D is a perfect 4th." Continue questioning in this manner until the students understand the concept. Remind them that the first note of a five-finger pattern is the "keynote," so they should think of the five-finger pattern that begins on that note.

Specific Page Suggestion: Spirito p. 68–Be sure to provide crayons or colored pencils. This page is too difficult to correct without color.

Suggested Games: ***Perfect One*** (without M6, M7 and P8 cards), ***Slap Me Silly, Kreative Keyboard®***—Intellectual intervals, What's Your Line or Space?, Interval Investigators, In-Tune Intervals.

Teacher Note: Now is a great time to discuss the "sound" of each of these intervals by introducing the familiar or popular songs that begin with the intervals (see page 145). Students should learn to sing the first two notes of these songs beginning on any pitch.

Listening Unit 19: page 134 "Fast or Slow and Steady or Unsteady"; page 145 "Intervals"; page 146 "Intervals"

Unit 10: Quarter, Half, and Whole Rests

Activity: Have students construct measures of rhythms in $\frac{2}{4}$, $\frac{3}{4}$, and $\frac{4}{4}$ with the note transparencies from the Kreative Keyboard® Game Materials. Clap and count the rhythms they create. Substitute rests for the quarter, half, and whole notes, then clap the rhythms again, but have the students throw their hands apart when "clapping" a rest.

Suggested Games: ***Rockin' Rhythms (Beginning), Tapping Telephones*** (Levels A and B), ***Kreative Keyboard®***—Arresting Rhythms.

Listening Unit 19: page 147 "Intervals"

Unit 11: Dotted Quarter and Eighth Notes

Activity 1: Use Hershey's® chocolate bars to make rhythms with the dotted quarter-eighth rhythm. (See Unit 4 discussion about eighth notes.) Use three sections of chocolate to represent the dotted quarter note, and one section to represent the eighth note.

Give each student eight sections of chocolate bar and instruct them to plan out one measure of $\frac{4}{4}$ time, then break their bar apart to construct that rhythm out of the chocolate sections. Give each student a paper plate on which to display their measure. Require that they use at lease one dotted quarter-eighth note rhythm. Place the "measure" of chocolate in front of the class and have the class clap and count the rhythms together as a class.

Activity 2: Most students struggle to understand the dot because they have not yet studied fractions. One of the best ways we have found to reinforce this concept is to have the students play *War* using the ***Crazy Eighths*** cards. Have the students count using eighth beats as they are comparing the total counts on each card.

Specific Page Suggestion: Spirito p. 78–Have students play and count the rhythms on the piano, then change the pitches to compose melodies.

Specific Page Suggestion: Spirito p. 80–This page can be especially difficult. You may want to work through a few of the problems as a class before assigning this page as homework.

Suggested Games: ***Kreative Keyboard®–Rad Rhythms, Tapping Telephones®*** (Level B), ***Rockin' Rhythms*** (Elementary)

Listening Unit 19: page 148 "Intervals"; page 138 "What do you hear?"

Unit 12: Review #2

Activity: Divide the class into two teams. Have the teams stand in line, one behind the other, so that one person from each team is competing with each other. Show the two competing players a card from the ***Flashy Fingers*** card deck. The two players race to identify which group (Snowman, Hamburger, Ice Cream Sandwich, or Oddball) the chord or five-finger pattern belongs to by calling out the answer. The first student to answer earns the card–placed in a stack to be counted later–for their team. The two students move to the back of their team's line and play proceeds. At the end, the team with the most cards wins.

Suggested Games: ***Scale Scramble, Music Blitz, Musical Spoons®–Triads, Kreative Keyboard®***—Five Finger Frenzy, Tasty Triads, Tic-Tac Triads, Trivial Triads, What's Your Line or Space?

Listening Unit 19: page 135 "Crescendo or Decrescendo"; page 140 "Rhythmic Dictation"

Unit 13: Minor Five-Finger Patterns and i Chords

Activity: Using the cards from ***Music Blitz***, have the students spell a major five-finger pattern, then remove the third and have them replace it with the "lowered third" card. Reinforce the concept that a lowered third for a sharped note becomes a natural, and that a natural becomes a flat. (There are no double flats in this book.) Continue spelling Major/minor five-finger patterns until the students understand the concept, then spell minor five-finger patterns without first spelling the Major. Do the same with Major and minor I/i chords.

Suggested Games: ***Scale Scramble, Music Blitz, Musical Spoons®–Triads, Kreative Keyboard®***—Five Finger Frenzy, Tasty Triads, Tic-Tac Triads, Trivial Triads, Minor Madness, What's Your Line or Space?

Listening Unit 19: page 143B "Minor Five-Finger Patterns"; page 144B "Minor I Chords"

Unit 14: Review #3

Specific Page Suggestion: Spirito pg 98-103—Some of these mazes are tricky. Encourage students to use erasable pencil because many answers come to dead ends.

Suggested Games: ***Scale Scramble, Kreative Keyboard®***—Minor Madness, Arresting Rhythms, Interval Investigator

Listening Unit 19: page 129 "Same or Different Triad"; page 141 "Rhythmic Dictation"

Unit 15: Signs and Terms

Specific Page Suggestion: Spirito p. 107–To help the students come up with answers for this page, first come up with a list of things that the students "do not like to do" as a class. Then match those to the terms.

Suggested Games: ***Screamin' Match, Slap Me Silly***, *Memory* using the ***Screamin' Match*** cards

Listening Unit 19: page 136 "Ascending or Descending and Crescendo or Decrescendo"; page 142 "Rhythmic Dictation"

Unit 16: Composition–Rhythm

Teacher Note: This is a wonderful unit to assign during Halloween. Composing during this time of year works well because it is easy for students to create musical pictures. After students compose, you may wish to hold a composition recital. Halloween composition recitals are especially fun where students can dress in costume to match their composition. In addition, you may want to create a book for each student that includes all of the recital's compositions.

Some ways to make a composition sound scary: Use a minor five-finger pattern, include the augmented 4th (tritone) interval, use the whole-tone scale, employ sudden dynamic changes.

Listening Unit 19: page 149 "Intervals"

Unit 17: Composition–Melody

Activity: Create a simple pattern at the piano and have the students play it in sequence and repetition on the piano. Show them simple songs that use repetition and sequence in their melodies (e.g., "Three Blind Mice," "Row, Row, Row Your Boat," "Peter, Peter Pumpkin Eater," "Heart and Soul")

Listening Units 19 & 20: page 150 "Intervals in Any Major Five-Finger Position"; page 153 "Singing Solfeggio"

Unit 18: Review #4

Activity: Play the pieces in this unit for the students. Help them find a few of the items in the music before they begin to analyze on their own.

Suggested Games: ***Scale Scramble, Musical Spoons®–Triads, Tapping Telephones®*** (Levels A and B), ***Flashy Fingers***, ***Perfect One*** (without the M6, M7, and P8 cards)

Listening Units 19 & 20: page 143C "Major or Minor Five-Finger Patterns"; page 144C "Major or Minor I Chords"; page 154 "Solfeggio in Duet"

Unit 19: Listening

Teacher Note: You may use the pages in this unit more than once by having the students mark their answers with a different color for each time they do a page. (This will require making up different examples for each page or playing the given examples in a different order each time.) Use these exercises along with the other units as the student progresses through Spirito. The listening examples in this unit are also available as audio clips. See page 44 for more information.

Specific Page Suggestions: Spirito pp. 137, 138–Have the students clap and count the rhythms on each page before your begin.

Specific Page Suggestions: Spirito pp. 143, 144, 145–Have the students sing these five-finger patterns, I/i chords, and intervals before they do these pages.

Specific Page Suggestion: Spirito p. 145–Offer to pay Music Money to students who can sing different songs to you that begin with these intervals.

Suggested Game: ***Kreative Keyboard®***—In Tune Intervals

Unit 20: Solfeggio

Activity: Use the Kreative Keyboard® and five round markers to reinforce "Do-Re-Mi-Fa-Sol" on the staff. Place the markers to represent Do, Re, Mi, Fa, and Sol and then sing them as a group—first as "1-2-3-4-5" and then as "Do-Re-Mi-Fa-Sol." Have the students mix up the five markers and then sing them as a group (always beginning on "Do").

Offer to pay Music Money to students who bring and sing one of their lesson book melodies using solfeggio.

Unit 21: Ludwig van Beethoven

Specific Page Suggestion: Spirito p. 157–Look over the timeline events before reading the story. Fill in the missing events as a class as you read.

Specific Page Suggestion: Spirito p. 158–Play a recording of Für Elise for the students before they reconstruct the theme.

Specific Page Suggestion: Spirito p. 159–Use colors to mark the sequences and repetitions in Beethoven's Fifth.

Music Listening List of Works by Ludwig van Beethoven

1. Für Elise, WoO 59, for Piano
2. Symphony No. 5 in C Minor, Op. 67, 1st Movement
3. Piano Sonata in C Minor, Op. 13 ("Pathetique"), all movements
4. Quartet in C for Piano & String Trio, WoO 36, No. 3, 3rd Movement
5. Piano Concerto No. 5 in Eb Major, Op. 73 ("The Emperor")
6. Piano Sonata in C# Minor, Op. 27, No. 2 ("Moonlight"), 1st Movement
7. Ruins of Athens, Op 113, No. 4 ("Turkish March")
8. Symphony No. 9, Op.125, 4th Movement-coda

GRAB A PENCIL!

1. Trace the brace. Then, begin at the dot and complete each treble clef and bass clef sign.

2. Draw three treble clefs and three bass clefs.

3. Draw the parts of the grand staff: brace, two barlines, double bar, treble clef, bass clef, and repeat sign.

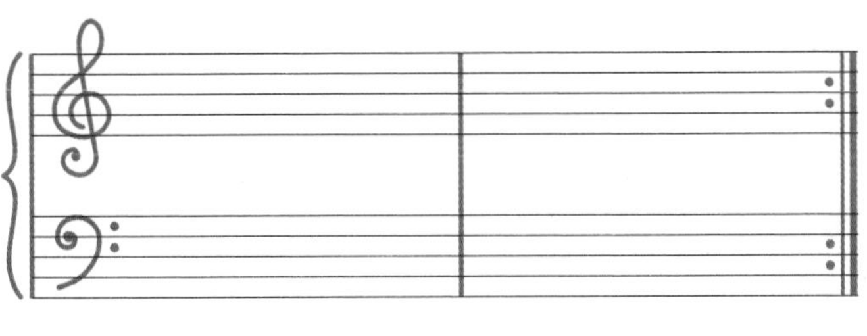

GRAND STAFF PUZZLER

Using the clues below, fill in the blanks and solve the puzzle.

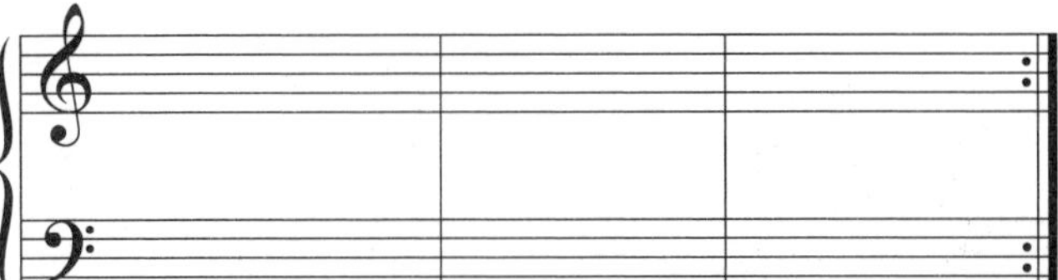

1. These divide the staff into measures.

2. The bass clef is sometimes called the

3. This sign wraps around the G line.

4. This is placed at the beginning of each grand staff.

5. Barlines are drawn all the way through both

6. This sign starts with a dot on the **F** line.

7. Barlines divide the staff into

8. The treble clef is sometimes called the

9. This is placed at the end of the grand staff.

10. This sign means, "play it again."

Use your answers to solve the puzzle.

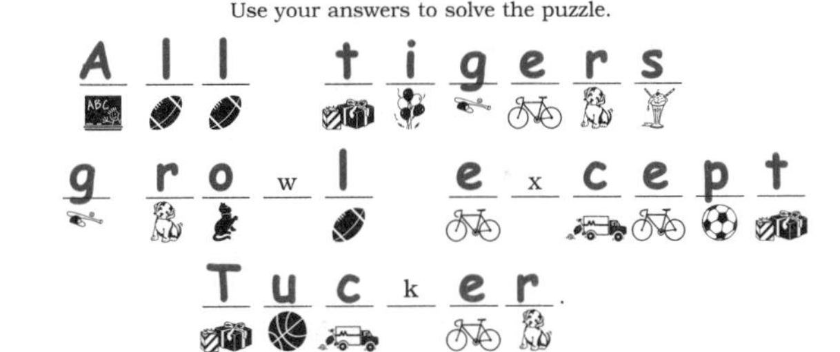

SOMETHING'S MISSING!

There are two things missing from each grand staff below. Draw the missing parts.

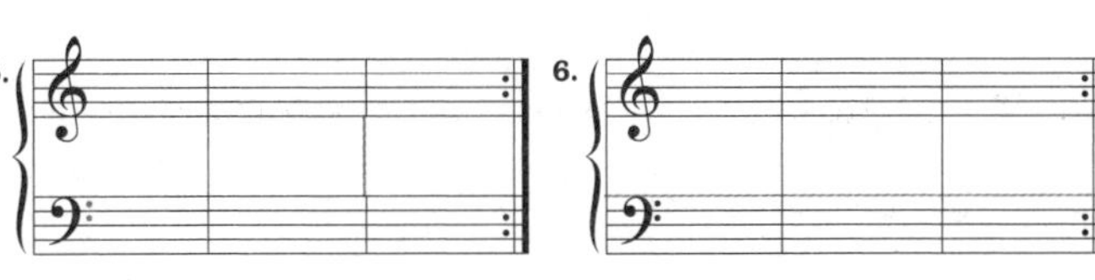

Drawing and Naming Guideposts

A. The Guidepost C's: Draw a line from each guidepost name to its matching key on the keyboard and its matching note on the staff. Use a different color for each line that you draw.

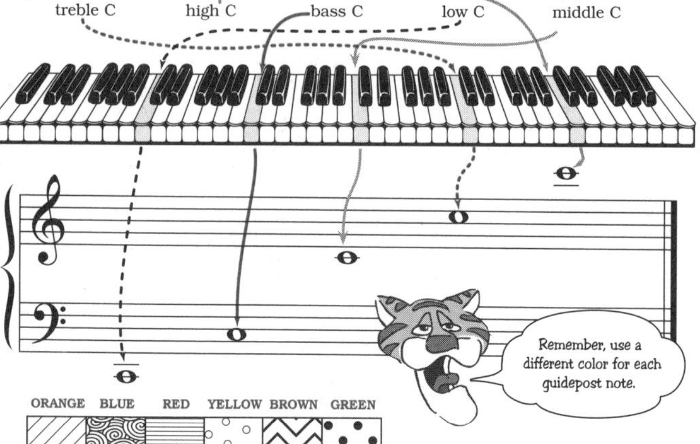

B. The Guidepost G's and F's: For each guidepost, shade the correct key on the keyboard and draw the note on the staff. Draw lines connecting each guidepost key to its place on the staff. (Use a different color for each line that you draw.)

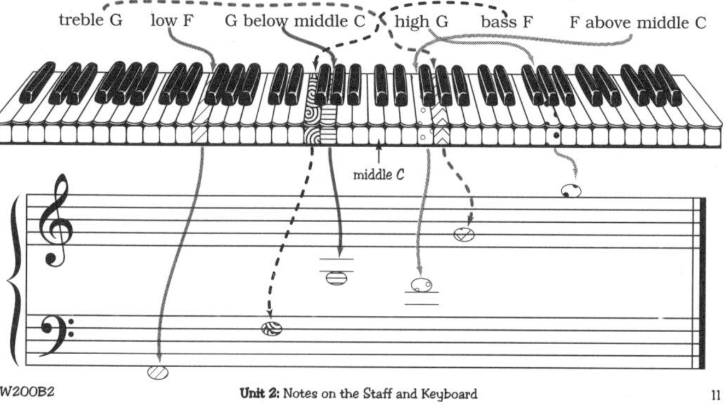

– Page 12 – 14

Pick a Color

Create your own color key by coloring each box a different color. Color the notes between and around the guideposts using the colors you chose.

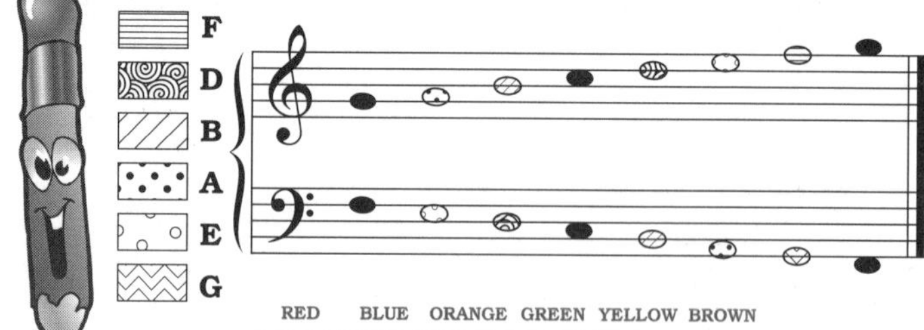

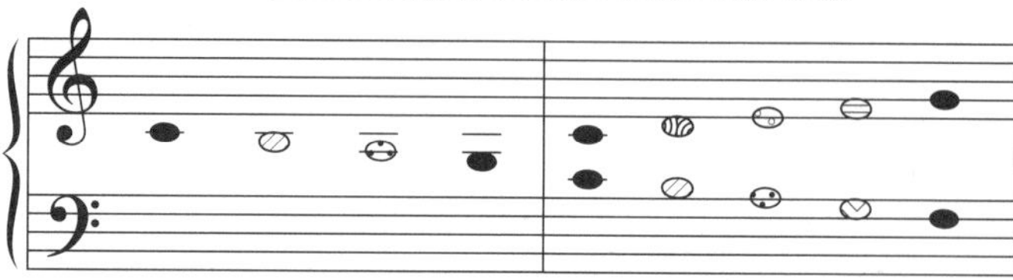

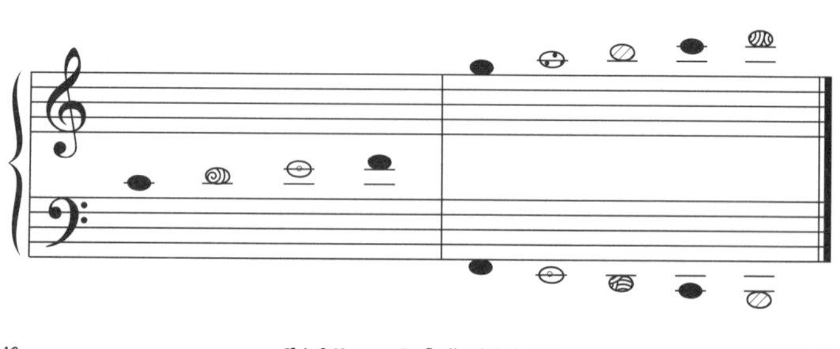

– Page 13 –

Nuts About Guideposts

Sigmund Squirrel is *nuts* about acorn guideposts. A storm is coming and he needs to gather his acorns quickly, or he'll go hungry for the winter! Help him by coloring all of the **guidepost** acorn notes brown. Of the remaining notes, color all of the **D**'s red, the **A**'s yellow, the **G**'s blue, the **B**'s orange, the **E**'s green, and the **F**'s purple.

– Page 14 –

In The Doghouse

Name the notes inside each paw print. *Unscramble the letters* to finish the story of Max, the dog.

1. Max likes to hide things. He hid Dad's S O C K S

2. He hid Mom's N E C K L A C E

3. He even hid my goldfish in the G A R A G E !

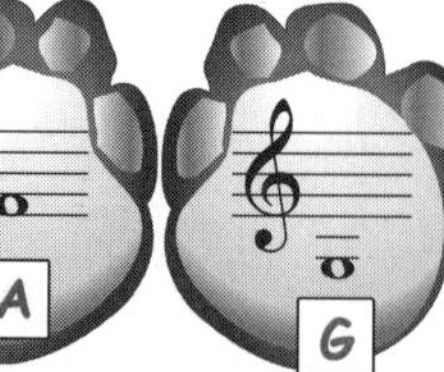

– Page 15 –

In The Doghouse cont.

4. One day, I told Max that if he would stop hiding things, I would give him a B E E F flavored frozen pop every night after dinner.

B F E E

5. Not only does he not hide things anymore, he helps us L O C A T E things when they are lost!

C A E

Good dog, Max!

TW200B2 **Unit 2:** Notes on the Staff and Keyboard 15

– Page 16 –

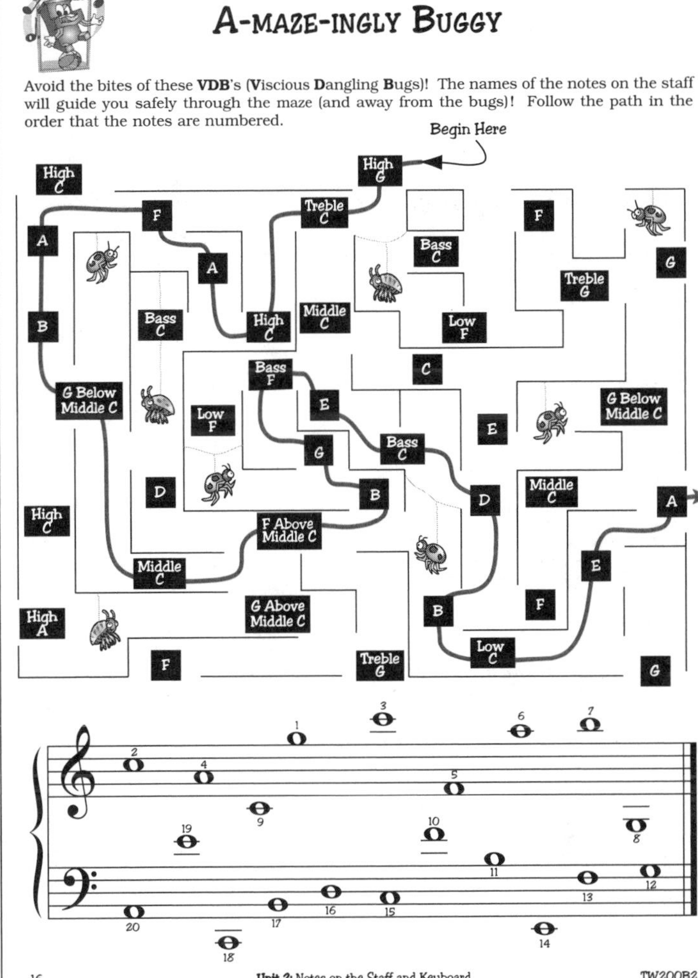

A-maze-ingly Buggy

Avoid the bites of these **VDB**'s (**V**iscious **D**angling **B**ugs)! The names of the notes on the staff will guide you safely through the maze (and away from the bugs)! Follow the path in the order that the notes are numbered.

16 **Unit 2:** Notes on the Staff and Keyboard TW200B2

– Page 17 –

Slippery Guideposts

Each of these guideposts has slipped one line or space up or down from where it is supposed to be. Fix each one by drawing the guidepost it was meant to be next to it.

TW200B2 **Unit 2:** Notes on the Staff and Keyboard 17

– Page 20 –

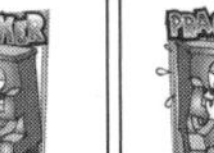

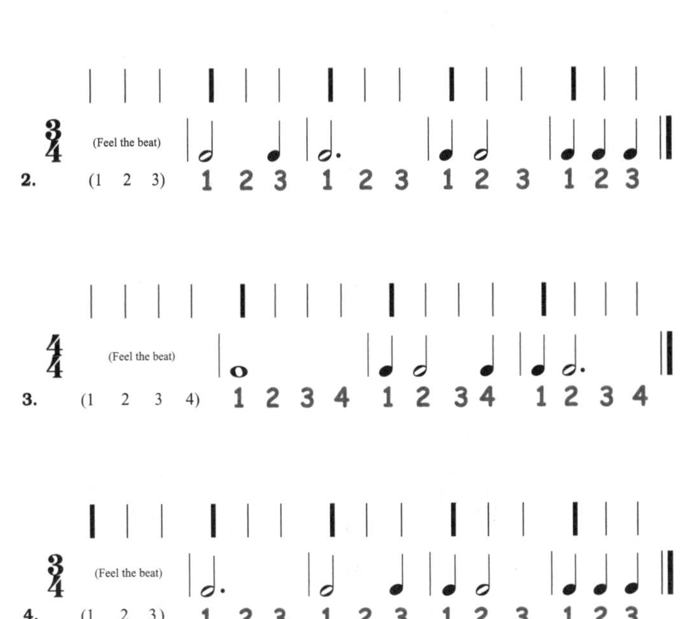

Count On It!

Write in the counts beneath the notes, then clap and count the rhythms. Remember to feel the steady beat before you begin.

1. (Feel the beat) (1 2) 1 - 2 1 2 1 2 1 - 2 1 - 2 1 2

2. (Feel the beat) (1 2 3) 1 2 3 1 2 3 1 2 3 1 2 3

3. (Feel the beat) (1 2 3 4) 1 2 3 4 1 2 3 4 1 2 3 4

4. (Feel the beat) (1 2 3) 1 2 3 1 2 3 1 2 3 1 2 3

20 **Unit 3:** Note Values and Time Signatures TW200B2

– Page 21 –

Missing One

A. Some of these measures are missing beats. Add *only one note* to each measure with missing beats to complete the measure. Then, clap and count the rhythms. Remember to feel the steady beat before you begin.

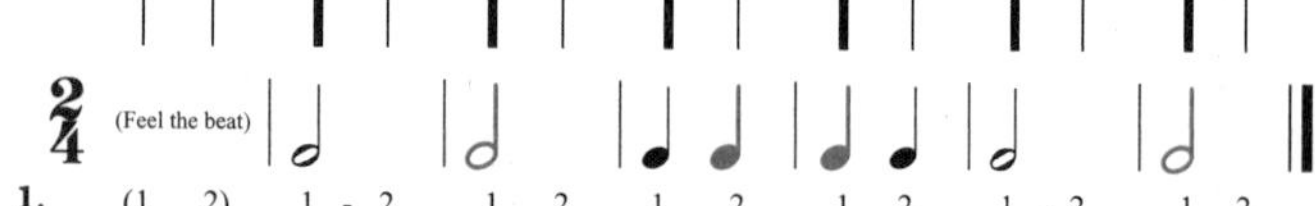

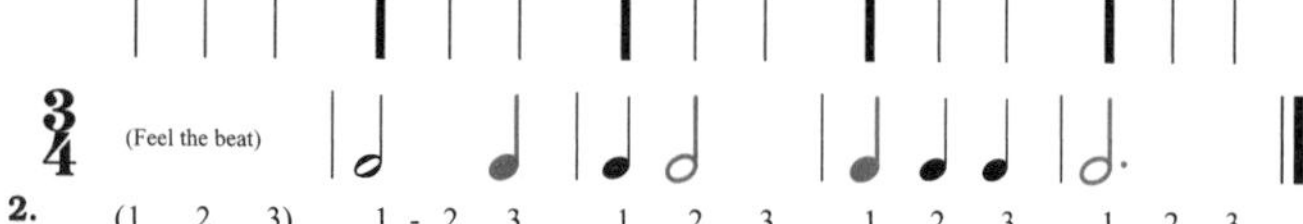

B. Add notes to fill these measures. You may use any combination of quarter notes, half notes, dotted half notes, and whole notes. **Use each type of note at least once**. Clap and count the rhythms you create.

Answers will vary.

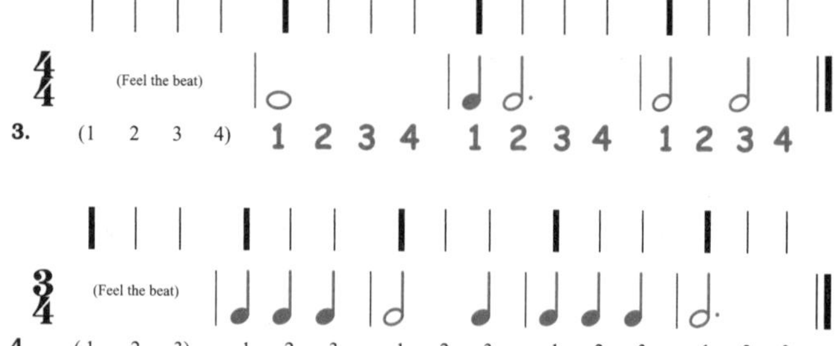

– Page 22 –

Rhythm Basketball

Each basketball represents one measure of rhythm. Color each basketball and its matching backboard the same color. Use green for $\frac{2}{4}$ time, purple for $\frac{3}{4}$ time, and orange for $\frac{4}{4}$ time.

– Page 23 –

Heat Wave

The highest temperature ever recorded in the United States was in Death Valley, California. In order to determine which of these dates holds the true record, add up the note values in each thermometer and color the temperature gauge to match.

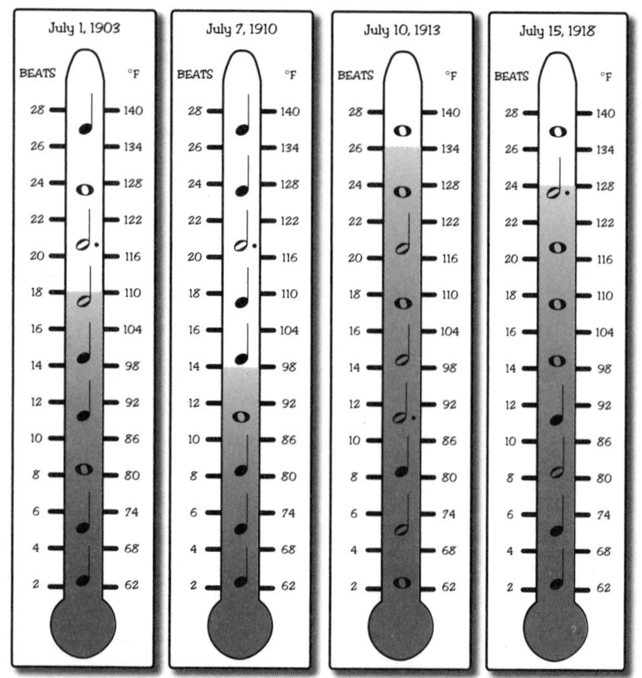

Record Breaking Date:

On July 10, 1913 it was 134 °F in Death Valley, California.

– Page 24 –

Hit the Trail

1. Write the total number of beats given within each shape.
2. Add up the values as you go through the trail. (The first two have been done for you.) When you get to the box with the question mark, fill it with note values that will make the grand total eighty!

Answers in the final box may vary.

– Page 26 –

Got Rhythm?

Write in the counts beneath the notes then clap and count the rhythms. Remember to feel the steady beat before you begin and clap only once for each note. If there are eighth notes in a rhythm, use the word "and" (+) when counting.

1. (Feel the beat) (1 + 2 +) 1 + 2 + 1 + 2 + 1 + 2 + 1 + 2 + 1 + 2 +

2. (Feel the beat) 1+2+3+ 1+2+3+ 1+2+3+ 1+2+3+ 1+2+3+

3. (Feel the beat) 1+2+3+4+ 1+2+3+4+ 1+2+3+4+ 1+2+3+4+

4. (Feel the beat) 1+2+3+4+ 1+2+3+4+ 1+2+3+4+ 1+2+3+4+

– Page 27 –

Eighth Notes Only

Some of these measures are missing beats. Using only eighth notes, fill up the incomplete measures. Write in the counts beneath each rhythm. Clap and count. Remember to use "and" (+) when counting rhythms with eighth notes.

1. (Feel the beat) 1+2+3+ 1+2+3+ 1+2+3+ 1+2+3+ 1+2+3+

2. (Feel the beat) 1+2+3+4+ 1+2+3+4+ 1+2+3+4+ 1+2+3+4+

Music Math

Circle the correct statements. Fix incorrect statements by crossing out or adding eighth notes.

1. ? =
2. ? =
3. ? =
4. ? =
5. ? =
6. ? =

– Page 28 –

More or Less

Add up the counts for each set of notes and write your answer on the blank next to it. Draw a box around the set of notes in each example with the most number of counts.

1.	6	or	12
2.	6	or	5
3.	4	or	5
4.	9	or	5
5.	2	or	4
6.	8	or	6
7.	4	or	5
8.	7	or	6
9.	7	or	8
10.	14	or	12

– Page 29 –

Homesick

1. Show the carriage the way to the castle by using a path made up of note values that adds up to **18 beats**.
2. Show the car the way home by using a path made up of note values that adds up to **10 beats**. **Hint:** Each path is separate; they do not cross.

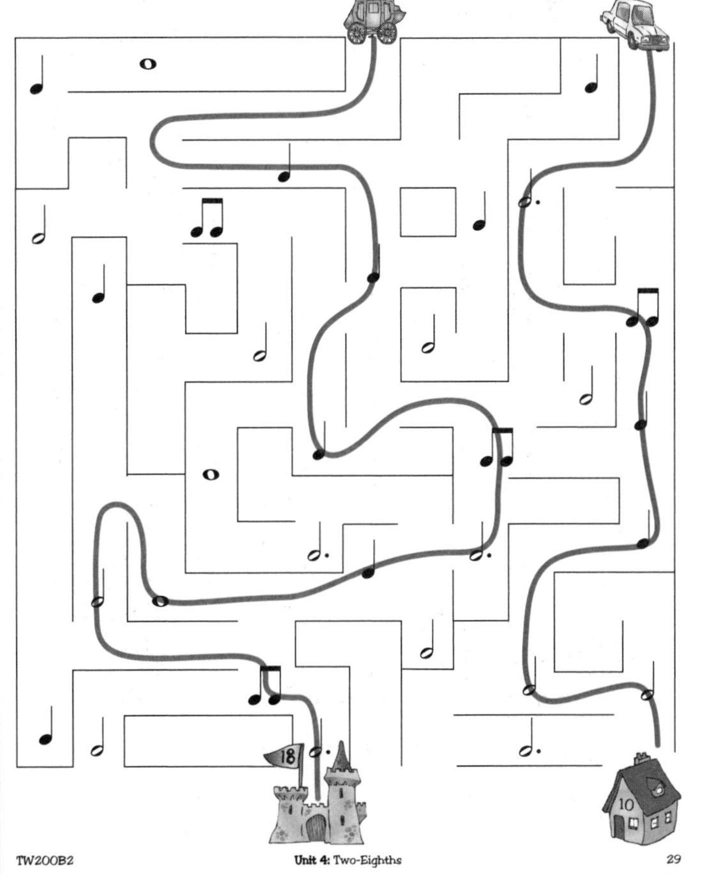

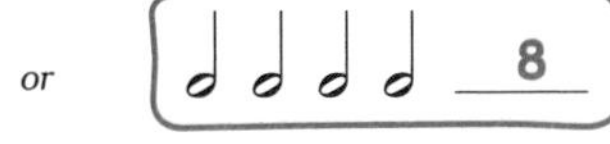

– Page 32 –

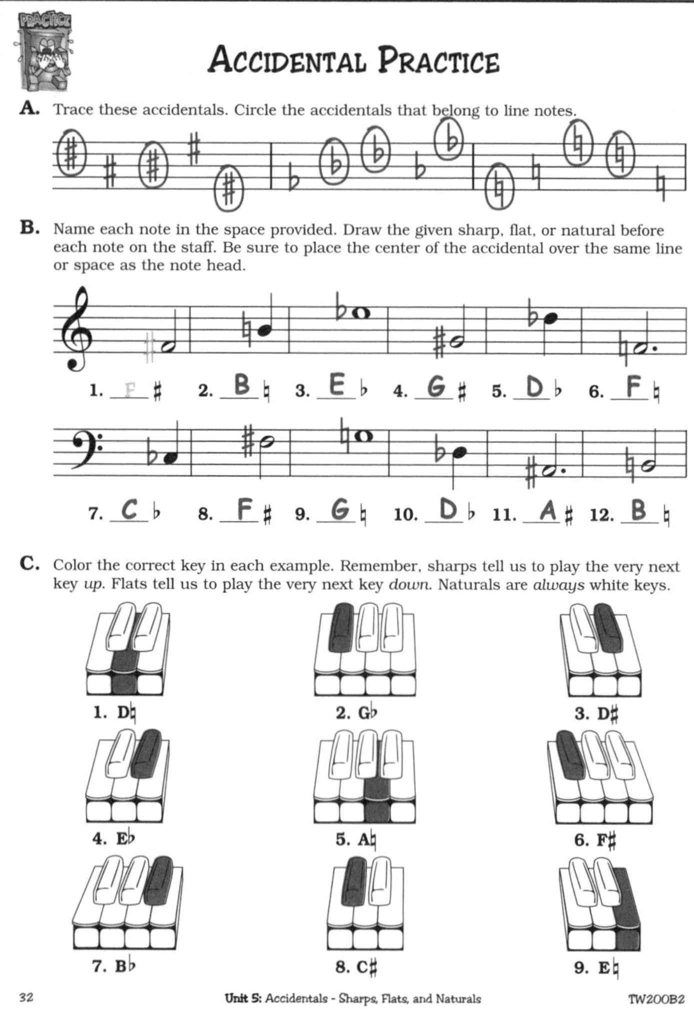

Accidental Practice

A. Trace these accidentals. Circle the accidentals that belong to line notes.

B. Name each note in the space provided. Draw the given sharp, flat, or natural before each note on the staff. Be sure to place the center of the accidental over the same line or space as the note head.

1. F ♯ 2. B ♮ 3. E ♭ 4. G ♯ 5. D ♭ 6. F ♮

7. C ♭ 8. F ♯ 9. G ♮ 10. D ♭ 11. A ♯ 12. B ♮

C. Color the correct key in each example. Remember, sharps tell us to play the very next key *up*. Flats tell us to play the very next key *down*. Naturals are *always* white keys.

1. D♮ 2. G♭ 3. D♮

4. E♭ 5. A♮ 6. F♯

7. B♭ 8. C♯ 9. E♮

32 **Unit 5:** Accidentals - Sharps, Flats, and Naturals TW200B2

– Page 33 –

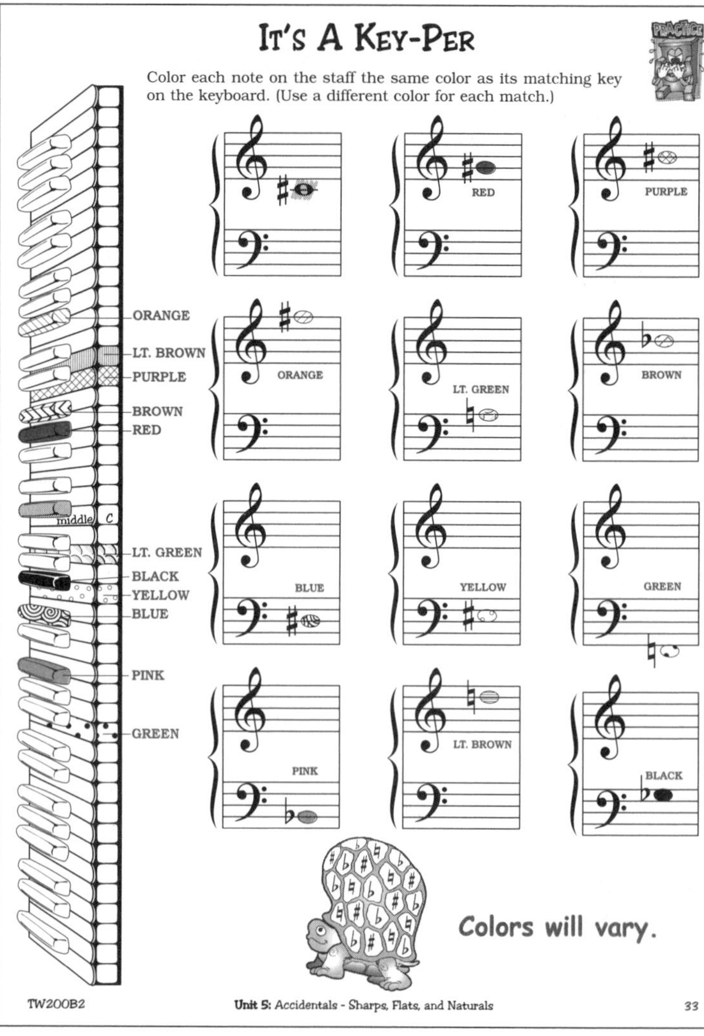

It's A Key-Per

Color each note on the staff the same color as its matching key on the keyboard. (Use a different color for each match.)

Colors will vary.

TW200B2 **Unit 5:** Accidentals - Sharps, Flats, and Naturals 33

– Page 34 –

A Hard Day's Work

Joel works hard building roads in his town and he has many pairs of boots for work. Yesterday, Joel came home from work and discovered his boots strung all over the yard! Help Joel match his boots by coloring the enharmonics the same color. (Use a different color for each pair of boots. You will need eight colors.)

Colors will vary.

34 **Unit 5:** Accidentals - Sharps, Flats, and Naturals TW200B2

– Page 35 –

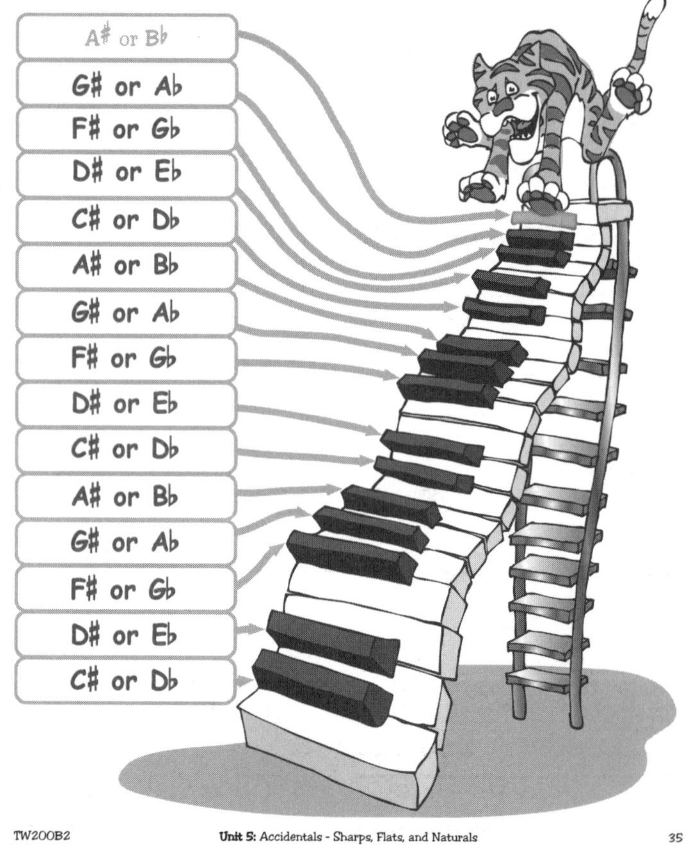

Enharmonic Slide

Tuck wants to slide down the keyboard, but first he has to do a little magic! Help him by providing two names for each of the black keys (enharmonics). Once that is done, the black keys will magically disappear, making a smooth ride for Tuck!

TW200B2 **Unit 5:** Accidentals - Sharps, Flats, and Naturals 35

– Page 38 –

Matching Steps and Skips

Match the circles to the circles, the squares to the squares, and the triangles to the triangles by drawing a line through the instructions. Use a different color for each note. The first one has been done for you.

Answers will vary.

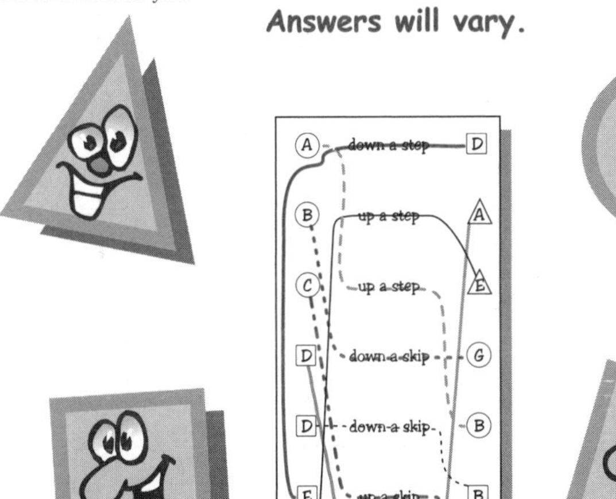

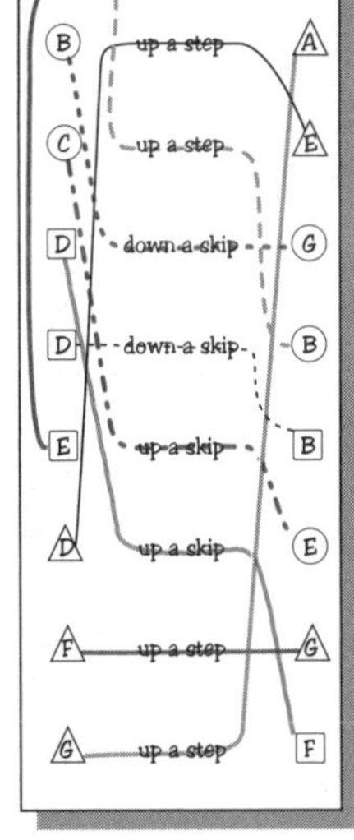

– Page 39 –

Secret Letter Treasure

Find your way to the treasure chest by *stepping* and *skipping* through the music alphabet. Write the letter name on which you land in each of the boxes as you work your way through the map.

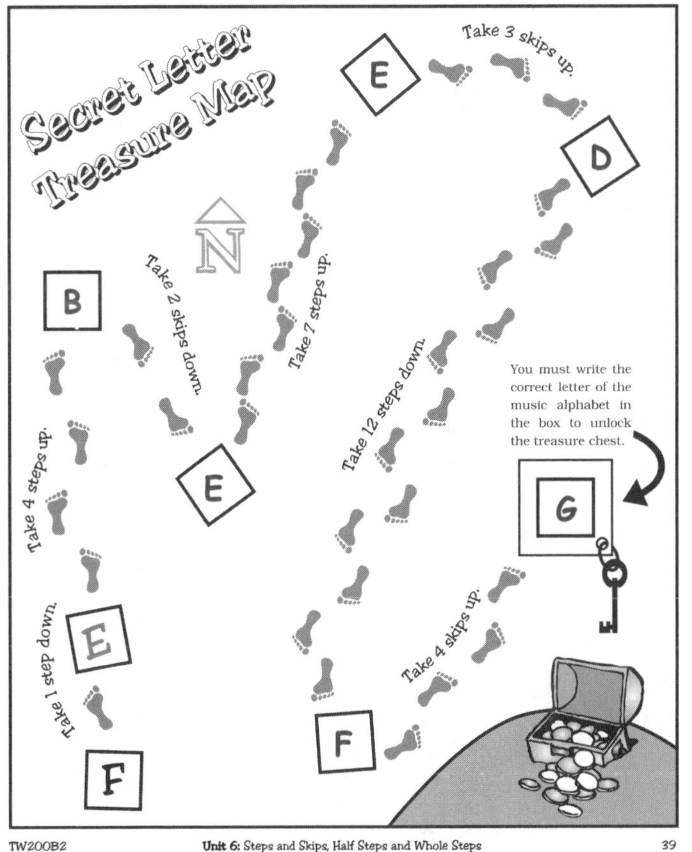

– Page 40 –

Harry Handstand

A. Harry Handstand is really good at doing handstands. Mark the half steps with an **H** and the whole steps with a **W**.

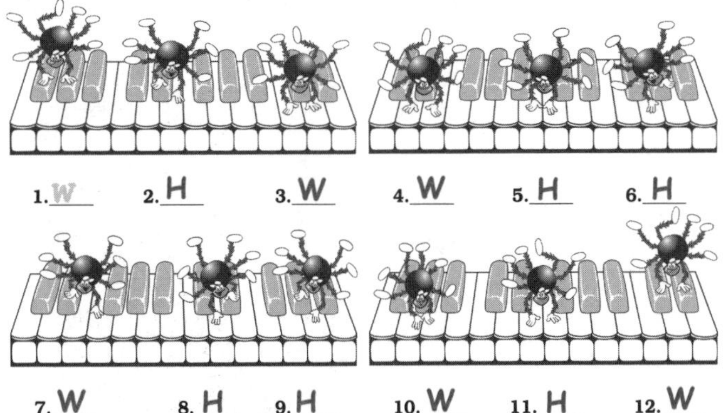

1. W 2. H 3. W 4. W 5. H 6. H

7. W 8. H 9. H 10. W 11. H 12. W

B. Harry Handstand is balancing on one hand. Mark the key where he should place his other hand.

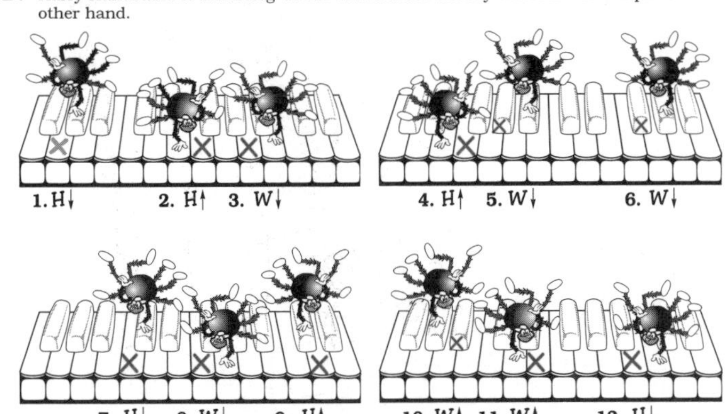

– Page 41 –

Half or Whole

A. Mark the keys on the keyboard to match the half or whole steps on the staff. Circle your answer.

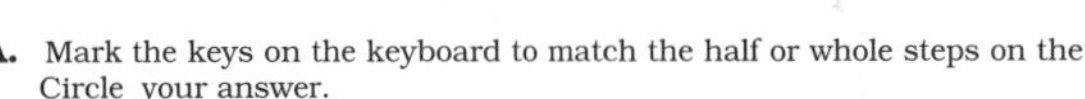

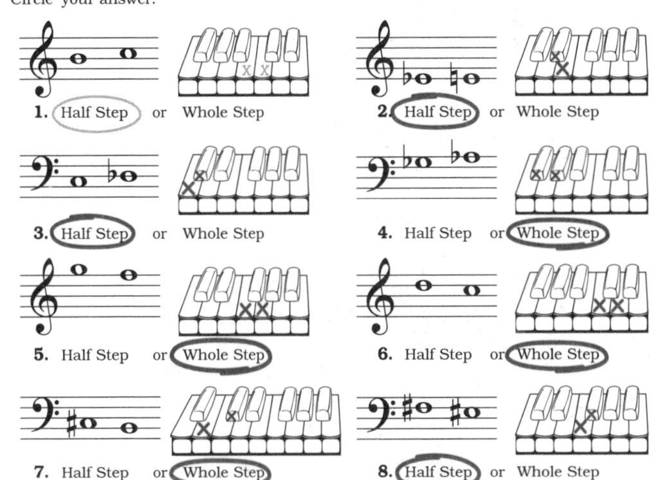

1. (Half Step) or Whole Step
2. (Half Step) or Whole Step
3. (Half Step) or Whole Step
4. Half Step or (Whole Step)
5. Half Step or (Whole Step)
6. Half Step or (Whole Step)
7. Half Step or (Whole Step)
8. (Half Step) or Whole Step

B. Draw a note that will complete the step, adding accidentals where needed. Use the keyboard to help you.

1. H↓ 2. W↑ 3. W↑ 4. W↓

– Page 42 –

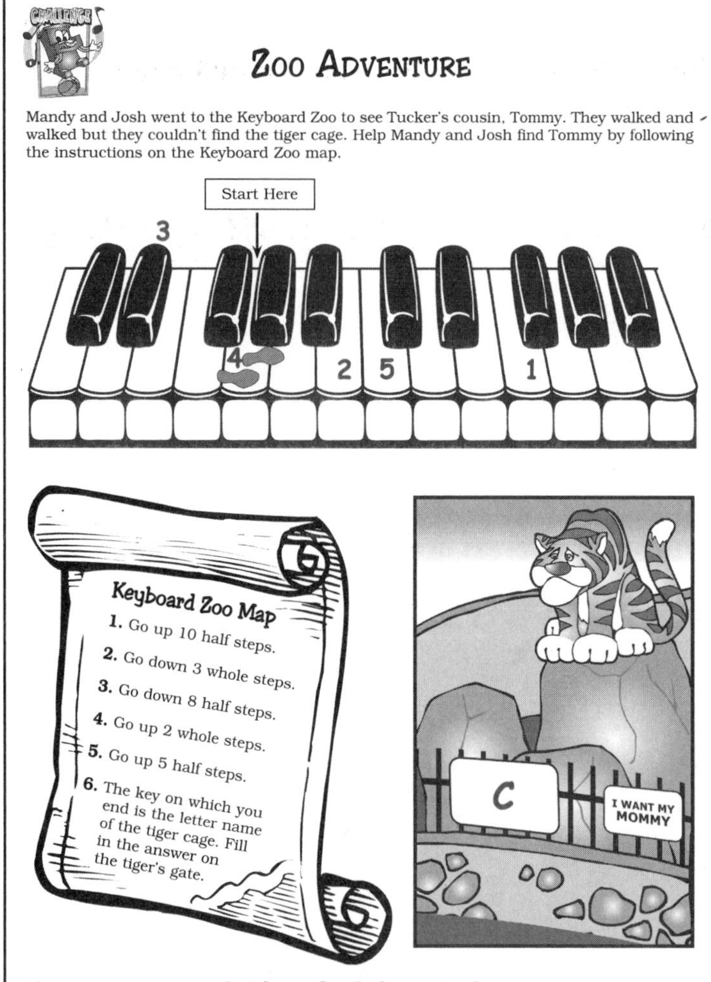

– Page 43 –

– Page 44 –

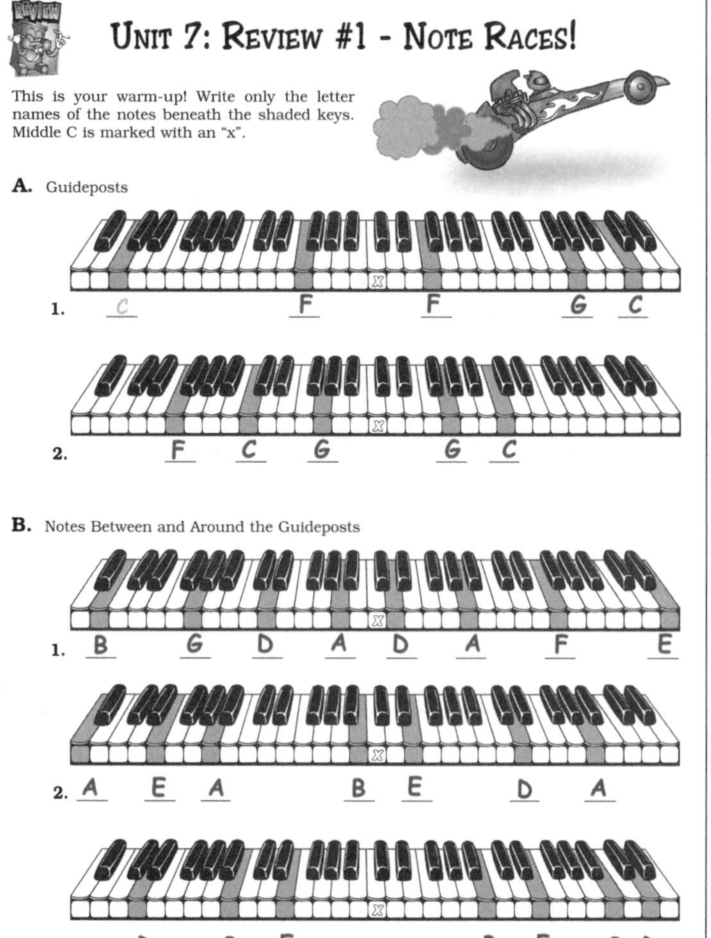

– Page 45 –

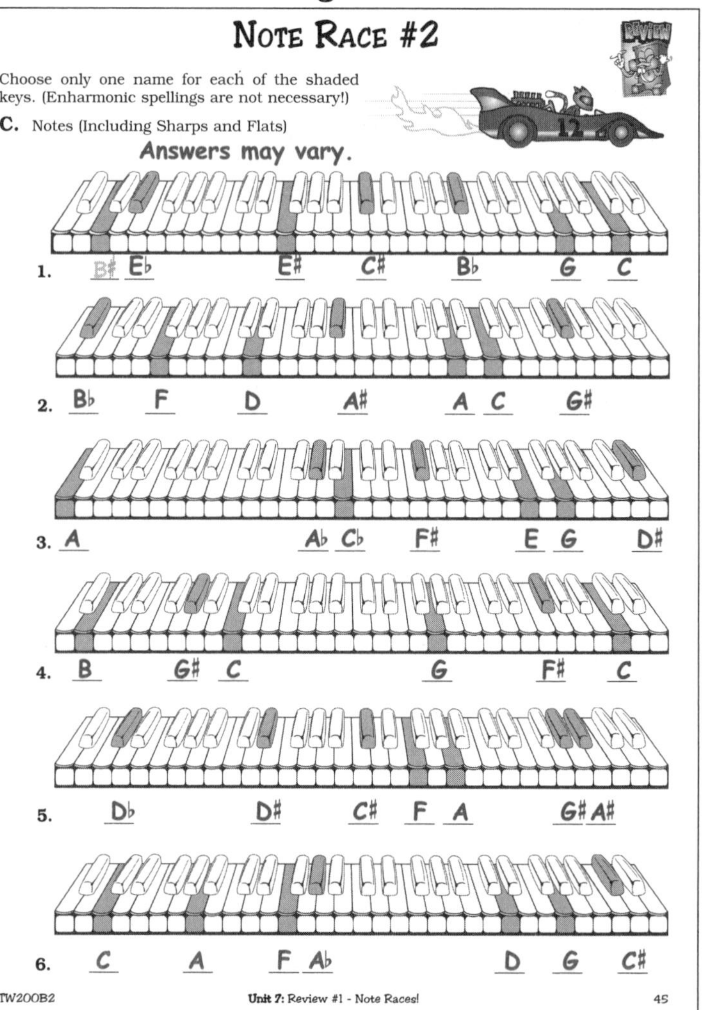

- Page 46 -

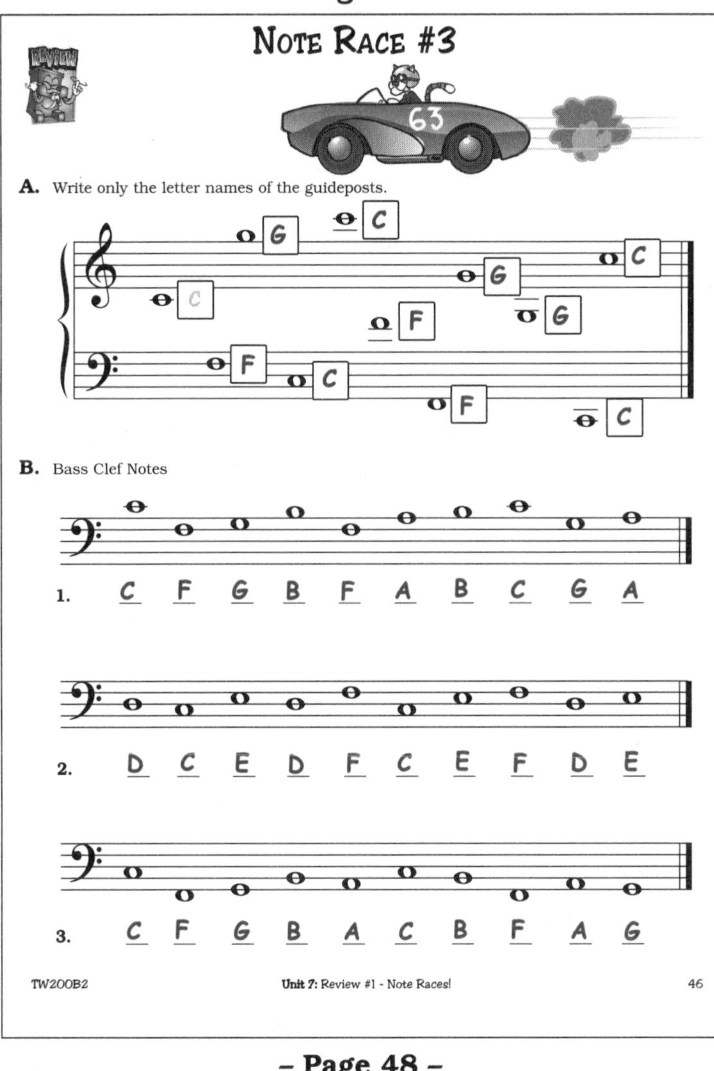

- Page 47 -

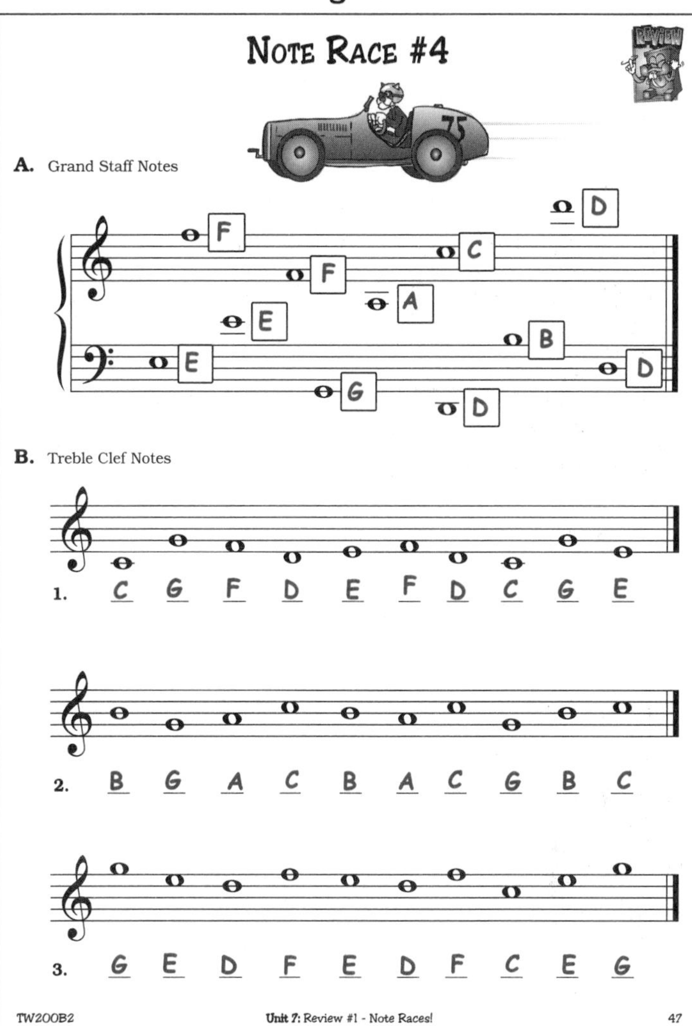

- Page 48 -

- Page 56 -

– Page 57 –

WHICH GROUP?

A. Write the names of the three keys that belong to each I chord group inside their square. Cross off the letter names as you assign them to a group.

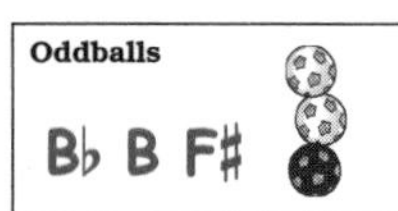

B. Write the names of the keys that look like the patterns below. Cross off the letter names as you assign them to a pattern.

1. C G
2. F
3. D A
4. E

5. D♭ A♭
6. E♭
7. B♭
8. B
9. F♯

– Page 58 –

ALL TOGETHER NOW

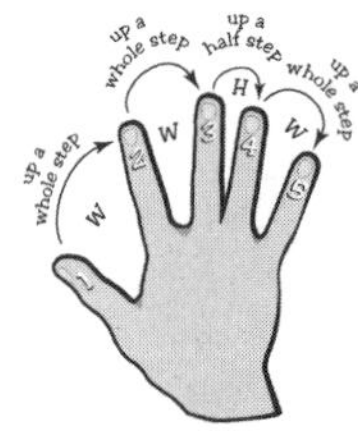

1. For each example, write the names of the notes in the five-finger pattern on the keyboard.
2. Color in the squares to represent the black key/white key pattern.
3. Draw the five-finger pattern and I chord on the staff.

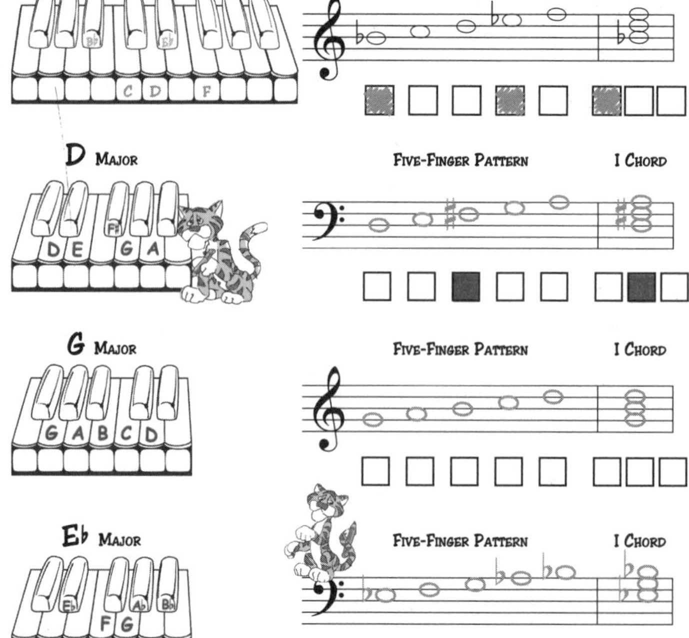

– Page 59 –

ALL TOGETHER NOW CONT.

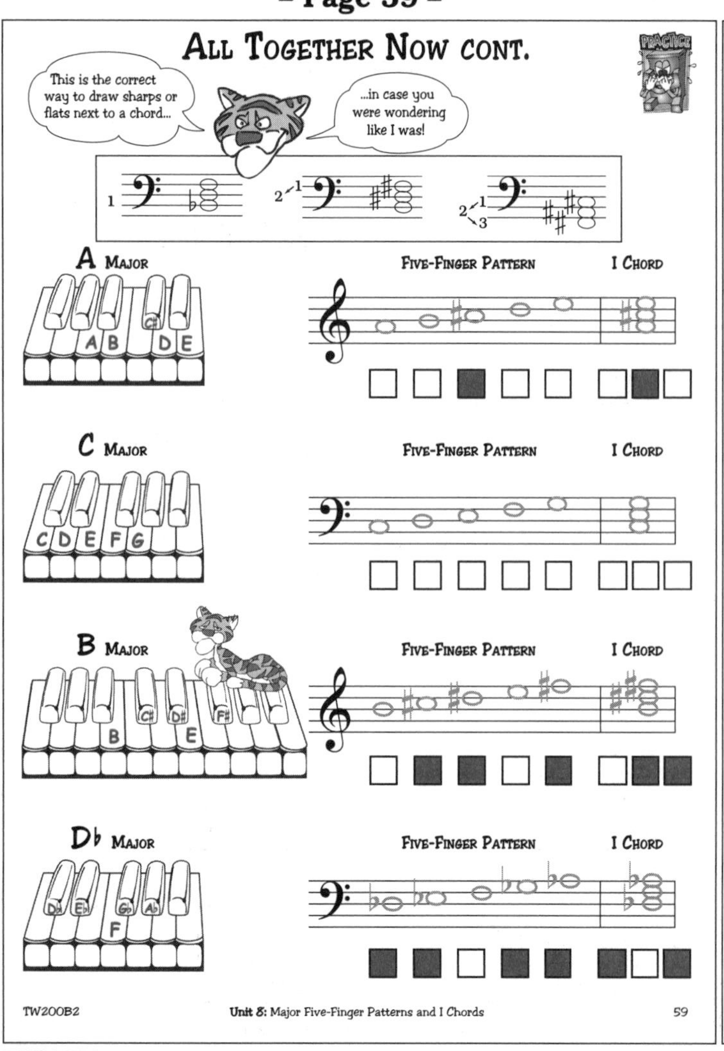

– Page 60 –

ALL TOGETHER NOW CONT.

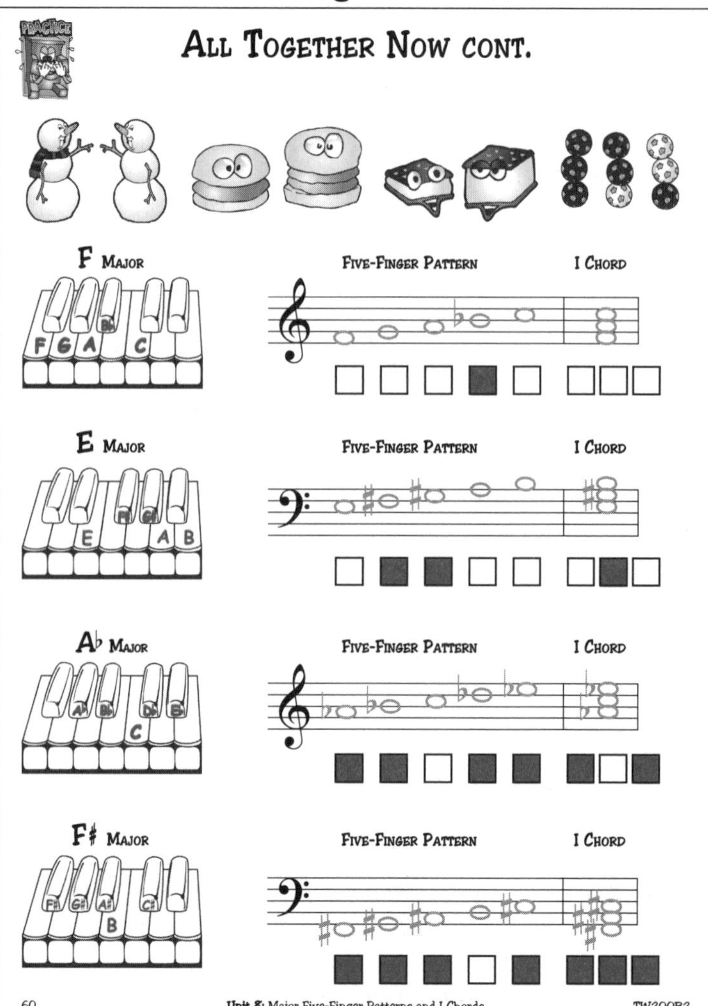

– Page 61 –

Alien Five-Finger Patterns

Aliens have invaded your piano room! Their fingers stuck to the keys when they were practicing their five-finger patterns, but their alien powers only transferred the keynote of each pattern. Fill in the rest of the patterns so when they go back to their home planet they can share their discovery of earthly five-finger patterns.

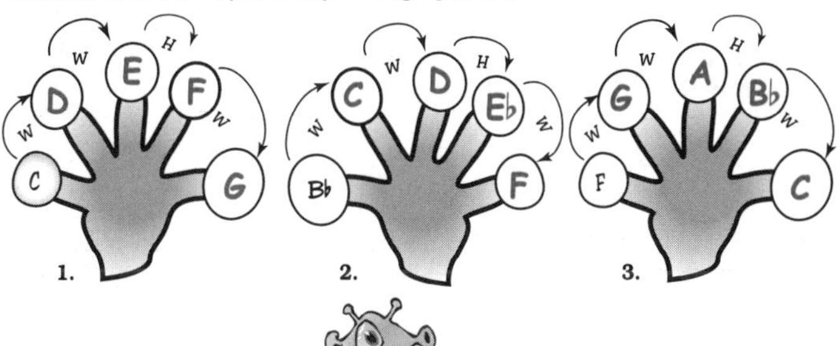

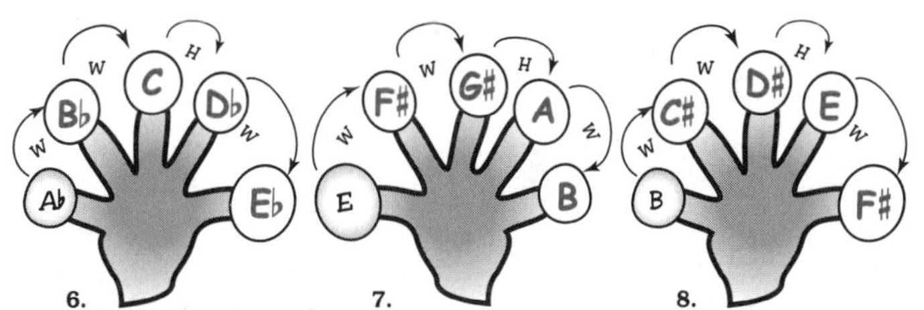

– Page 62 –

Scrambled Five-Finger Patterns

A. Unscramble the following Major five-finger patterns:

1. G B♭ F A C — F G A B♭ C
2. C F D G E — C D E F G
3. F♯ A D E G — D E F♯ G A
4. B C♯ D E A — A B C♯ D E
5. D♭ E♭ C B♭ A♭ — A♭ B♭ C D♭ E♭
6. C B A D G — G A B C D

Over-Easy I Chords

Unscramble the following Major I chords:

1. C♯ E A — A C♯ E
2. E G C — C E G
3. D B♭ F — B♭ D F
4. C♯ A♯ F♯ — F♯ A♯ C♯
5. A F C — F A C
6. A♭ E♭ C — A♭ C E♭
7. B♭ G E♭ — E♭ G B♭
8. B F♯ D♯ — B D♯ F♯
9. B G D — G B D
10. F♯ A D — D F♯ A
11. B G♯ E — E G♯ B
12. F D♭ A♭ — D♭ F A♭

– Page 63 –

We Are Number One! (Or 2...or 3...or 4...or 5?)

Fill in the blanks with the correct answers.

R.H. Major Five-Finger Patterns

When this right-hand finger:	is on this note:	The Major five-finger pattern is:
1	C	CM
3	G	E♭M
1	D♭	D♭M
2	G♯	F♯M
3	D♯	BM
4	D	AM

L.H. Major I Chords

When this left-hand finger:	is on this note:	The Major I Chord is:
5	G	GM
5	E♭	E♭M
3	A	FM
3	F♯	DM
1	F	B♭M
3	C	A♭M

– Page 66 –

Marking Intervals

A. For each five-finger pattern below, shade the boxes to indicate the black keys needed. Then, circle the square in each five-finger pattern that will form the given interval from the keynote.

1. D Major: **P4**
2. E Major: **M2**
3. F♯ Major: **M3**
4. F Major: **P5**
5. A♭ Major: **P1**
6. B♭ Major: **P4**

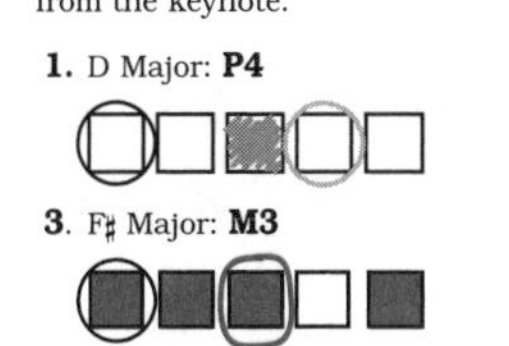

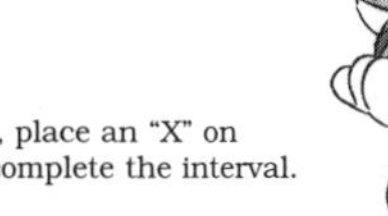

B. For each example, place an "X" on the key that will complete the interval.

1. A Major: **M2**
2. C Major: **M3**

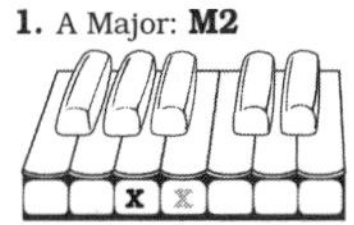

3. D♭ Major: **P5**
4. E♭ Major: **P1**

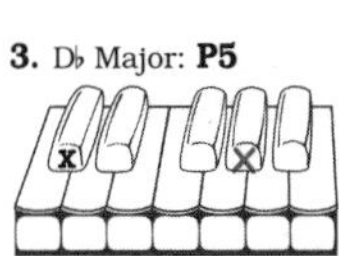

5. B Major: **P4**
6. G♭ Major (Enharmonic of F♯): **M3**

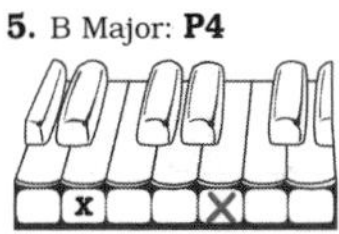

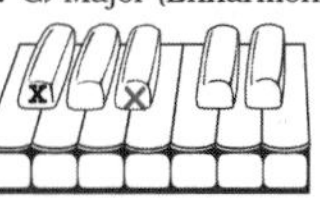

– Page 67 –

Note to Note

A. Add accidentals (sharps or flats) where needed to complete the Major five-finger patterns below. Then, circle the note in each five-finger pattern that will form the given interval from the keynote.

1. F Major: **M3** **2.** G Major: **P5**

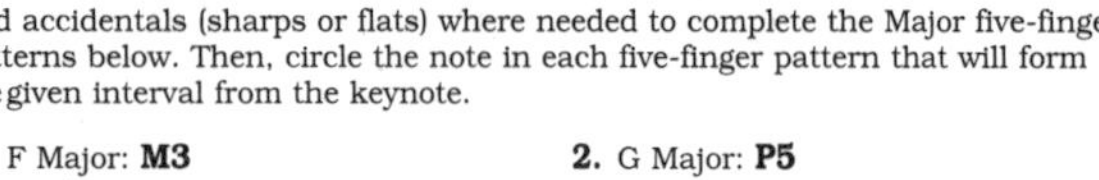

3. C Major: **P5** **4.** E Major: **P4**

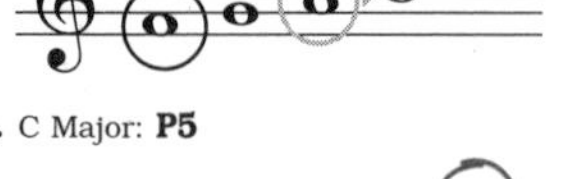

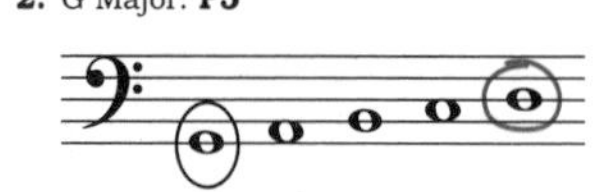

5. B Major: **M2** **6.** A Major: **M3**

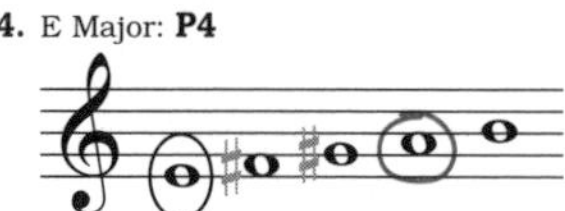

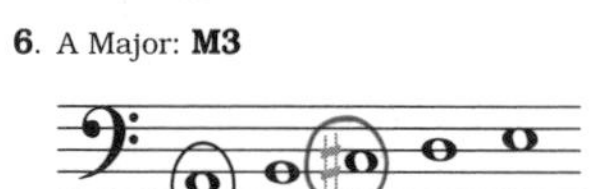

B. For each example, draw the note and accidental (if needed) to form the given interval.

1. C Major: **M2** **2.** A Major: **P5** **3.** E♭ Major: **M3**

4. B Major: **P5** **5.** G Major: **P5** **6.** D Major: **P4**

  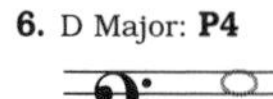

7. F♯ Major: **M3** **8.** E Major: **P4** **9.** B♭ Major: **M2**

– Page 68 –

Captain Long Johns and the Interval Islands

Help Captain Long Johns find as many successful routes as possible to the Interval Islands. Draw lines to show him all the possibilities. Use a different color for each island.
Sailor's Hint: Identify each interval as Major or Perfect before you navigate each route.

Answers may vary.

– Page 69 –

Save the Ship!

Captain Long Johns has encountered the evil interval pirates and needs your help! To break the code, find and circle only the buttons with true Major or perfect intervals. Arrange them in order from the smallest to the largest interval and write the code at the bottom of the page. This code will launch the firing power Captain Long Johns needs to defend the ship.

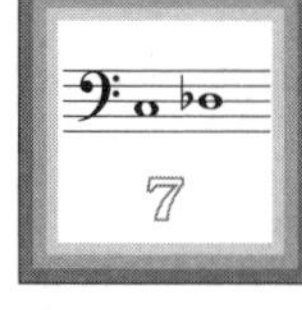

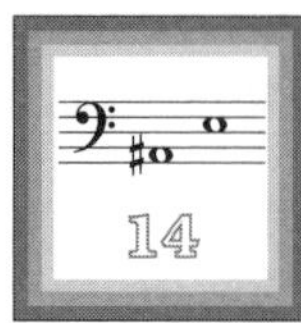

Code:

3	13	11	5	16
P1	M2	M3	P4	P5

– Page 71 –

Headin' to the Beach

Draw a line from each beach ball to the pair of fins with matching rest values. Count each whole rest in 4/4 time.

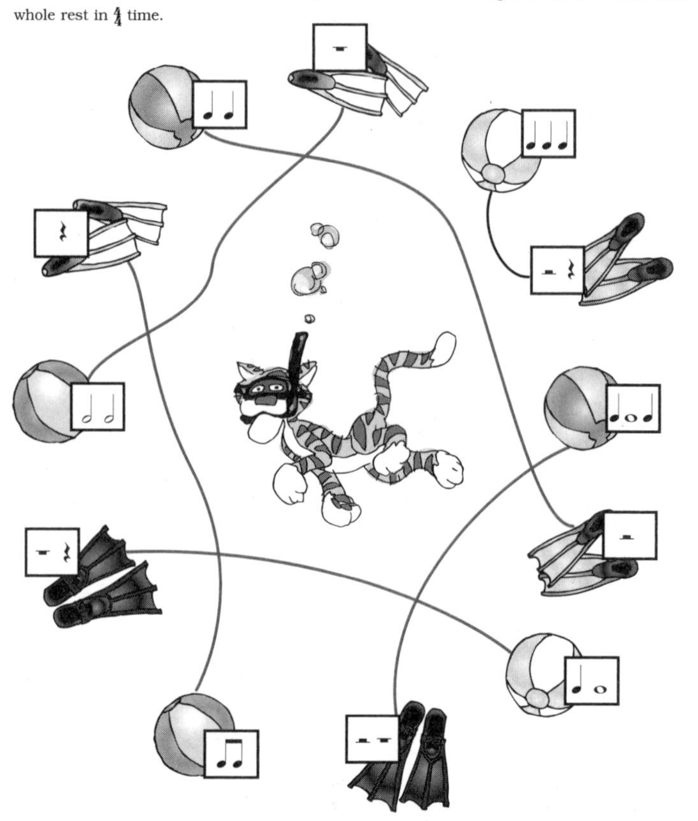

– Page 72 –

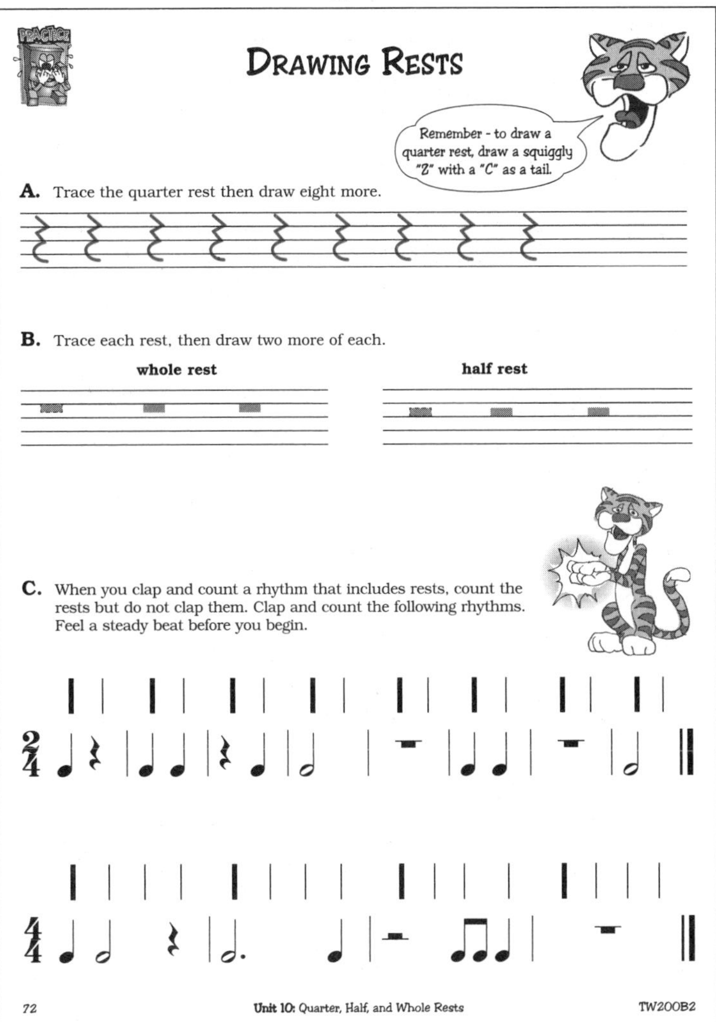

– Page 73 –

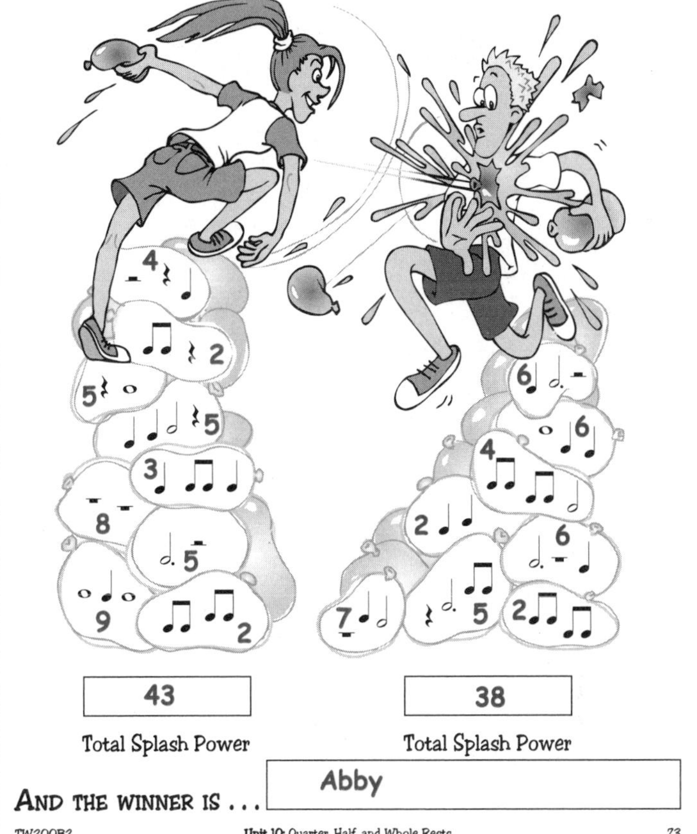

– Page 74 –

– Page 77 –

– Page 78 –

Counting the Eighths

For each example, write in the counts then clap and count the rhythms.

1. 1 + 2 + | 1 + 2 + | 1 + 2 + | 1 + 2 +
2. 1 + 2 + 3 + | 1 + 2 + 3 + | 1 + 2 + 3 + | 1 + 2 + 3 +
3. 1+2+3+4+ | 1+2+ 3+4+ | 1+2+3+4+ | 1+2+3+4+
4. 1 + 2 + | 1 + 2 + | 1 + 2 + | 1 + 2 +
5. 1 + 2 + 3 + | 1 + 2 + 3 + | 1 + 2 + 3 + | 1 + 2 + 3 +
6. 1+2+3+4+ | 1+2+3+4+ | 1+2+3+4+ | 1+2+3+4+

– Page 79 –

Super Heroes

Help these Super Heroes find their capes by matching the number of eighth beats on each cape to the number of eighth beats next to its Super Hero. Write the number of each matching cape in the box next to the Super Hero it belongs to.

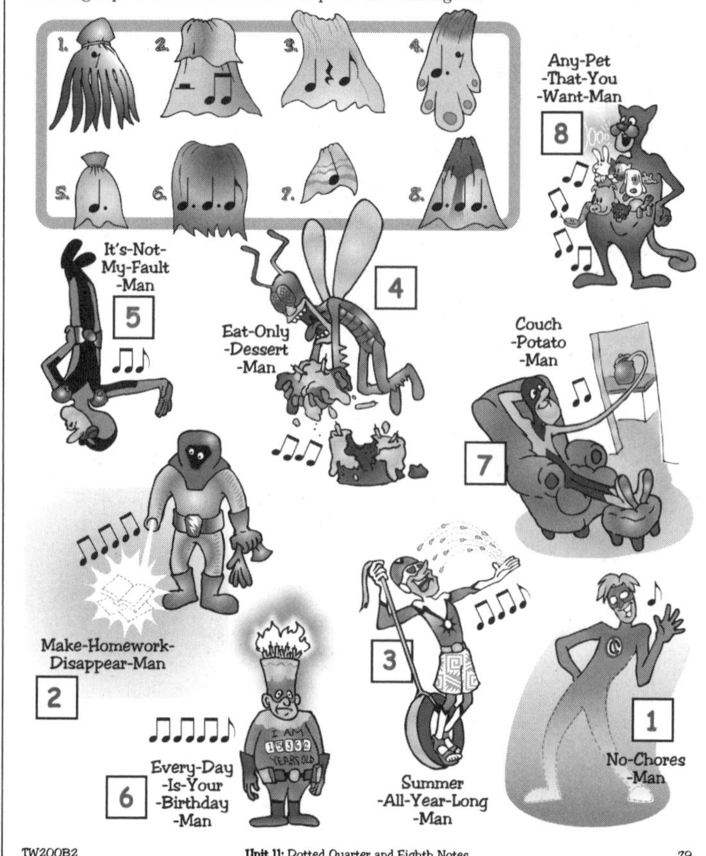

– Page 80 –

You Be the Teacher!

You be the teacher! Correct Tucker's music math. If the answer is correct, put a "**C**" by it. If the answer is incorrect, cross it out and write the correct answer next to it.

1. 4/4 = 8 C quarter notes *or* 16 C eighth notes
2. 3/4 = 3 C quarter notes *or* 6 C eighth notes
3. 4/4 = ~~X~~ 8 quarter notes *or* ~~X~~ 16 eighth notes
4. 2/4 = ~~X~~ 6 quarter notes *or* ~~X~~ 12 eighth notes
5. 4/4 = ~~X~~ 12 quarter notes *or* 24 C eighth notes
6. 2/4 = 4 C quarter notes *or* ~~X~~ 8 eighth notes
7. 4/4 = ~~X~~ 8 quarter notes *or* 16 C eighth notes
8. 3/4 = 6 C quarter notes *or* ~~X~~ 12 eighth notes

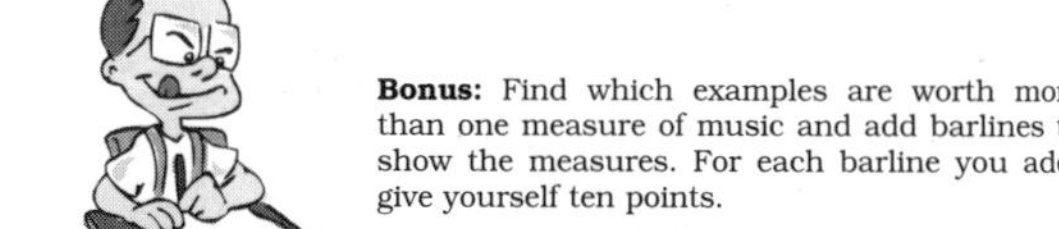

Bonus: Find which examples are worth more than one measure of music and add barlines to show the measures. For each barline you add, give yourself ten points.

Points Earned: 170

– Page 81 –

Hidden Picture

Find the hidden picture by coloring all the notes, rests, or combinations of notes and/or rests (vertical or horizontal) that equal a dotted quarter note.

♪	𝅝	𝅗𝅥	♩.	♩	𝄾	𝄽	𝄾	▬	♪	𝄾	𝅗𝅥.	𝄽
𝅗𝅥	▬	♩.	▬	𝄽	𝅗𝅥	▬	𝅗𝅥	♩.	𝅗𝅥.	𝅝	▬	𝅗𝅥
𝅗𝅥	♩	▬	𝅗𝅥	𝄽	𝅗𝅥	𝅝	♩	𝅗𝅥	♪	𝄾	𝅗𝅥.	♩.
𝅗𝅥.	𝄾	𝅝	♪	▬	𝅗𝅥.	𝄽	▬	𝅝	♩	𝅗𝅥.	𝅝	▬
♪	𝅗𝅥	♩.	▬	𝅗𝅥.	▬	𝅝	♪	𝄾	𝅗𝅥.	𝄾	▬	𝅝
▬	▬	𝄾	♪	𝅗𝅥	𝄾	𝅗𝅥	𝅝	▬	𝅗𝅥.	𝄾	▬	♩.
𝄽	𝅗𝅥	▬	▬	𝅝	𝅗𝅥	♩	▬	𝅝	𝅗𝅥	♪	▬	𝄽
▬	♪	𝅗𝅥.	𝅗𝅥	♪	𝅗𝅥.	▬	♪	▬	𝄾	▬	𝅗𝅥.	♩
♩	𝅗𝅥.	▬	𝄽	𝅗𝅥	▬	𝄽	𝅗𝅥.	𝄾	♪	𝅗𝅥	𝅗𝅥.	𝅗𝅥
𝅗𝅥	𝄾	♪	𝅗𝅥.	▬	𝄾	▬	▬	𝅗𝅥	𝄾	𝅝	▬	♪
▬	▬	𝅗𝅥	♩	𝅗𝅥.	𝅗𝅥	𝅝	♪	𝄾	▬	▬	♩	𝅝
♪	𝅗𝅥.	𝄽	▬	♪	▬	𝄾	𝅗𝅥.	𝄽	▬	𝅝	𝅗𝅥.	𝄾
▬	♩	𝅗𝅥	𝅗𝅥.	𝅝	♩	𝅝	♩.	▬	𝅗𝅥	▬	𝅗𝅥	𝅗𝅥.
𝄾	𝅝	▬	♪	𝅗𝅥	𝄽	♩.	♩	𝄽	▬	𝅗𝅥.	▬	𝅗𝅥.
𝅗𝅥	♪	𝅝	𝅗𝅥.	𝄽	♩.	▬	𝄽	▬	♩	▬	𝄾	♪

– Page 82 –

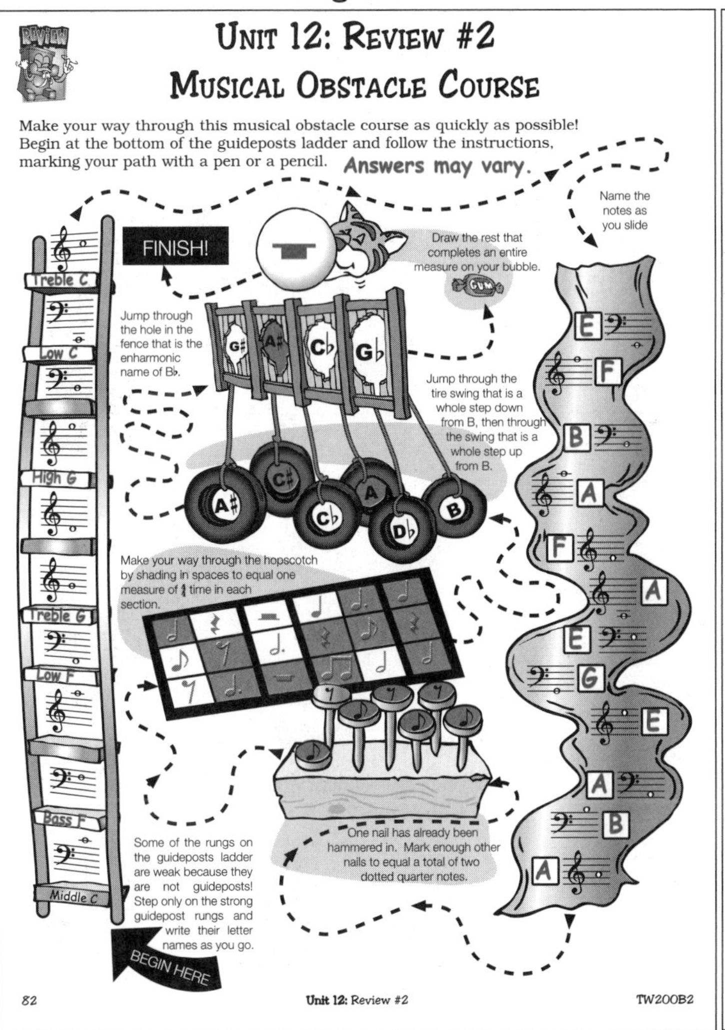

– Page 83 –

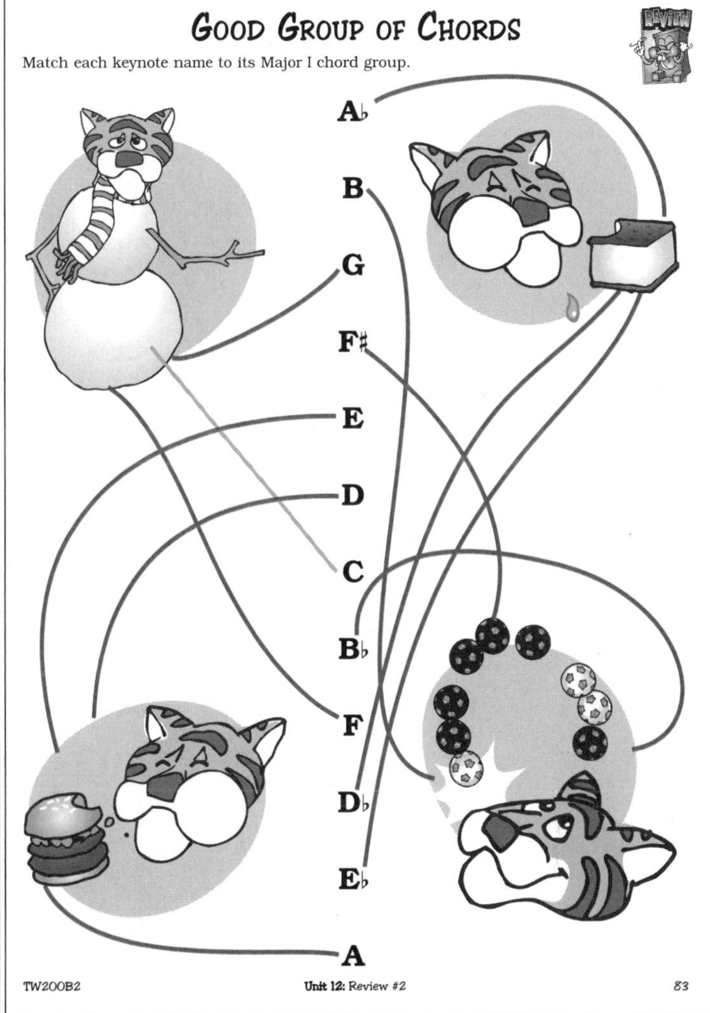

– Page 84 –

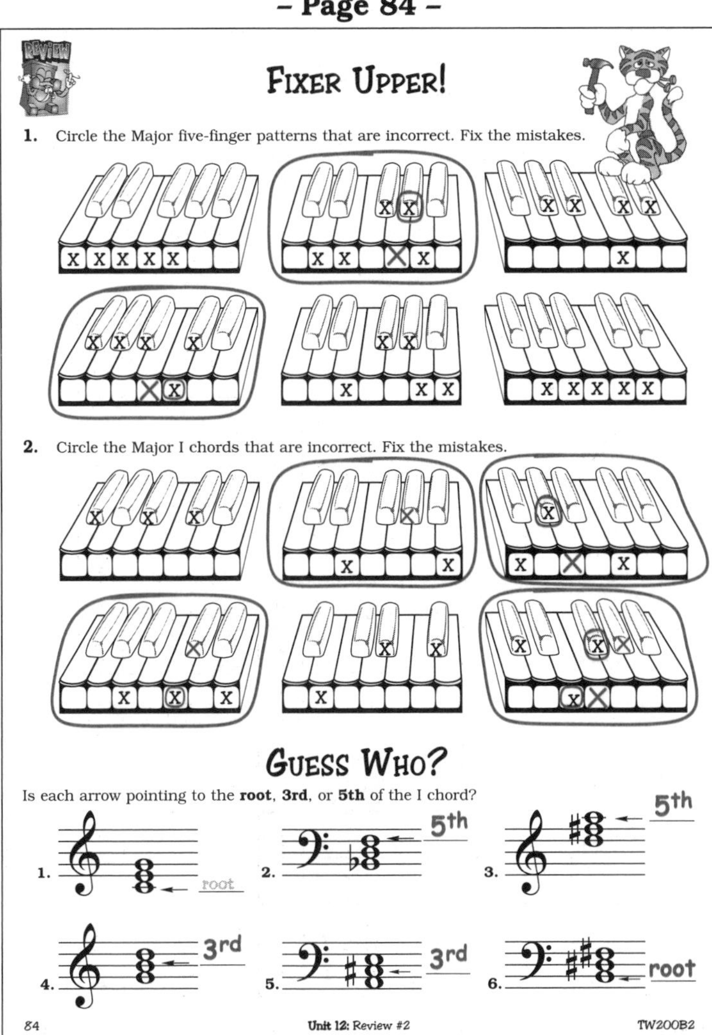

– Page 85 –

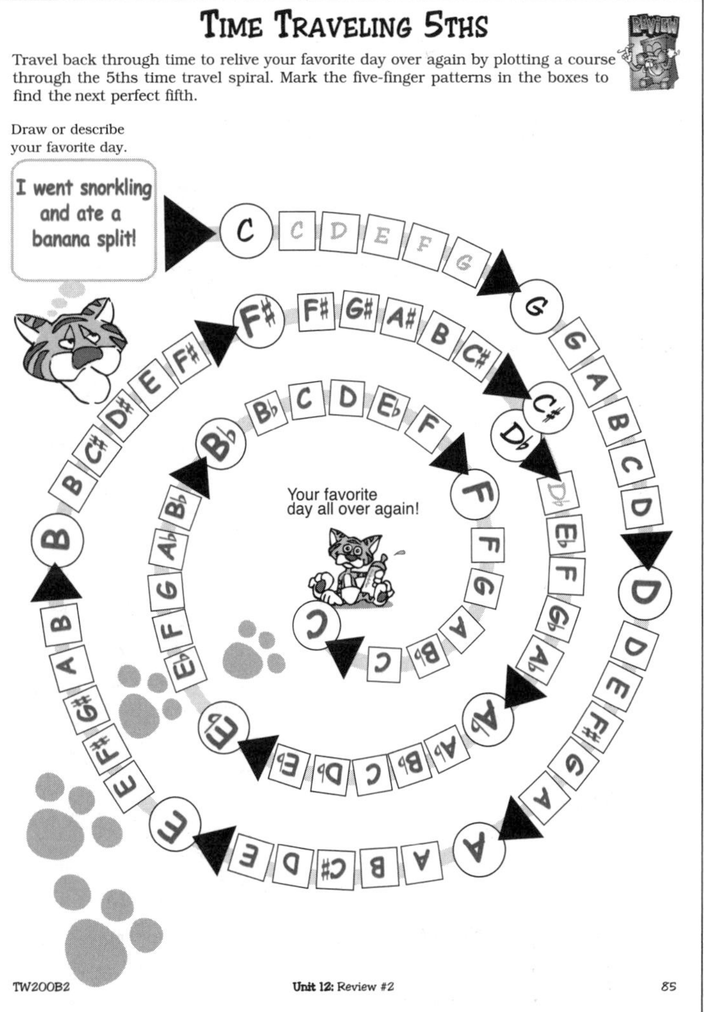

– Page 86 –

Painting Pitfalls

Tucker has been painting all day. He wrote you an important message, but his paint ladder slipped and he spilled paint all over the note. Find out which letters got covered up by answering the questions below. Use your answers to fill in the missing letters. **Hint:** Fill the letters in as you go.

1. The 4th note of a C Major five-finger pattern is: F
2. The 3rd note of a C Major five-finger pattern is: E
3. The 2nd note of a D Major five-finger pattern is: E
4. The 5th note of a G Major five-finger pattern is: D
5. The 4th note of a B Major five-finger pattern is: E
6. The 3rd note of an E♭ Major five-finger pattern is: G
7. The keynote of a B Major five-finger pattern is: B
8. The 5th note of an A Major five-finger pattern is: E
9. The 5th of a D Major I chord is: A
10. The root of an E Major I chord is: E
11. The 3rd of an A♭ Major I chord is: C
12. The 3rd of a B♭ Major I chord is: D
13. The 5th of a C Major I chord is: G
14. The root of an A Major I chord is: A
15. The 3rd of a C Major I chord is: E
16. The 5th of a B♭ Major I chord is: F

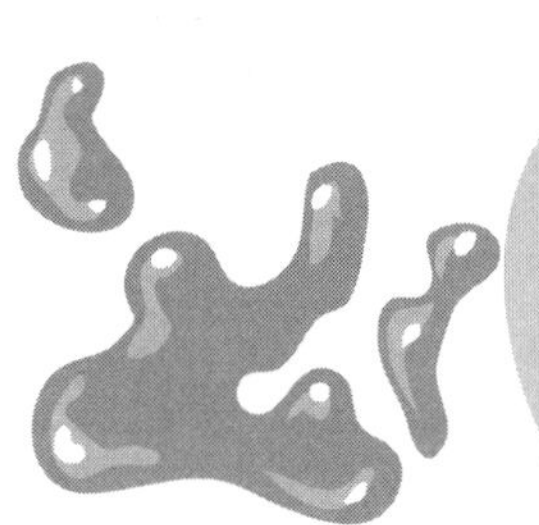

– Page 87 –

I Can Do That!

Tucker likes to challenge his friends to draw five-finger patterns with just a few notes as clues to help them. See if you can keep up with Tucker and his friends by taking the challenge!

Four-Note Clues

1. C Major 2. B Major 3. A Major

B. Three-Note Clues

1. F Major 2. E♭ Major 3. D Major

C. Two-Note Clues

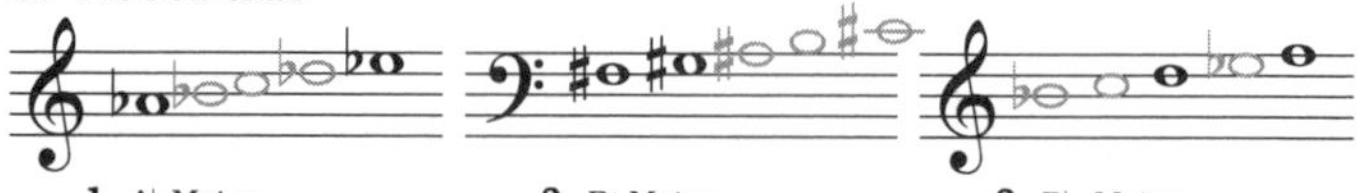

1. A♭ Major 2. F♯ Major 3. B♭ Major

D. One-Note Clues

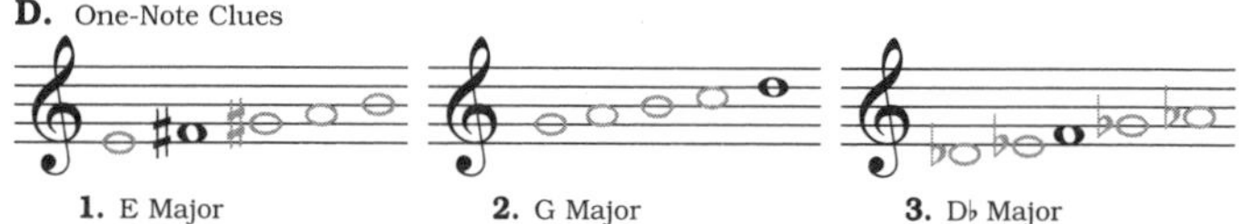

1. E Major 2. G Major 3. D♭ Major

– Page 88 –

Steppin' Up and Skippin' Over

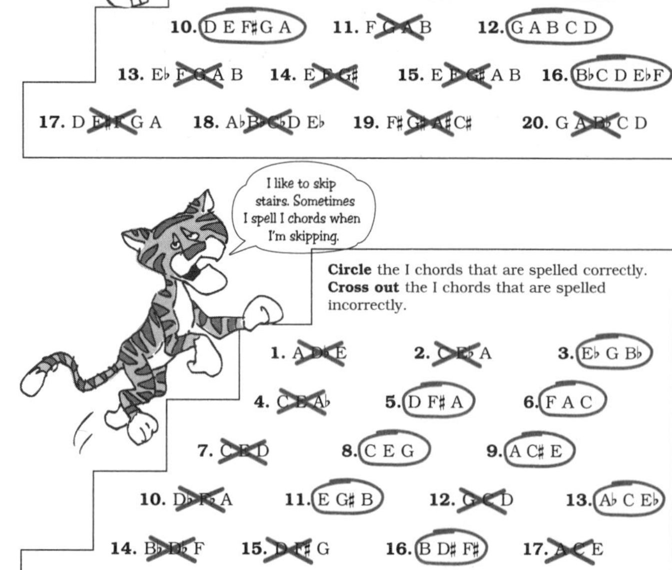

Circle the Major five-finger patterns that are spelled correctly. **Cross out** the five-finger patterns that are spelled incorrectly.

1. A B C♯ D E (circled)
2. C D E F (crossed out)
3. C E F G♭ A (crossed out)
4. A B C D♭ E (crossed out)
5. A B C D E (crossed out)
6. D♭ E♭ F G♭ A♭ (circled)
7. C E G B D (crossed out)
8. F G A B♭ C (circled)
9. E♭ F G A♭ B♭ (circled)
10. D E F♯ G A (circled)
11. F G A B (crossed out)
12. G A B C D (circled)
13. E♭ F G A B (crossed out)
14. E F G♯ (crossed out)
15. E F G♯ A B (crossed out)
16. B♭ C D E♭ F (circled)
17. D E♯ F G A (crossed out)
18. A♭ B♭ C♭ D E♭ (crossed out)
19. F♯ G♯ A♯ C♯ (crossed out)
20. G A B♭ C D (crossed out)

Circle the I chords that are spelled correctly. **Cross out** the I chords that are spelled incorrectly.

1. A D♭ E (crossed out)
2. C E♭ A (crossed out)
3. E♭ G B♭ (circled)
4. C E A♭ (crossed out)
5. D F♯ A (circled)
6. F A C (circled)
7. C E D (crossed out)
8. C E G (circled)
9. A C♯ E (circled)
10. D♭ F♭ A (crossed out)
11. E G♯ B (circled)
12. G C D (crossed out)
13. A♭ C E♭ (circled)
14. B♭ D♭ F (crossed out)
15. D F♯ G (crossed out)
16. B D♯ F♯ (circled)
17. A C E (crossed out)
18. F♯ A♯ C♯ (circled)
19. E B♭ C (crossed out)
20. E G B (crossed out)
21. B♭ D F (circled)

– Page 91 –

The 3rd Goes Down

Provide the lowered 3rd for each minor five-finger pattern and i chord.

1. F Major: F B A B♭ C — F minor: f g **a♭** b♭ c
2. A Major: A B C♯ D E — A minor: a b **c** d e
3. F♯ Major: F♯ G♯ A♯ B C♯ — F♯ minor: f♯ g♯ **a** b c♯
4. E♭ Major: E♭ F G A♭ B♭ — E♭ minor: e♭ f **g♭** a♭ b♭
5. G Major: G A B C D — G minor: g a **b♭** c d
6. B Major: B C♯ D♯ E F♯ — B minor: b c♯ **d** e f♯
7. D♭ Major: D♭ F A♭ — D♭ minor: d♭ **f♭** a♭
8. B♭ Major: B♭ D F — B♭ minor: b♭ **d♭** f
9. E Major: E G♯ B — E minor: e **g** b
10. A♭ Major: A♭ C E♭ — A♭ minor: a♭ **c♭** e♭

– Page 92 –

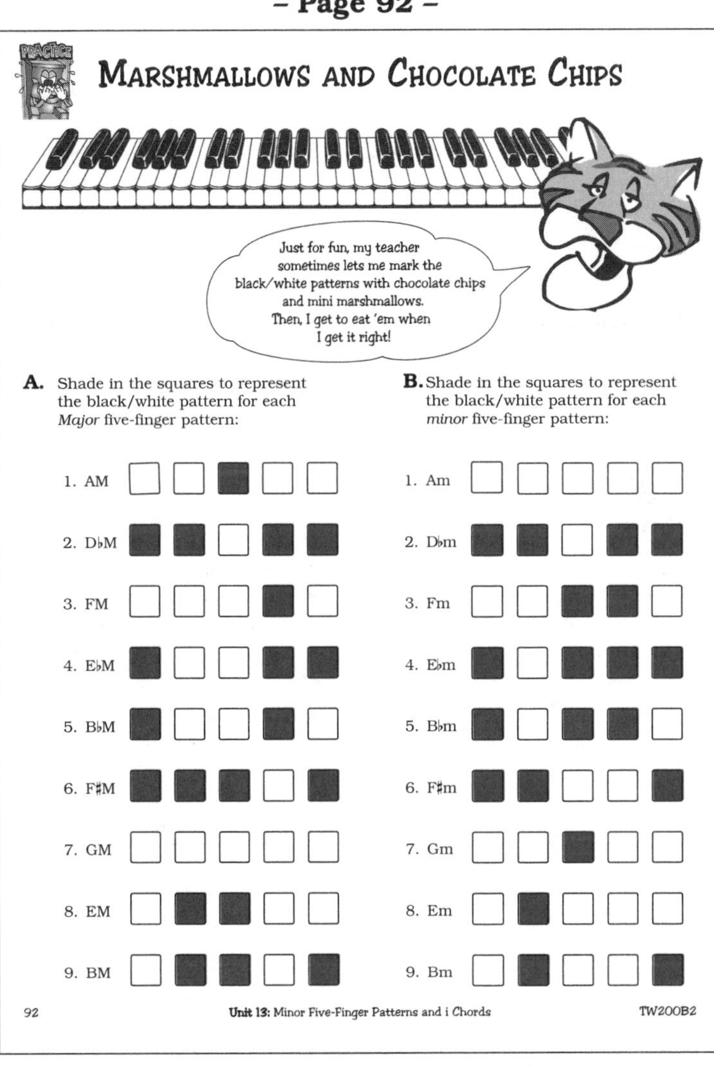

Marshmallows and Chocolate Chips

A. Shade in the squares to represent the black/white pattern for each *Major* five-finger pattern:

1. AM
2. D♭M
3. FM
4. E♭M
5. B♭M
6. F♯M
7. GM
8. EM
9. BM

B. Shade in the squares to represent the black/white pattern for each *minor* five-finger pattern:

1. Am
2. D♭m
3. Fm
4. E♭m
5. B♭m
6. F♯m
7. Gm
8. Em
9. Bm

92 **Unit 13:** Minor Five-Finger Patterns and i Chords TW200B2

– Page 93 –

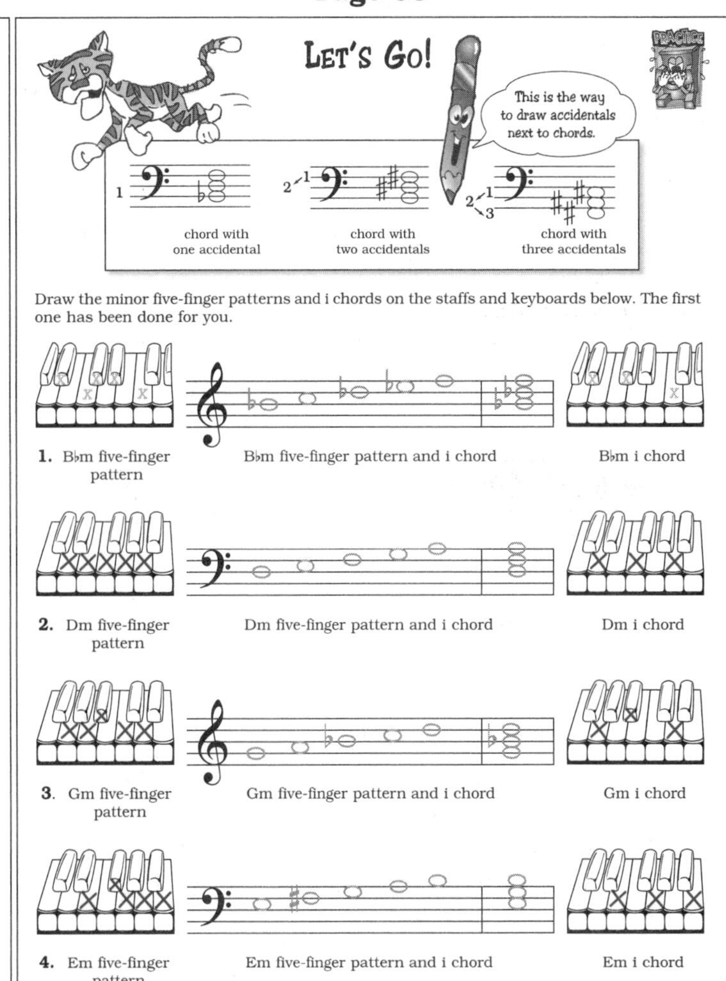

Let's Go!

Draw the minor five-finger patterns and i chords on the staffs and keyboards below. The first one has been done for you.

1. B♭m five-finger pattern — B♭m five-finger pattern and i chord — B♭m i chord
2. Dm five-finger pattern — Dm five-finger pattern and i chord — Dm i chord
3. Gm five-finger pattern — Gm five-finger pattern and i chord — Gm i chord
4. Em five-finger pattern — Em five-finger pattern and i chord — Em i chord

TW200B2 **Unit 13:** Minor Five-Finger Patterns and i Chords 93

– Page 94 –

– Page 95 –

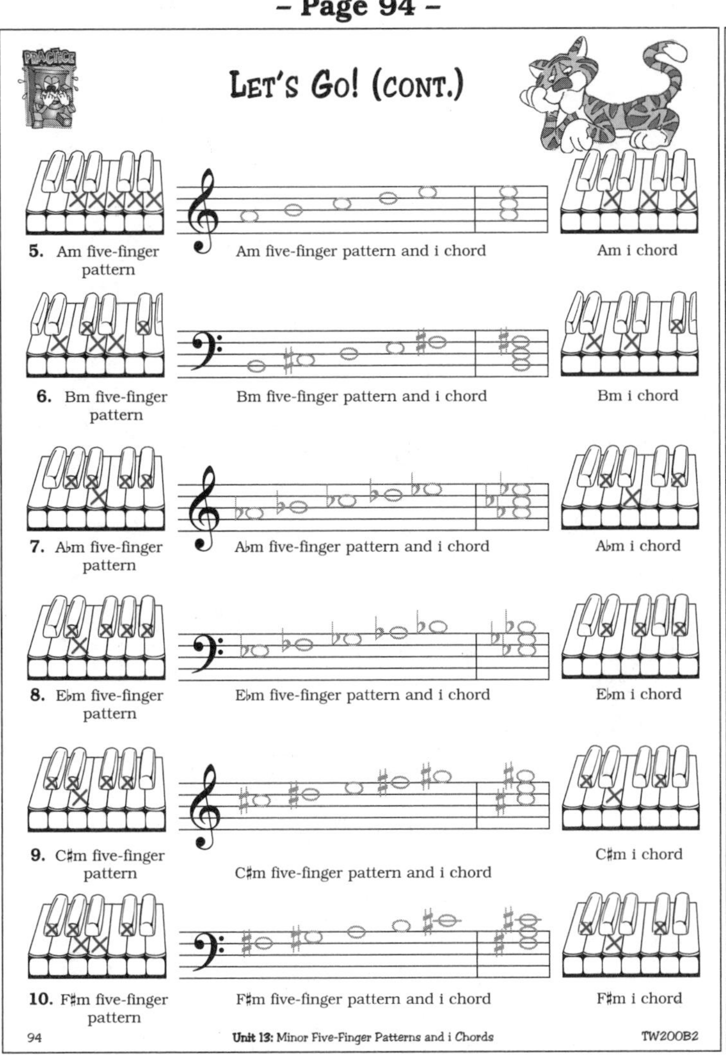

Let's Go! (cont.)

5. Am five-finger pattern — Am five-finger pattern and i chord — Am i chord
6. Bm five-finger pattern — Bm five-finger pattern and i chord — Bm i chord
7. A♭m five-finger pattern — A♭m five-finger pattern and i chord — A♭m i chord
8. E♭m five-finger pattern — E♭m five-finger pattern and i chord — E♭m i chord
9. C♯m five-finger pattern — C♯m five-finger pattern and i chord — C♯m i chord
10. F♯m five-finger pattern — F♯m five-finger pattern and i chord — F♯m i chord

94 **Unit 13:** Minor Five-Finger Patterns and i Chords TW200B2

Roots and Keynotes

A. Fill in the missing root for each Major I chord. Then, draw the minor i chord that is built on the same root next to it.

Major minor Major minor

1. 2. 3. 4. 5. 6.

B. Fill in the missing keynote for each minor five-finger pattern. Use the keyboard to help you visualize the patterns.

1. 2. 3. 4. 5. 6.

TW200B2 **Unit 13:** Minor Five-Finger Patterns and i Chords 95

– Page 96 –

Minor Five-Finger Pattern Search

Find and circle both the hidden minor five-finger patterns and i chords down or across using the color key. The first one has been done as an example.

F	A♭	C	G	A	B♭	C	D	D
A	B	C	D	E	D	F	A	E
F	G	A♭	B♭	C	D	G	C♯	F
G	E	A	C♯	D	F	C	E♭	G
A♭	G	C	G	E♭	F♯	E	B	A
B♭	B♭	E	D	F	G	G	D	F
C	D	E	F♯	G	A	B	B♭	C

Color Key

- Fm - gray
- Cm - orange
- Gm - blue
- Dm - purple
- Am - yellow
- Em - red

A♭	B♭	C♭	D♭	E♭	G♭	B♭	C♯	D
E♭	F♯	G♯	A	B	C♯	C	B♭	F♯
D♭	E♭	F	G♭	A♭	B♭	D	D♭	A
C♭	D	E	F♯	G♯	A	E	F	C♯
B♭	C♯	B♭	C	D♭	E♭	F	G	E
A♭	C♭	E♭	B	C♯	D♯	E	F♯	G♯
B	C♯	D	E	F♯	A	B	D	F♯

Color Key

- Bm - green
- F♯m - orange
- C♯m - blue
- A♭m - purple
- E♭m - yellow
- B♭m - red

– Page 97 –

Hat Day

Tommy is very style-conscious! Find out which hat he prefers to wear with each hairstyle. Follow the directions below each hat and write the number of the hat in one of the squares below Tommy. The first one has been done for you. Be careful, some are Major and some are minor.

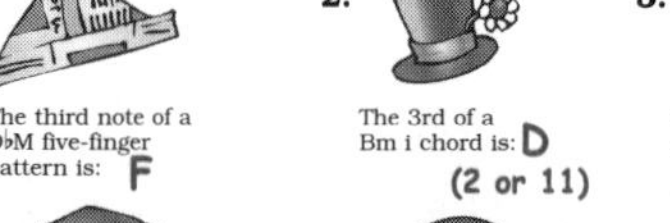

1. The third note of a D♭M five-finger pattern is: F
2. The 3rd of a Bm i chord is: D (2 or 11)
3. The fifth note of an Am five-finger pattern is: E
4. The 3rd of an A♭m i chord is: C♭

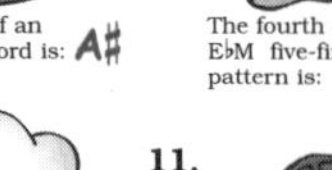

5. The second note of an F♯M five-finger pattern is: G♯
6. The 3rd of an F♯M I chord is: A♯
7. The fourth note of an E♭M five-finger pattern is: A♭
8. The 5th of an E♭M I chord is: B♭

9. The fourth note of a Bm five-finger pattern is: E
10. The root of the D♭m i chord is: D♭
11. The third note of a B♭M five-finger pattern is: D (2 or 11)
12. The 5th of an Em i chord is: B

F	D	A♯	E	A♭	G♯
1	2	6	3	7	5

D♭	D	E	B♭	B	C♭
10	11	9	8	12	4

– Page 98 –

Unit 14: Review # 3 - The Musical Rain Forest

Major I Chords Tree

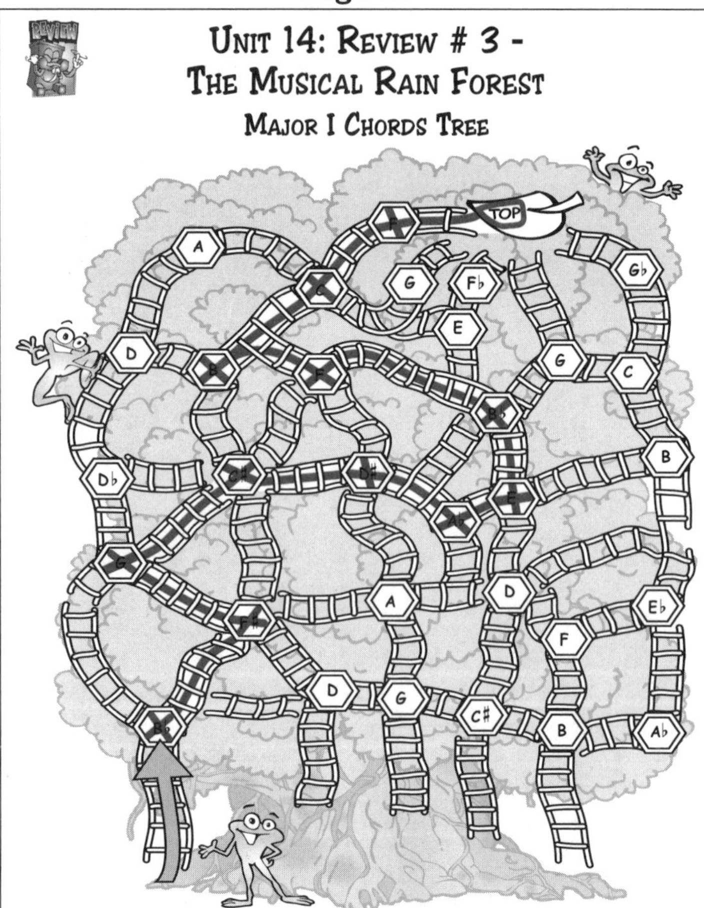

Welcome to the musical rain forest! To get safely to the top of the tree, climb through the root, 3rd, or 5th of each Major I chord in this order, crossing them out as you go: (1) Root of B♭M. (2) 3rd of DM. (3) 5th of CM. (4) 5th of F♯M. (5) 3rd of BM. (6) Root of A♭M. (7) Root of EM. (8) 5th of E♭M. (9) 3rd of D♭M. (10) 3rd of GM. (11) 5th of FM. (12) 5th of B♭M.

– Page 99 –

Mossy Minor Thirds Tree

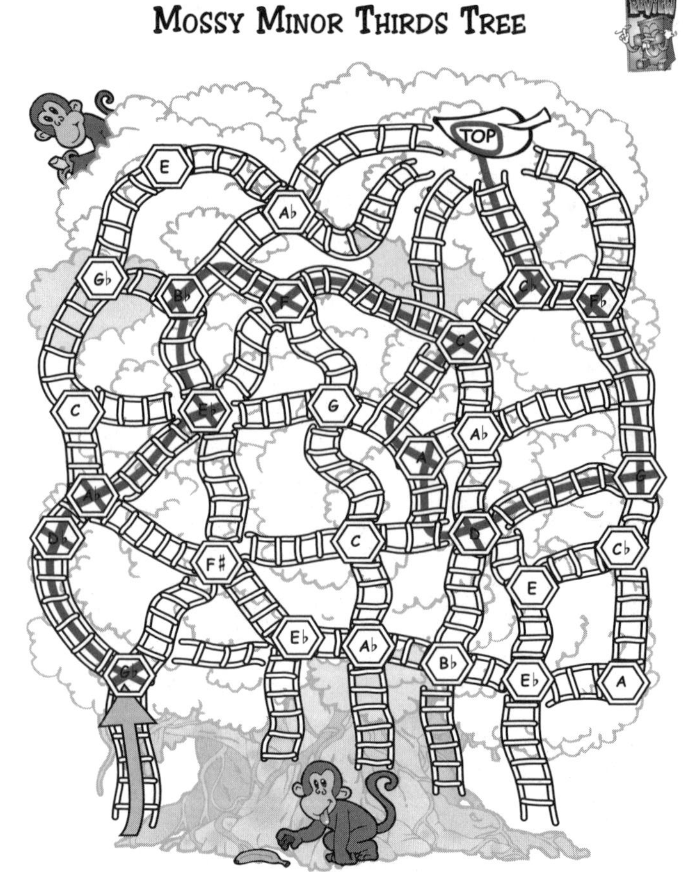

To get safely to the top, climb through the 3rd of each minor i chord in the following order, crossing them out as you go: (1) E♭m. (2) B♭m. (3) Fm. (4) Cm. (5) Gm. (6) Dm. (7) Am. (8) F♯m. (9) Bm. (10) Em. (11) D♭m. (12) A♭m.

– Page 100 –

Dripping Rhythms Tree

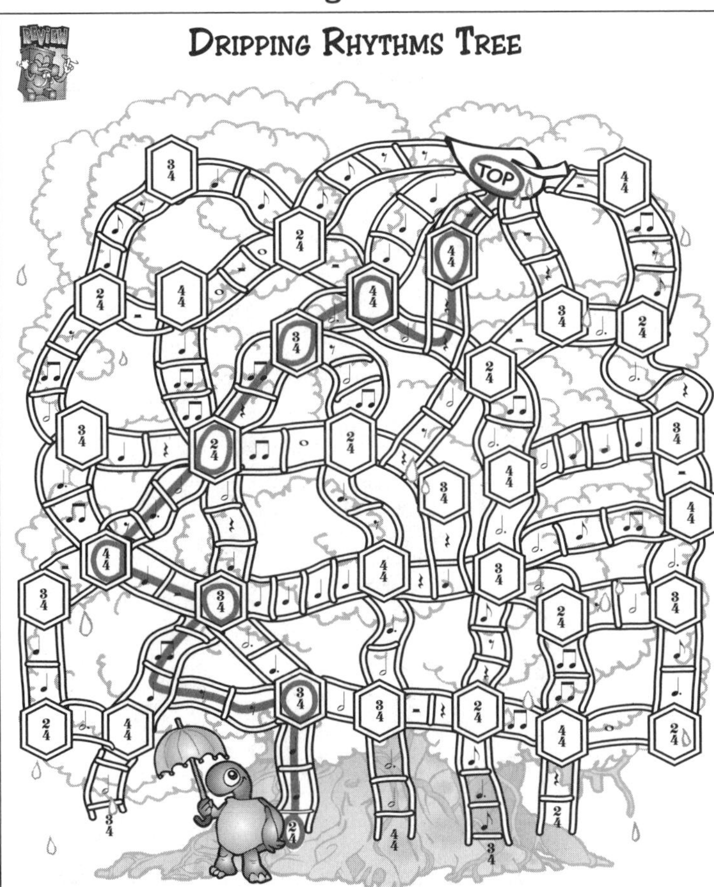

To get to the top, choose a rope ladder at the bottom of the tree and climb through a time signature. Next choose the rope ladder with the correct number of notes and rests to equal one measure in that time signature before you reach the next time signature. (If the first time signature you climb through doesn't work, try a different one.) Continue in this way until you reach the top safely!

– Page 101 –

Minor i Chords Tree

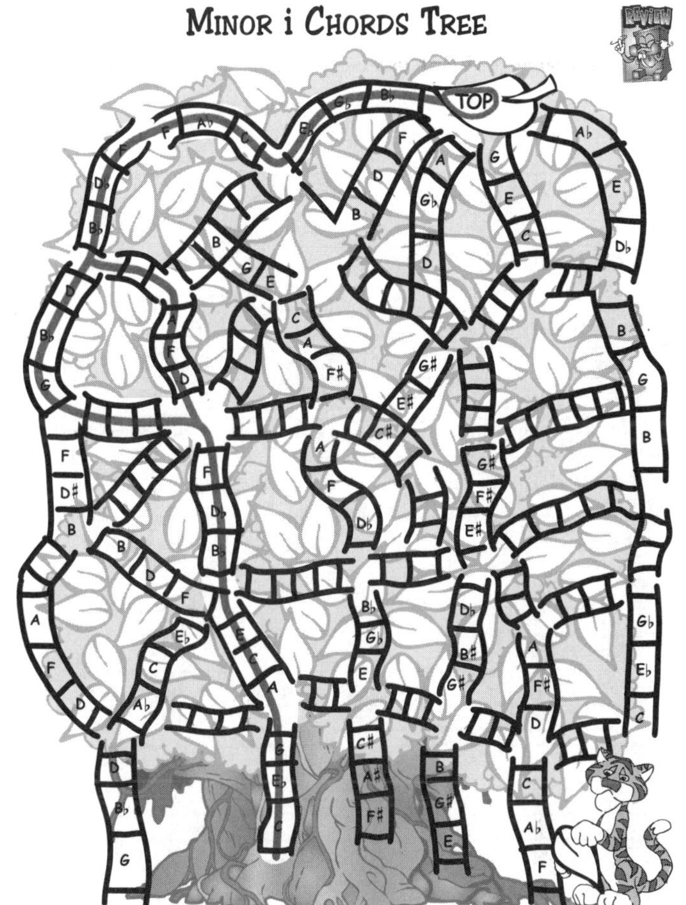

Choose a rope ladder at the bottom of the tree and make your way to the top by climbing only the ladders with correctly spelled minor i chords. (**Hint:** The first ladder you try may not work!) **Answers may vary.**

– Page 102 –

Minor Five-Finger Pattern Tree

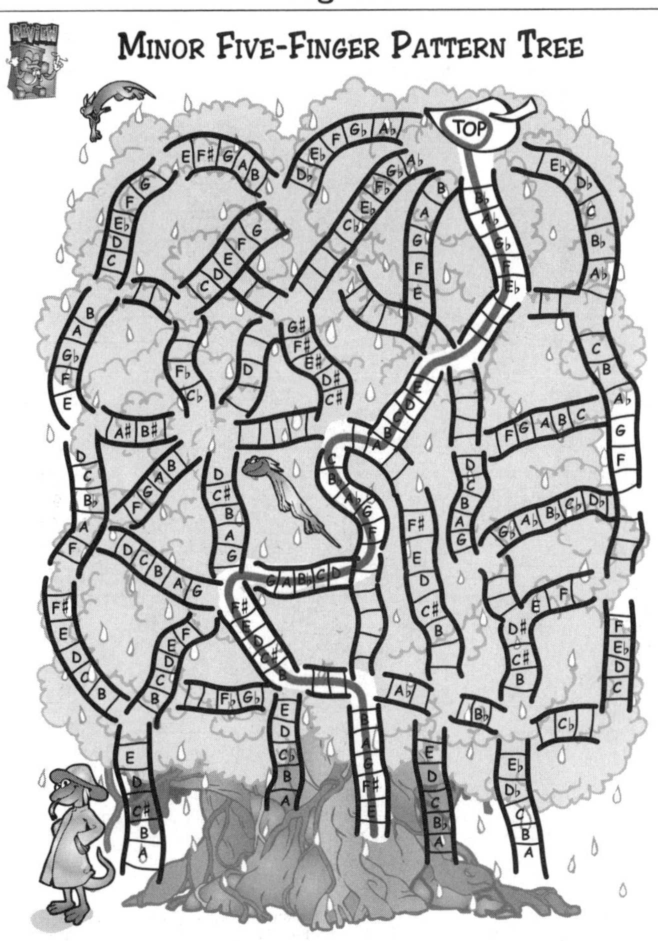

Choose a rope ladder at the bottom of the tree and make your way to the top by climbing only the ladders with correctly spelled minor five-finger patterns.

– Page 103 –

Petrified Intervals Tree

Begin on a rope ladder at the bottom of the tree and climb to the top by determining the note from one rope ladder to the note on the next rope ladder by the interval through which you climb. There is only one path that works and it never crosses.

– Page 105 –

On Joking Terms

Use this code to answer the jokes below.

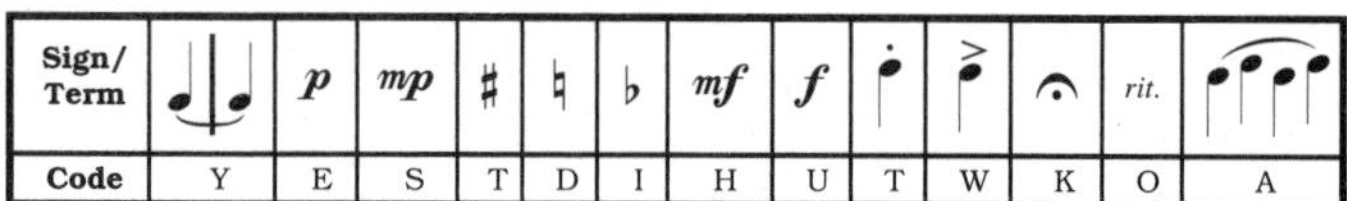

Sign/Term	(tie)	*p*	*mp*	♯	♮	♭	*mf*	*f*	(staccato)	(accent)	(fermata)	*rit.*	(slur)
Code	Y	E	S	T	D	I	H	U	T	W	K	O	A

Q: Which side of a tiger has the most stripes?

The back side?

Definition	Raises a note a half step	Moderately loud	Soft
Sign/Term	♯	*mf*	*p*
Code	T	H	E

Definition	Gradually slowing	Loud	Detached	Medium soft	Lowers a note a half step	Cancels a sharp or flat	Soft
Sign/Term	*rit.*	*f*	(staccato)	*mp*	♭	♮	*p*
Code	O	U	T	S	I	D	E

Q: What do you call a cat that tells jokes?

Definition	Slur	Emphasized	Lowers a note a half step	Raises a note a half step	Detached	Tie
Sign/Term	(slur)	(accent)	♭	♯	(staccato)	(tie)
Code	A	W	I	T	T	Y

Definition	Fermata	Flat	Sharp	Staccato	Curved line connecting two notes of the same pitch
Sign/Term	(fermata)	♭	♯	(staccato)	(tie)
Code	K	I	T	T	Y

Q: What has more lives than a cat?

A frog, because it croaks every night!

– Page 106 –

Terms Got You Down? Try Across!

Across

1. Lowers a note one half step
2. A curved line joining two of the same pitches. Play the first one and add the value of the second note to hold it that much longer.
6. Cancels a sharp or flat
8. Detached
11. Smooth and connected.
12. Emphasized
14. Medium soft
15. With spirit!
17. Gradually louder

Choose from: Flat, Sharp, Crescendo, Decrescendo, Ritardando, Forte, Piano, Mezzo forte, Mezzo piano, Tie, Slur, Accent, Legato, Staccato, Spirito, Natural, Allegro, Andante, Fermata

Answers: 1. FLAT; 2. TIE; 6. NATURAL; 8. STACCATO; 11. LEGATO; 12. ACCENT; 14. MEZZOPIANO; 15. SPIRITO; 17. CRESCENDO; Down: 1. FERMATA; 3. SLUR; 4. ALLEGRO; 5. ANDANTE; 7. DECRESCENDO; 9. FORTE; 10. MEZZOFORTE; 13. RITARDANDO; 16. SHARP

Down

1. Hold
3. A line that curves over or under two or more notes. Play these notes smooth and connected.
4. Quickly
5. Walking tempo
7. Gradually softer
9. Loud
10. Medium loud
13. Gradually slowing
16. Raises a note one half step

– Page 107 –

Do NOT Make Me Do That!

Next to each example, write one thing you do **NOT** like to do that reminds you of the sign or term. Be prepared to defend your answers. One has been done as an example.

Here are a few ideas.

1. *p* Mom always tells me, "Be quiet, the baby is sleeping!"
2. *mp* Being quieter in class
3. *mf* Give the dog a bath
4. *f* Vacuuming the living room
5. (decrescendo) Turn off the T.V.
6. (crescendo) Starting up the lawn mower
7. > Getting scared by my sister and shrieking
8. Allegro Running from my brother
9. Andante Walking to school
10. *ritard.* Ending my ride on the rollercoaster
11. ♯ Sitting on a nail and getting up
12. ♭ Letting out the air in my intertube
13. ♮ Putting away all my toys...returning my room to normal
14. *legato* Wiping down the kitchen counter
15. *staccato* Clinking dishes together while washing
16. fermata Waiting for a movie to start
17. tie Pausing my video game
18. slur Waxing my dad's car

I do **NOT** like waking up early in the morning!

– Page 109 –

My Son, John

I got it started for you. Don't forget the time signature!

Add rhythms to this nursery rhyme using the steps described on page 108.

Rhythms may vary.

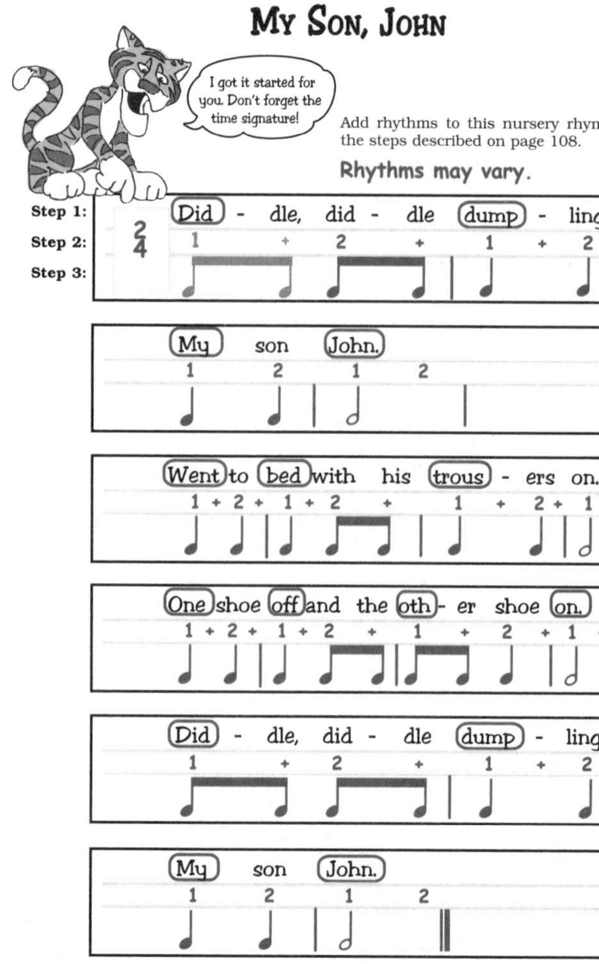

– Page 110 –

Teach Her Some More!

Rhythms may vary.

Step 1:
Step 2:
Step 3:

In - ter - vals, I chords and five fin - ger pat - terns.
1 2 3 1 2 3 1 2 3 1 2 3

Half steps, whole steps, brac - es and mea - sures.
1 2 3 1 2 3 1 2 3 1 2 3

Bar - lines and eighth rests, mi - nor and Ma - jor.
1 2 3 1 2 3 1 2 3 1 2 3

Teach her some more, noth - ing can faze her!
1 2 3 1 2 3 1 2 3 1 2 3

110 **Unit 16:** Composition: Rhythm TW200B2

– Page 111 –

Is the First Beat Really the First Beat?

Sometimes the first beat you come to isn't the *strongest* beat.

See 'ya lat - er al - li - ga - tor!
2 + 1 + 2 + 1 +

Take care griz - zly bear!
2 + 1 + 2 + 1 + 2

Answers may vary.

1. Mañ - AN - a i - GUAN - a!
3 1 2 3 1 2 3

2. See `ya ROUND grey - HOUND!
2 + 1 + 2 + 1 + 2 +

3. See ya SOON ya big ba - BOON!
3 + 4 + 1 + 2 + 3 + 4 + 1 + 2 + 3 + 4

4. Be right back black yak!
2 + 1 + 2 + 1 + 2 +

5. In a while croc - o - dile!
2 + 1 + 2 + 1 + 2 +

TW200B2 **Unit 16:** Composition: Rhythm 111

– Page 114 –

Repetition and Sequence

A. Label each musical example with "R" for repetition or "S" for sequence in the box beside it.

1. R
2. S
3. R
4. S
5. R

B. Write your own musical examples according to the label.

Sequence answers may vary.

1. repetition
2. sequence
3. sequence
4. sequence

114 **Unit 17:** Composition: Melody TW200B2

– Page 115 –

Look Around You

There are examples of repetition and sequence all around us. In the city street below, circle examples of repetition in blue. Circle examples of sequences in orange. Many different answers are possible. Discuss this page with your teacher.

Answers may vary.

TW200B2 **Unit 17:** Composition: Melody 115

– Page 116 –

My Tiger

Compose your own melody for this poem. The rhythm for the poem is written above the staff but feel free to change it if you like. Use these steps to help you compose:

1. Choose any five-finger pattern, Major or minor.
2. Use repetition, sequence, or both.
3. Surprise your listener with something unexpected!
4. Add signs and terms to describe how you want your music to sound.

Title Suckers for Tucker

– Page 117 –

Unit 18: Review #4

Tucker and his friends are at it again, but this time they're reviewing their minor five-finger patterns. The challenge is even greater this time because they've decided to begin with only three notes as clues and work their way to zero notes as clues. Are you up to the challenge?

A. Using only three notes as clues:

1. Gm:

2. F♯m:

B. Using only two notes as clues:

1. A♭m:

2. Em:

C. Using only one note as a clue:

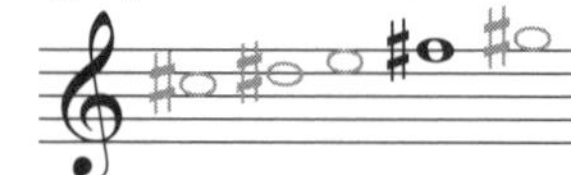

1. C♯m:

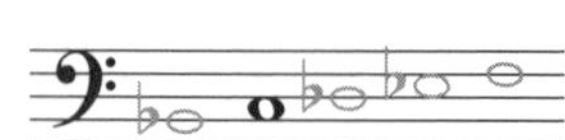

2. B♭m:

D. Using zero notes as clues:

1. Fm:

2. E♭m:

– Page 118 –

The local hot dog stand has just hired Tommy. Tommy can never seem to put the right food items in the correct bag. Help him by writing note names of the root, 3rd, and 5th on the food items to match the chord name on the bag. Remember, "M" is for Major, and "m" is for minor.
Hint: See the menu for help.

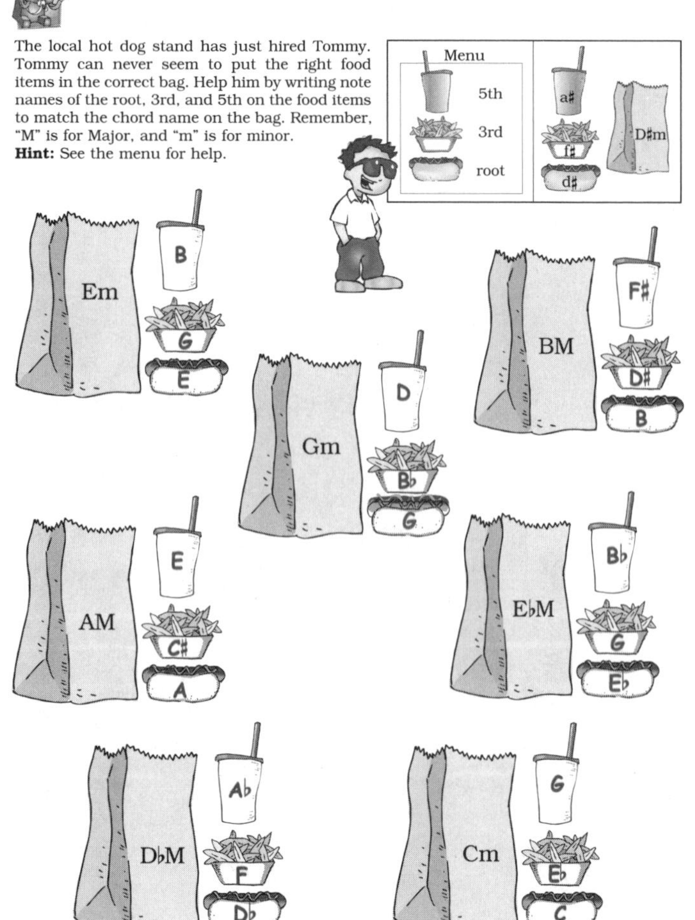

– Page 119 –

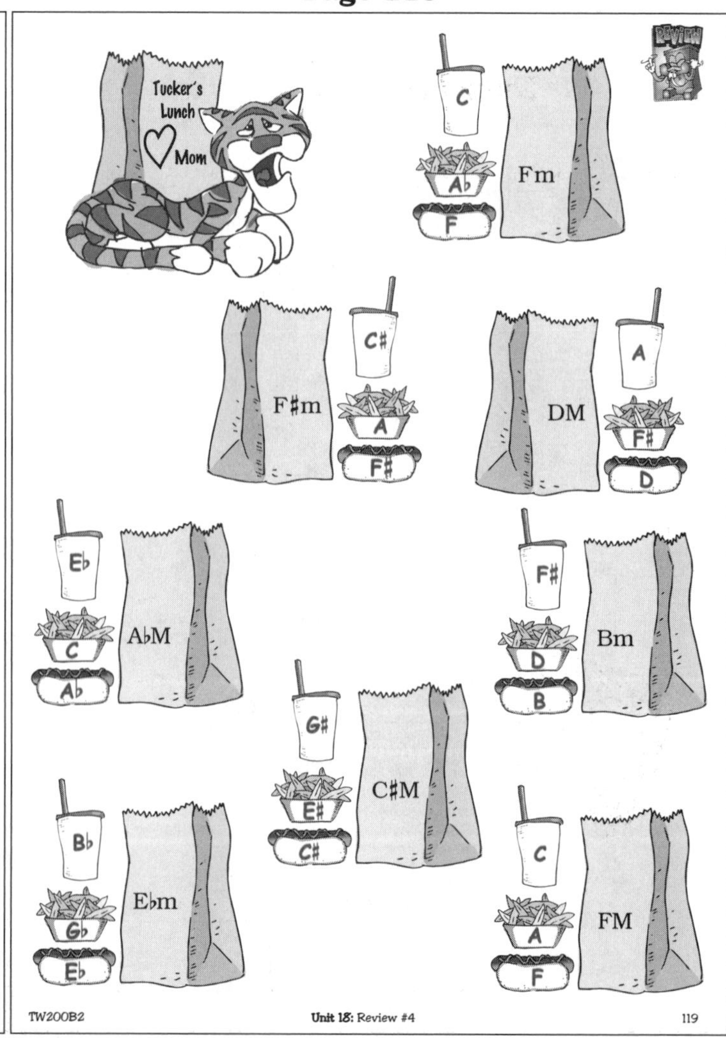

– Page 120 –

Music Detective

Be a music detective! Find these things hidden in the music score on the next page. **Number** and **circle** each one you find. You score ten points for each correct answer. Time yourself - how many points can you get in fifteen minutes?

Answers may vary.

1. This is the guidepost “F above middle C.”
2. This is a quarter rest.
3. This is a perfect 5th.
4. This is a whole step.
5. This is a low F♯.
6. This is a Major 2nd.
7. This is a perfect 4th.
8. This is a whole rest.
9. This is a G Major I chord.
10. This is a repetition.
11. This is a dotted quarter note.
12. This is a barline. It separates the measures.
13. This means “running” tempo.
14. This is a single eighth note.
15. This is a fermata. It means to hold the note.

I scored **150** points in 15 minutes!

– Page 121 –

I'm Gonna Go Eat Worms!

– Page 122 –

Music Detectives Hall of Fame

Now try this music detective game at a more difficult level. Find these things hidden in the music score on the next page. **Number** and **circle** each one you find. Each item is worth 25 points. You only get 15 minutes . . . Go!

Some answers will vary.

1. This is an accent.
2. This is a G Major I chord.
3. This is an eighth rest.
4. This is a half rest.
5. This is a Major 3rd.
6. This is a double bar.
7. This is a half step.
8. This is a brace.
9. This is a staccato.
10. This is a Major 2nd.
11. This is a flat. It tells you to play the note down a half step.
12. This is a *ritardando.* It means to play gradually slower.
13. This is a sign that means to play loudly.
14. This is a decrescendo. It means to play gradually softer.
15. This is a slur. Play these notes smoothly.
16. This is a sign that means to play medium soft.
17. This is a tie. Play the first note and hold through the value of the second note.
18. This is a bass clef sign. Sometimes it is called the F clef.
19. This is a sign that means play medium loud.
20. This is a treble clef sign. Sometimes it is called the G clef.

HALL OF FAME

Name	Score
Charlene	375
Kathleen	475
Laura	425
Tucker the Tiger	450
(your name here)	(your score)

– Page 123 –

Yankee Doodle

– Page 124 –

Rhythm Waterslide Park

For each ticket, add up the total number of eighth note counts and write that number on the ticket. Match the number of each ticket to the slide it will allow you to ride. Can you ride all four slides?

– Page 125 –

Points for Intervals!

A. In *August's Melody*, circle at least five half steps with red, five whole steps with blue, three 3rds with yellow, and two 4ths with orange. Circle more to earn more points! **Answers will vary.**

I like to use the keyboard to picture half steps and whole steps.

Color Key	
red	———
blue	———
yellow	....
orange	———
green	------

August's Melody

B. In *The Determined Waltz*, circle at least ten 3rds with yellow and at least five 5ths with green. Circle more to earn more points!

The Determined Waltz

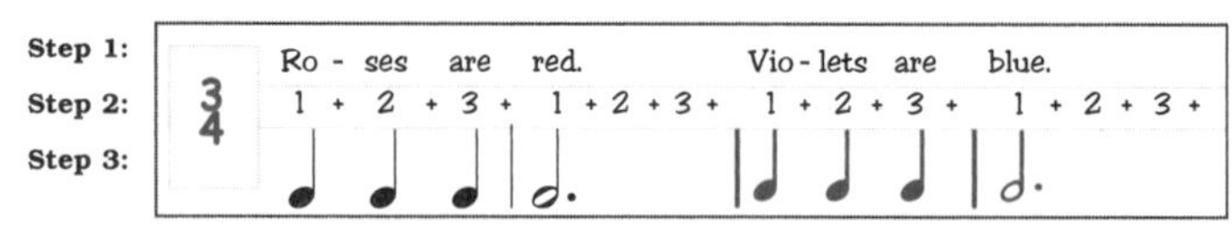

Scorecard
1 point for every half step
2 points for every whole step
3 points for every 3rd
4 points for every 4th
5 points for every 5th

Circle the B Major five-finger pattern in *The Determined Waltz* for a 10-point bonus!

Your Score
152

– Page 126 –

Back to the Rain Forest!

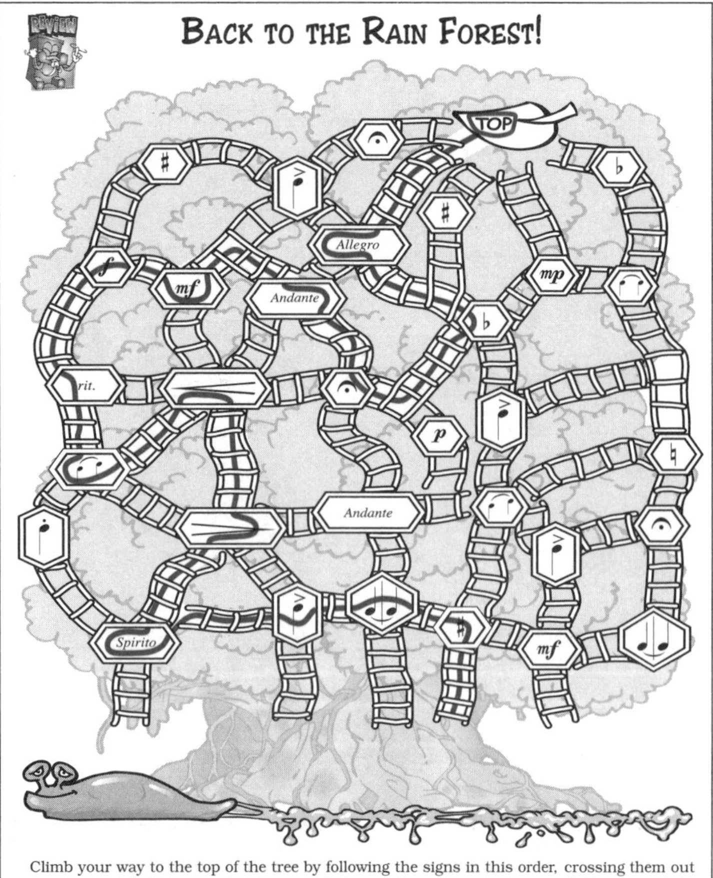

Climb your way to the top of the tree by following the signs in this order, crossing them out as you go: (1) Raises a note ½ step. (2) Curved line joining two notes of the same pitch. The second note is not played. (3) Emphasized. (4) "With Spirit." (5) Gradually softer. (6) Gradually louder. (7) Curved line joining two or more notes that are to be played legato. (8) Gradually slower. (9) Loud. (10) Medium loud. (11) "Walking tempo." (12) Hold. (13) Lowers a note ½ step. (14) "Quickly" – a running tempo.

– Page 127 –

Dune Buggy Rock

A. Compose a rhythm for this poem.

Step 1: Ro - ses are red. Vio - lets are blue.
Step 2: 1 + 2 + 3 + 1 + 2 + 3 + 1 + 2 + 3 + 1 + 2 + 3 +
Step 3:

Dune bug - gies real - ly rock and mu - sic does too!
1 + 2 + 3 + 1+2+ 3 + 1 + 2 + 3 + 1+2+3+

B. Compose a melody using your rhythm for the poem. (See pages 112 -113 for tips!)

– Page 128 –

Unit 19: Listening

You will hear two examples. If they sound the **same**, circle the small picture that matches the big picture. If they sound **different**, circle the small picture that looks different.

Pitch

1.
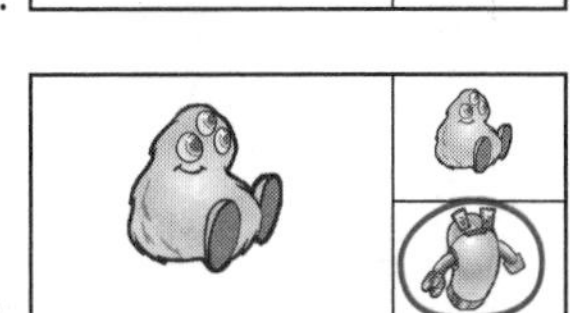
2.
3.
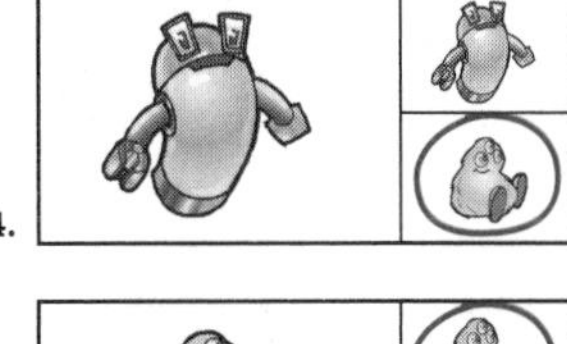
4.
5.

Melody

1.

2.

3.

4.

5.

– Page 129 –

Same or Different

You will hear two examples. If they sound the **same**, circle the small picture that matches the big picture. If they sound **different**, circle the small picture that looks different.

Major I Chord

1.

2.

3.

4.

5.

Minor i Chord

1.

2.

3.

4.

5.

– Page 130 –

High or Low

Circle the frog **pointing up** if the example is a **high sound**. Circle the frog **pointing down** if the example is a **low sound**.

1.

2.

3.

4.

Loud or Soft

Circle the picture of Tuck **roaring** if the example is a **loud sound**. Circle the picture of Tuck **smiling** if the example is a **soft sound**.

1.

2.

3.

4.

– Page 131 –

High or Low and Loud or Soft

Circle **two** pictures in each example that represent what you heard (high or low **and** loud or soft.)

1.
2.

3.
4.

5.

6.

– Page 132 –

Slow or Fast

Tempo indicates whether music should be played slow or fast.

You will hear four examples. Circle something moving **slowly** if you hear music played at a **slow tempo**. Circle something moving **fast** if you hear music played at a **fast tempo**.

Answers may vary.

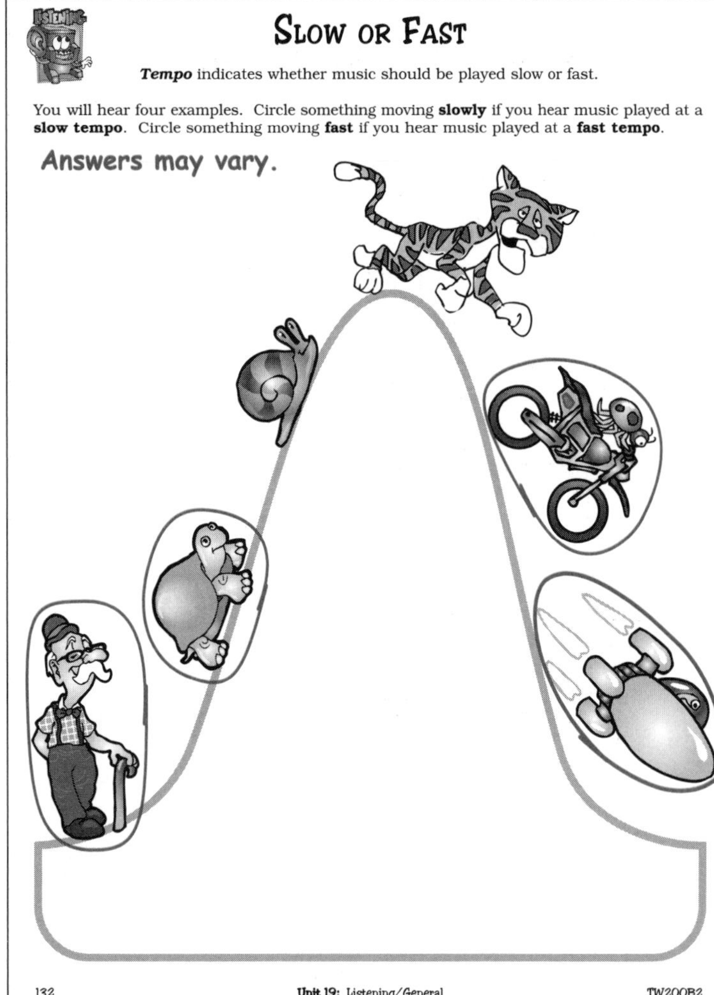

– Page 133 –

Steady or Unsteady

If you hear a **steady beat**, circle the spaceship with the **steady** acceleration. If you hear an **unsteady beat**, circle the worn out spaceship with **unsteady** acceleration.

1.

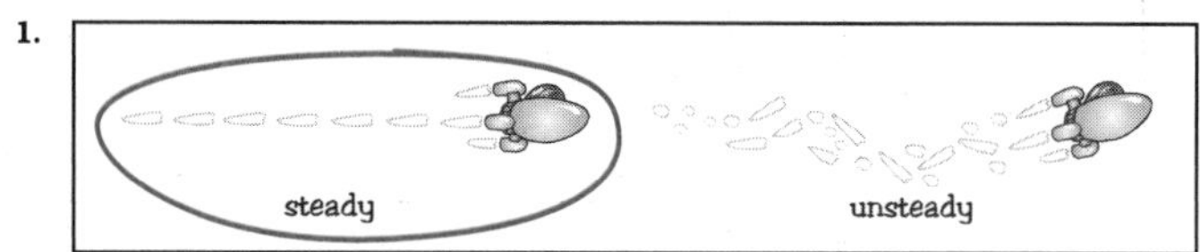

2.

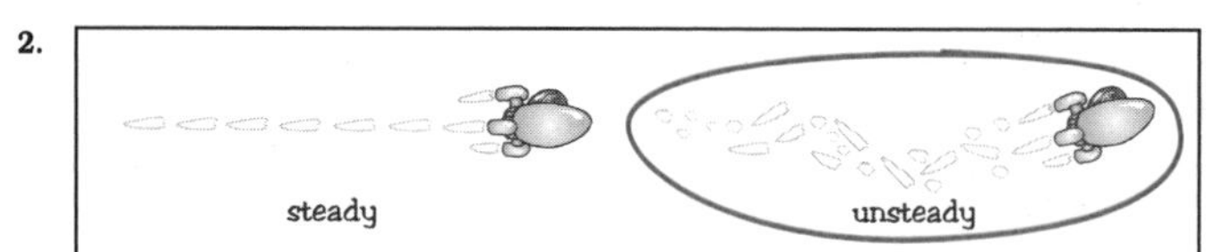

3.

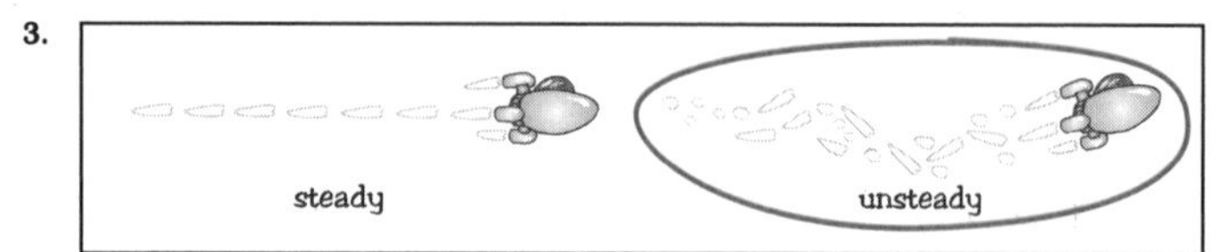

4.

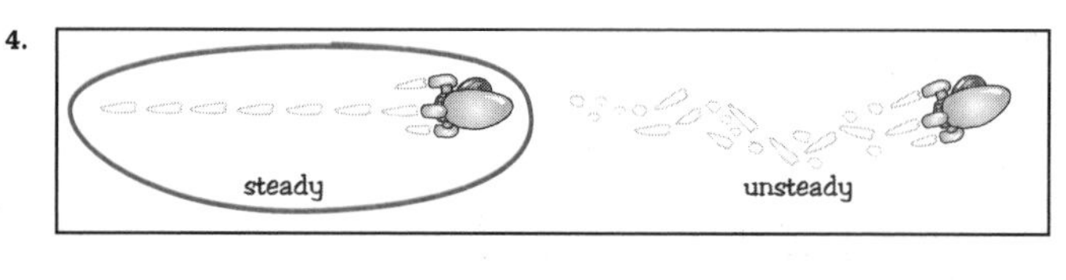

– Page 134 –

Fast or Slow and Steady or Unsteady

Each box below contains pictures that look like four different types of music. After you hear each example, color the box that looks like what you heard.

Color Key

Example #1 - Red Example #2 - Blue Example #3 - Yellow Example #4 - Green

RED BLUE YELLOW GREEN

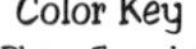

Fast and Steady

Fast and Unsteady

Slow and Steady

Slow and Unsteady

– Page 135 –

Crescendo or Decrescendo (Diminuendo)

For each example, circle a **crescendo** ( ) if the music gets **louder**, or a **decrescendo/diminuendo** ( ) if the music gets **softer**.

1. 2.

3. 4.

Ascending or Descending

If you hear notes that move **up**, circle the **ascending** notes. If you hear notes that move **down**, circle the **descending** notes.

1.

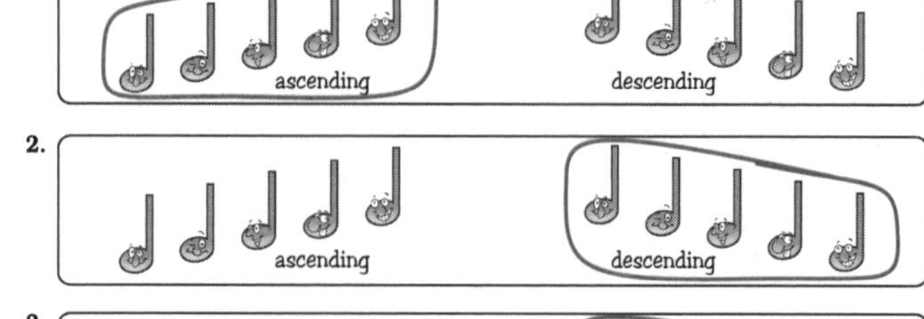

2. ascending descending

3. ascending descending

4.

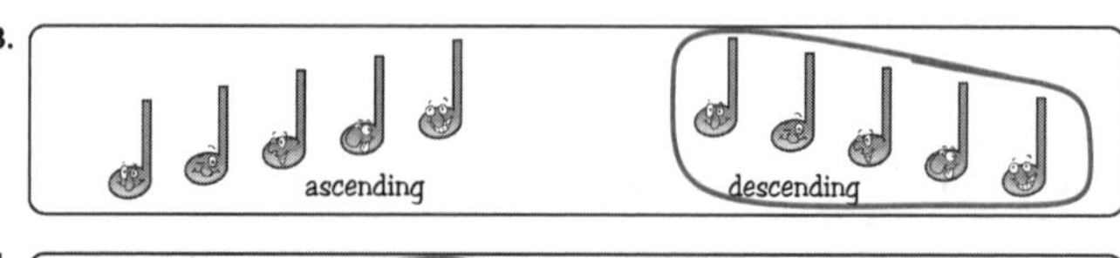

– Page 136 –

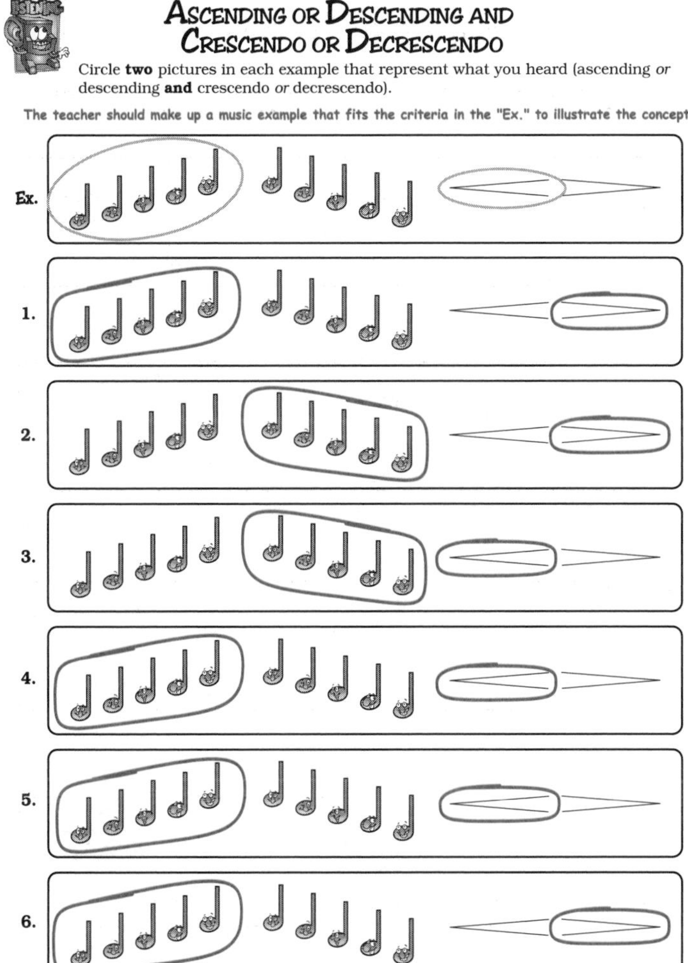

Ascending or Descending and Crescendo or Decrescendo

Circle **two** pictures in each example that represent what you heard (ascending *or* descending **and** crescendo *or* decrescendo).

The teacher should make up a music example that fits the criteria in the "Ex." to illustrate the concept.

– Page 137 –

Same or Different Rhythm

You will hear two rhythms. Decide if the second rhythm is the same or different. Circle the **second** rhythm that you hear.

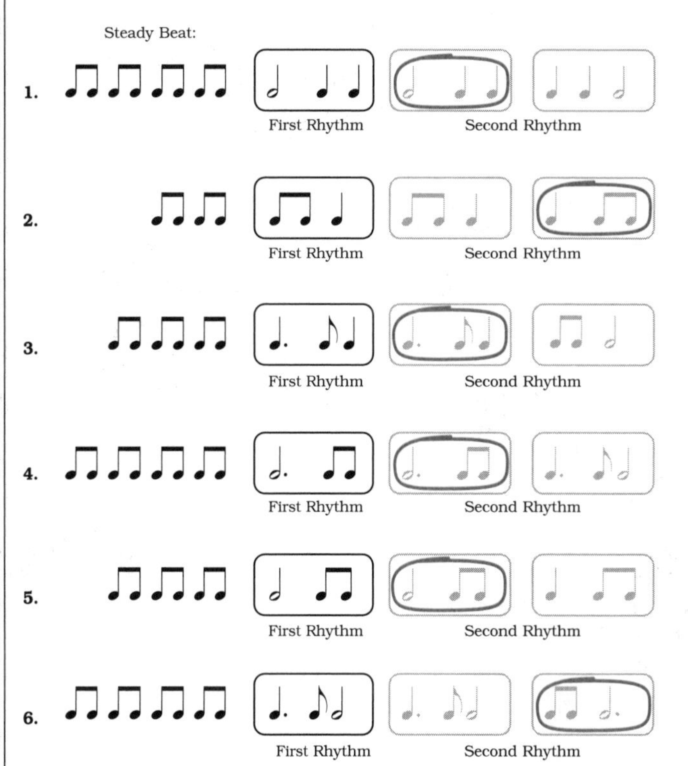

– Page 138 –

What Do You Hear?

For each example there are three rhythms to choose from. Circle the **one** rhythm that you hear.

– Page 139 –

Rhythmic Dictation

Follow these steps when taking rhythmic dictation:

1. The eighth notes for one measure of each time signature are written. As you listen to each example, follow along by counting out loud and pointing to each eighth note.
2. When you hear a note, draw a line through the eighth note you are pointing to.
3. Draw the note values to match the rhythm that you marked.

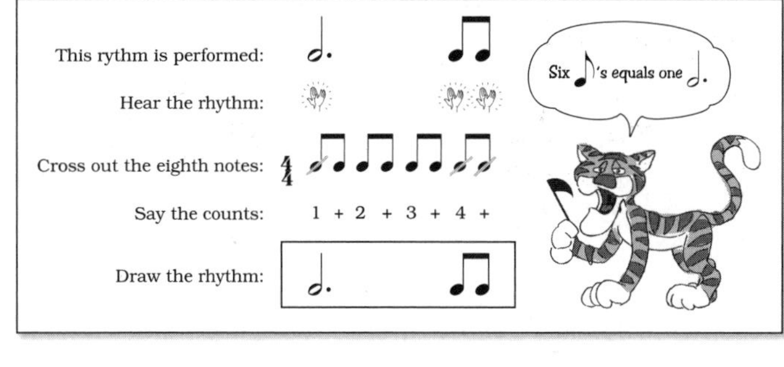

A. Tuck has already marked the eighth notes you will hear. Follow along by counting out loud and pointing to each eight note. Then, draw note values to match the rhythm in the box beside each note.

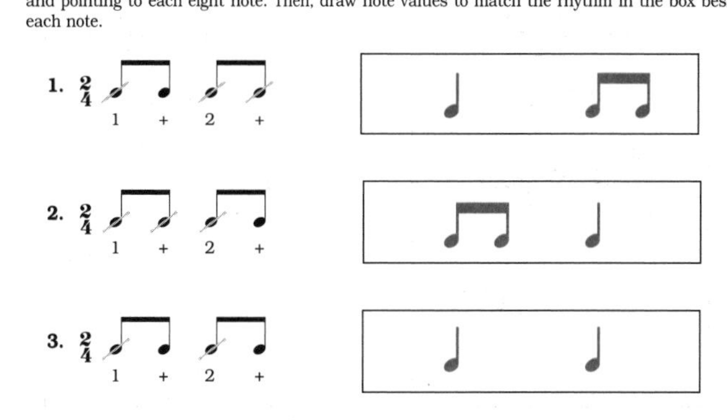

– Page 140 –

Rhythmic Dictation in $\frac{2}{4}$ Time

As you listen to each example, follow along by counting out loud and pointing to each eighth note. When you hear a note, draw a line through the eighth note you are pointing to. In the box beside each example, draw note values to match the rhythm you marked.

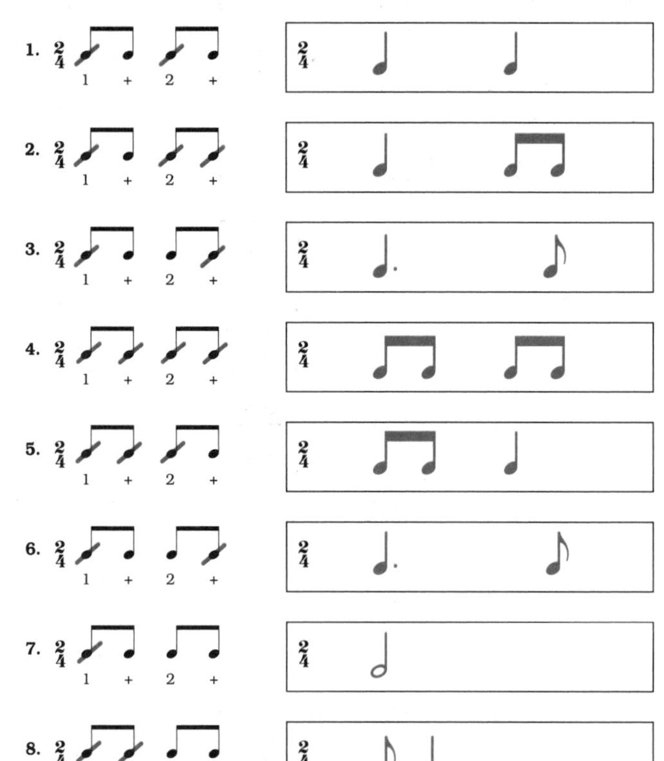

– Page 141 –

Rhythmic Dictation in $\frac{3}{4}$ Time

As you listen to each example, follow along by counting out loud and pointing to each eighth note. When you hear a note, draw a line through the eighth note you are pointing to. In the box beside each example, draw note values to match the rhythm you marked.

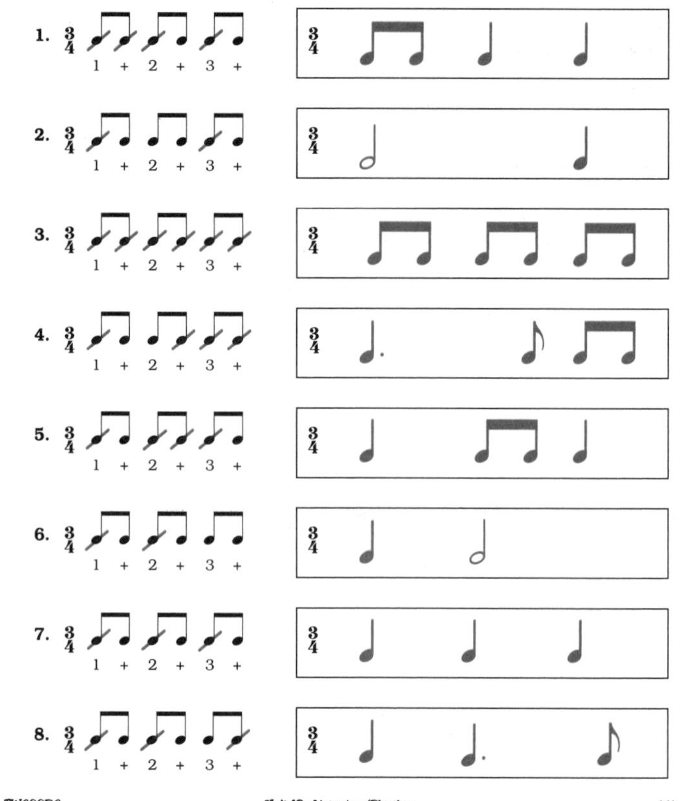

– Page 142 –

Rhythmic Dictation in $\frac{4}{4}$ Time

As you listen to each example, follow along by counting out loud and pointing to each eighth note. When you hear a note, draw a line through the eighth note you are pointing to. In the box beside each example, draw note values to match the rhythm you marked.

– Page 143 –

Major and Minor Five-Finger Patterns

A. Circle yes if you hear a **Major five-finger** pattern and no if you do not.

1.	**yes**	no	6.	**yes**	no
2.	yes	**no**	7.	**yes**	no
3.	yes	**no**	8.	yes	**no**
4.	**yes**	no	9.	yes	**no**
5.	yes	**no**	10.	**yes**	no

B. Circle yes if you hear a **minor five-finger** pattern and no if you do not.

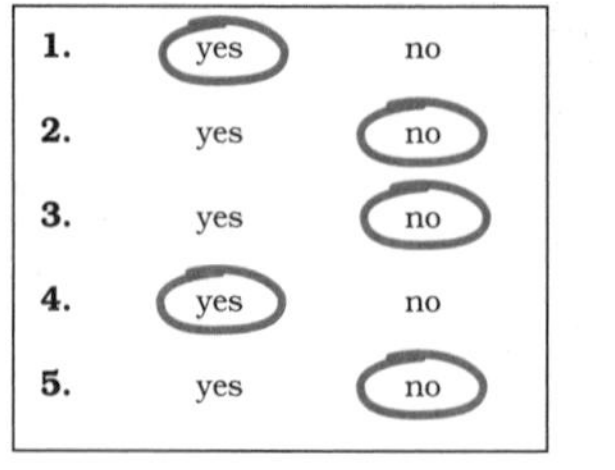

1.	**yes**	no	6.	**yes**	no
2.	yes	**no**	7.	yes	**no**
3.	yes	**no**	8.	**yes**	no
4.	**yes**	no	9.	**yes**	no
5.	yes	**no**	10.	yes	**no**

C. Identify each five-finger pattern you hear as **Major** or **minor**.

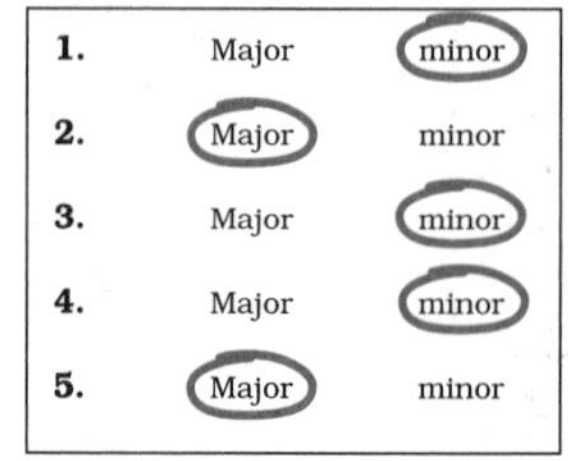

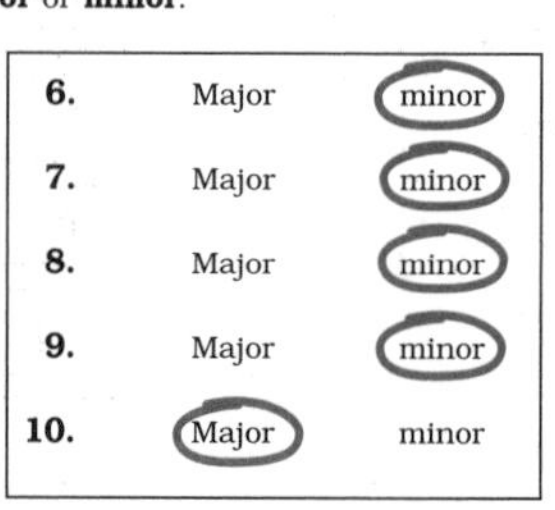

1.	Major	**minor**	6.	Major	**minor**
2.	**Major**	minor	7.	Major	**minor**
3.	Major	**minor**	8.	Major	**minor**
4.	Major	**minor**	9.	Major	**minor**
5.	**Major**	minor	10.	**Major**	minor

– Page 144 –

Major and Minor I/i Chords

A. Circle yes if you hear a **Major I chord** and no if you do not.

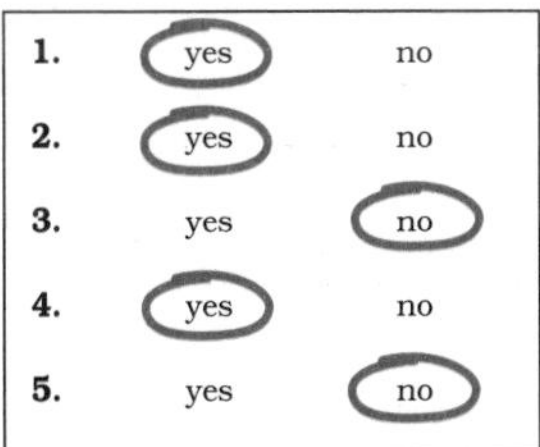

1.	**yes**	no	**6.**	**yes**	no
2.	**yes**	no	**7.**	yes	**no**
3.	**yes**	no	**8.**	yes	**no**
4.	yes	**no**	**9.**	**yes**	no
5.	yes	**no**	**10.**	**yes**	no

B. Circle yes if you hear a **minor i chord** and no if you do not.

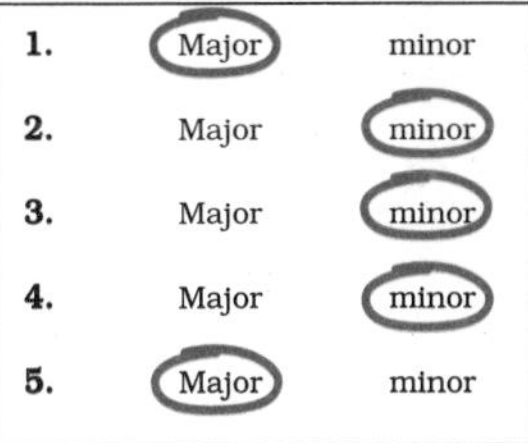

1.	**yes**	no	**6.**	**yes**	no
2.	**yes**	no	**7.**	yes	**no**
3.	yes	**no**	**8.**	yes	**no**
4.	**yes**	no	**9.**	**yes**	no
5.	yes	**no**	**10.**	yes	**no**

C. Identify each I/i chord you hear as **Major** or **minor**.

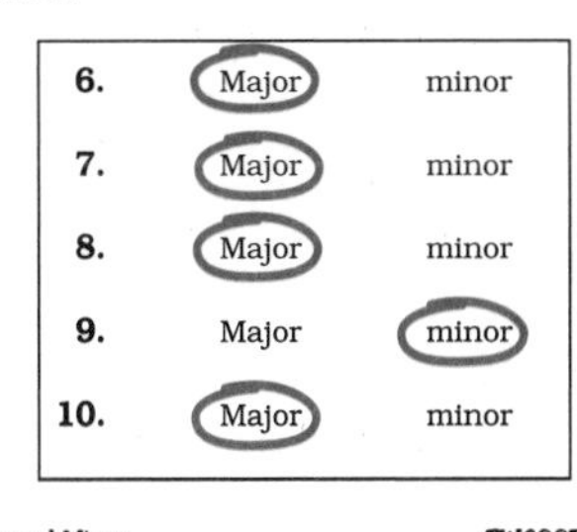

1.	**Major**	minor	**6.**	**Major**	minor
2.	Major	**minor**	**7.**	**Major**	minor
3.	Major	**minor**	**8.**	**Major**	minor
4.	Major	**minor**	**9.**	Major	**minor**
5.	**Major**	minor	**10.**	**Major**	minor

– Page 146 –

Intervals: P1, M2, M3

Identify the interval you hear by coloring the box with the correct answer.

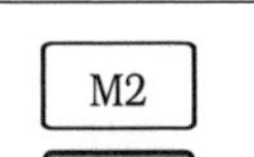

1.	P1	M2	**M3**
2.	P1	**M2**	M3
3.	P1	M2	**M3**
4.	**P1**	M2	M3
5.	P1	**M2**	M3
6.	P1	M2	**M3**
7.	P1	**M2**	M3
8.	P1	M2	**M3**
9.	P1	M2	**M3**
10.	P1	M2	**M3**
11.	P1	M2	**M3**
12.	P1	**M2**	M3
13.	P1	M2	**M3**
14.	**P1**	M2	M3
15.	P1	**M2**	M3

– Page 147 –

Intervals: P1, P4, P5

Identify the interval you hear by coloring the box with the correct answer.

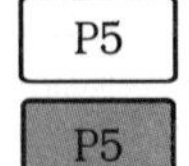
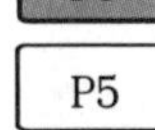

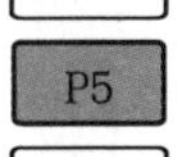

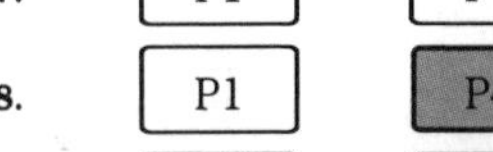
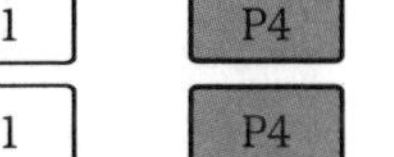
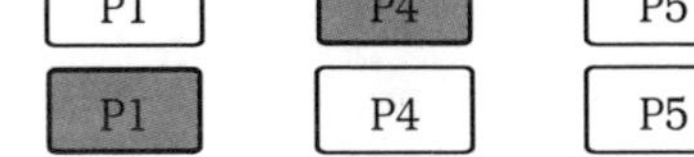
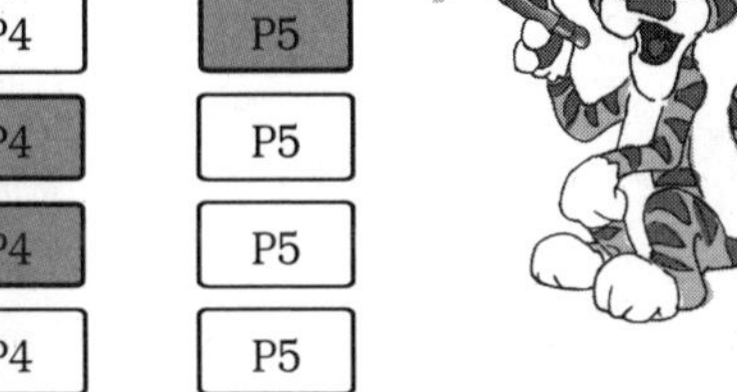
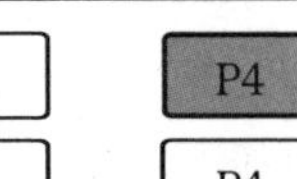

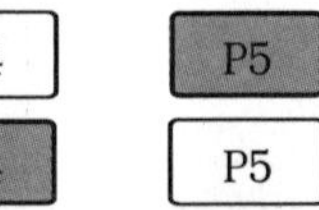
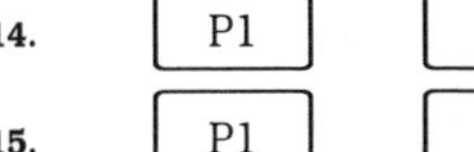
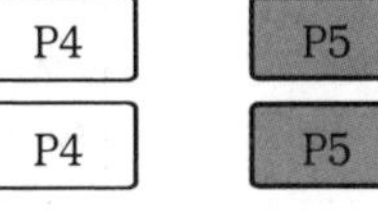

1.	P1	**P4**	P5
2.	P1	P4	**P5**
3.	**P1**	P4	P5
4.	P1	P4	**P5**
5.	P1	**P4**	P5
6.	P1	P4	**P5**
7.	P1	P4	**P5**
8.	P1	**P4**	P5
9.	P1	**P4**	P5
10.	**P1**	P4	P5
11.	P1	**P4**	P5
12.	P1	P4	**P5**
13.	P1	**P4**	P5
14.	P1	P4	**P5**
15.	P1	P4	**P5**

– Page 148 –

Intervals: P1, M2, M3, P4, P5

Identify the interval you hear by coloring the box with the correct answer.

1.	P4	M2	**M3**	**6.**	**P5**	M3	P4
2.	P5	M3	**P4**	**7.**	P1	M2	**P5**
3.	**P1**	M2	P5	**8.**	**M3**	P4	M2
4.	M3	P4	**M2**	**9.**	**M3**	P5	M2
5.	P4	**M2**	M3	**10.**	M2	**M3**	P4

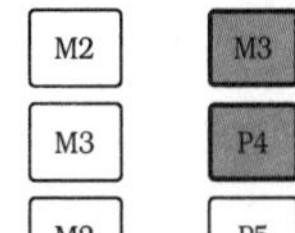
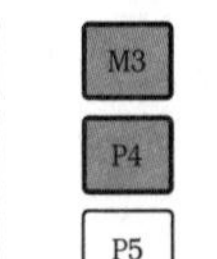
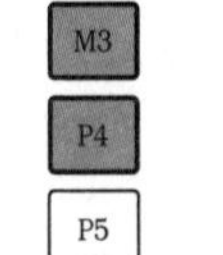
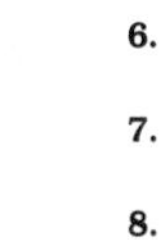
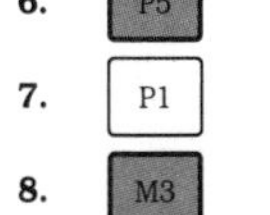
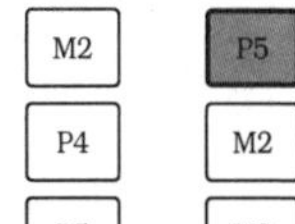
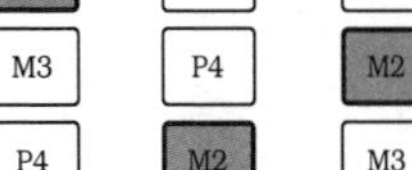
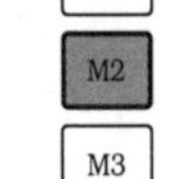
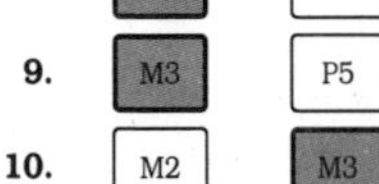

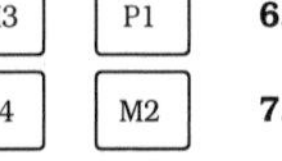
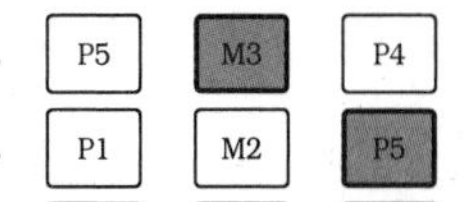
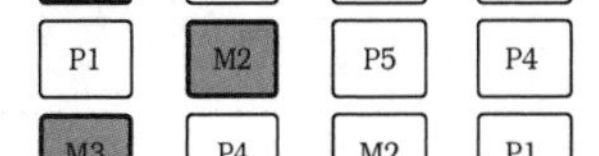
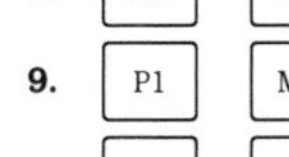
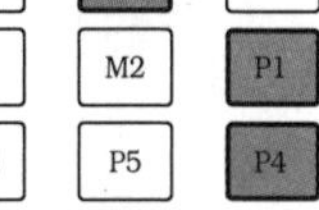
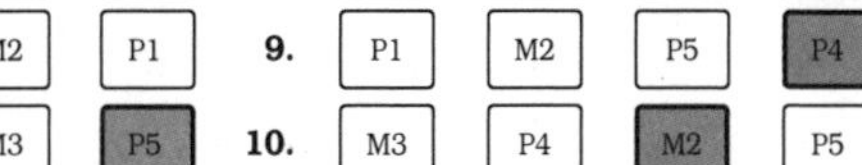

P5 Twinkle, Twinkle Little Star
(Remember: the first note of the interval happens two times.)

M2 Are You Sleeping?

P1 Yankee Doodle

P4 The Farmer in the Dell

M3 The Bear Went Over the Mountain

1.	**P4**	M2	M3	P1	**6.**	P5	**M3**	P4	M2
2.	**P5**	M3	P4	M2	**7.**	P1	M2	**P5**	P4
3.	P1	**M2**	P5	P4	**8.**	M3	P4	M2	**P1**
4.	**M3**	P4	M2	P1	**9.**	P1	M2	P5	**P4**
5.	P4	M2	M3	**P5**	**10.**	M3	P4	**M2**	P5

– Page 149 –

– Page 150 –

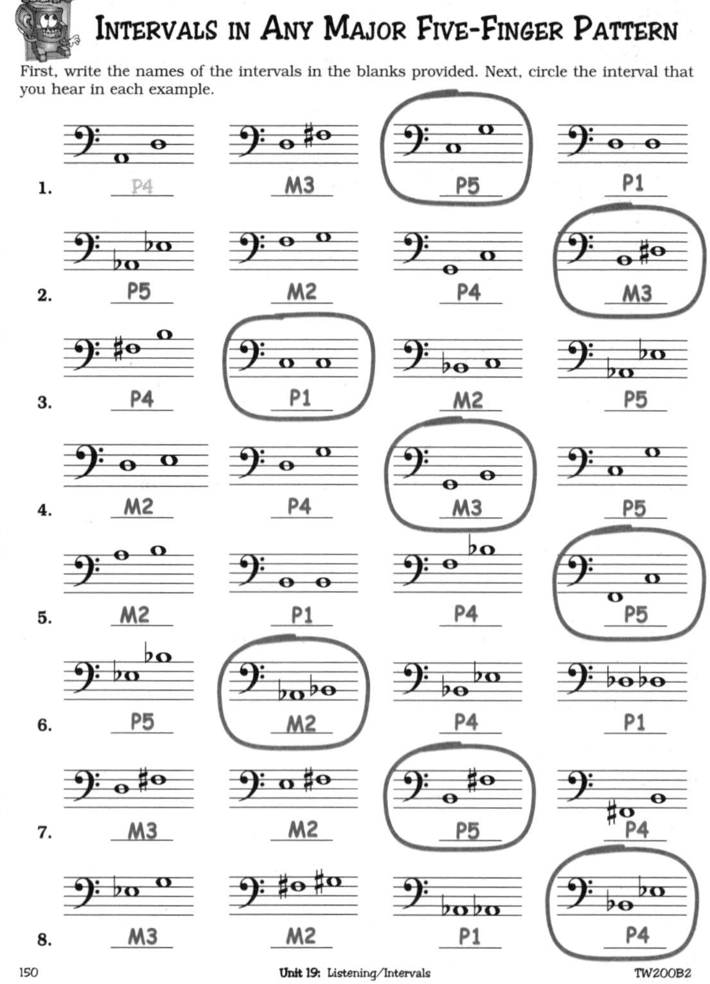

– Page 152 –

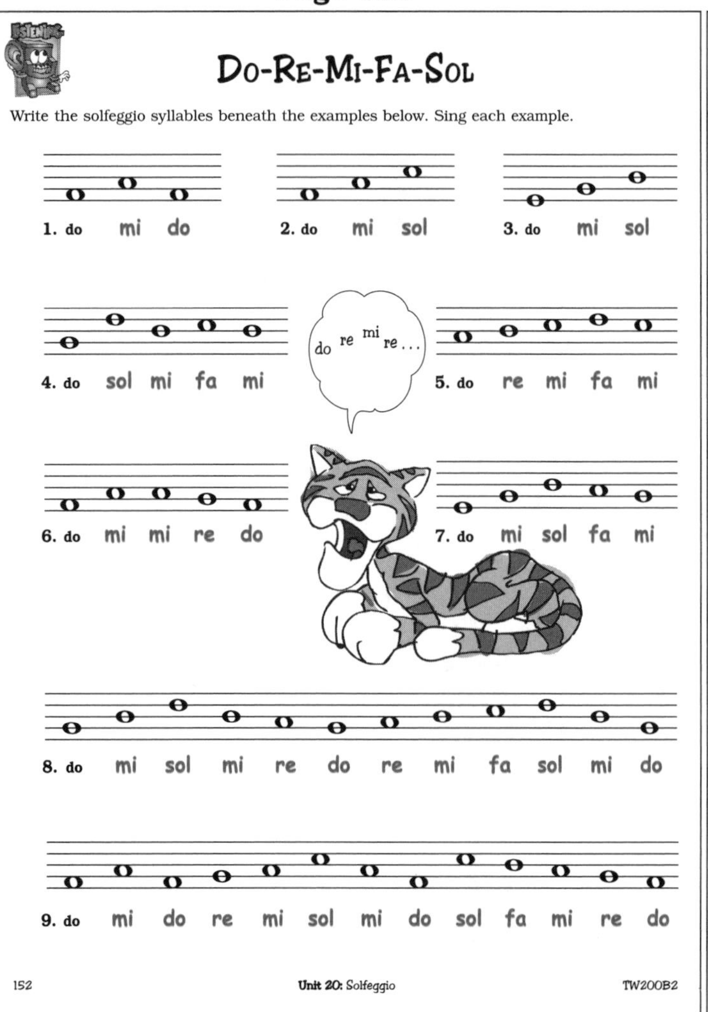

– Page 153 –

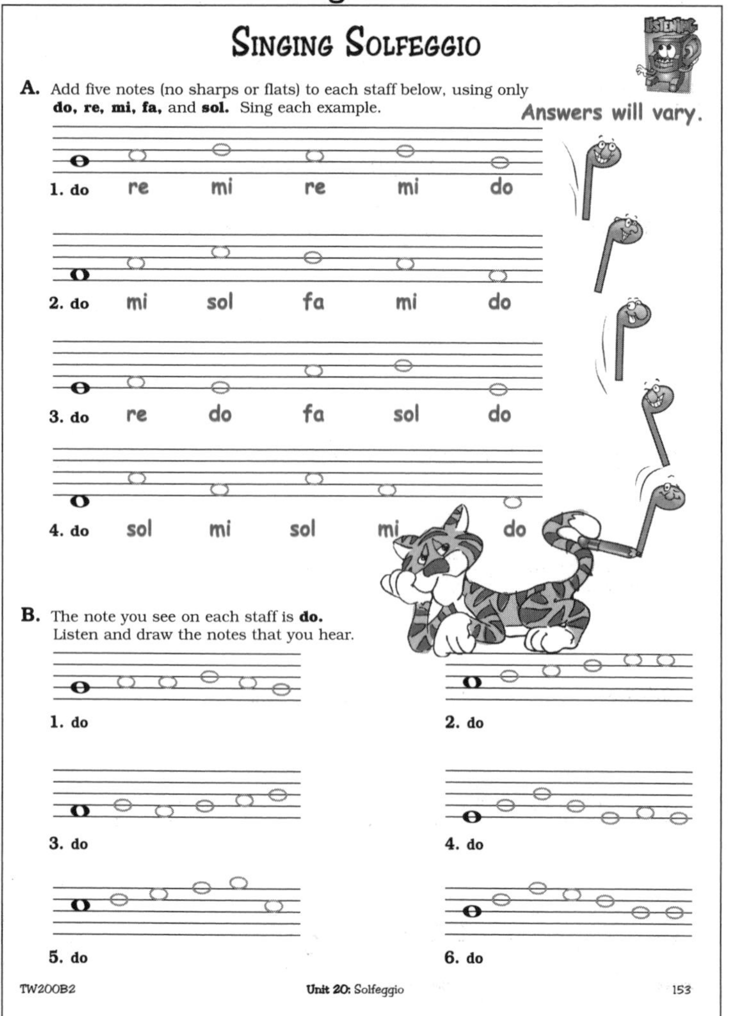

– Page 157 –

In 1823 the first performance of the Ninth Symphony was given. At the end of the concert Beethoven received standing ovations, but he did not hear them and did not see them standing. One of the soloists took the composer's hand and turned him to face the audience. The whole audience erupted. There were handkerchiefs in the air, hats and raised hands so that Beethoven could see the ovation. The theatre house had never seen such enthusiastic applause! At the time it was customary that the king and queen be greeted with three ovations as they entered the hall. Beethoven received five! This was unheard of and the police had to break off this spontaneous explosion of ovations. Beethoven left the concert deeply grateful for the audience's appreciation.

Three years later, Beethoven lay on his bed. There were heavy clouds in the sky. In the afternoon came a terrible blizzard. Thunder made the room shudder. Beethoven opened his eyes and raised his right arm towards the sky with his fist clenched. Then, his hand fell to the ground. His eyes closed. Beethoven died at age 56.

Beethoven was grand in many ways. His piano was big and sturdy. His music could be very soft to very, very loud. He used more lower and higher keys on the piano than anyone ever had. He added instruments to the orchestra for the biggest orchestra yet. He composed a symphony that included a large chorus of singers as well as all the instruments. He was one of the greatest composers to have ever lived!

Complete the timeline by filling in the letters of the events on the left.

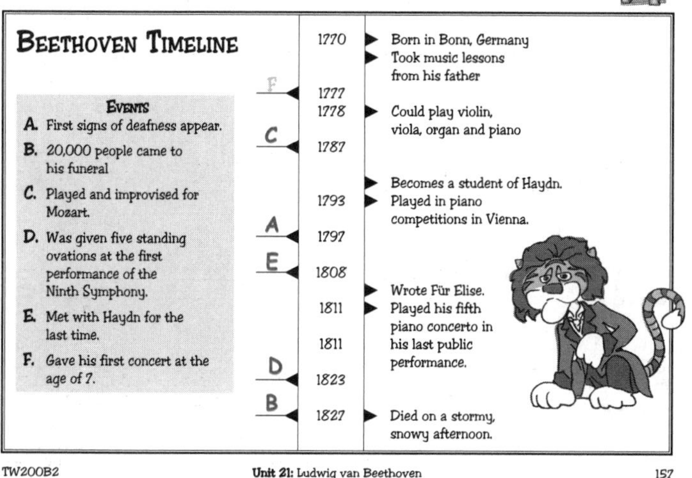

Beethoven Timeline

Events

- **A.** First signs of deafness appear.
- **B.** 20,000 people came to his funeral
- **C.** Played and improvised for Mozart.
- **D.** Was given five standing ovations at the first performance of the Ninth Symphony.
- **E.** Met with Haydn for the last time.
- **F.** Gave his first concert at the age of 7.

Answer	Year	Event
	1770	Born in Bonn, Germany
		Took music lessons from his father
F	1777	
	1778	Could play violin, viola, organ and piano
C	1787	
		Becomes a student of Haydn.
	1793	Played in piano competitions in Vienna.
A	1797	
E	1808	
		Wrote Für Elise.
	1811	Played his fifth piano concerto in his last public performance.
	1811	
D	1823	
B	1827	Died on a stormy, snowy afternoon.

– Page 158 –

Für Elise or Therese?

There is an interesting story about the famous piece *Für Elise* that may or may not be true. When Beethoven was forty years old, he fell in love with a beautiful young student named Therese Malfatti. He was invited to the Malfatti household for a party thrown by Therese's father. Beethoven composed a piece especially for Therese and he planned to propose to her on that night. As the night progressed he became so nervous that he was unable to play the piece *or* propose to her. All he could do was write Therese's name on the music – "Für Therese." After Therese died, the manuscript was found among her things and a publisher who recognized the handwriting as Beethoven's published the work. Unfortunately, Beethoven had very poor handwriting and it was mistakenly read as "Für Elise," which is what it has been called ever since.

Reconstruct this music to be the theme of the famous piece by Beethoven. Number your choices in order from one through seven.

Answers 2 and 5 are interchangable.

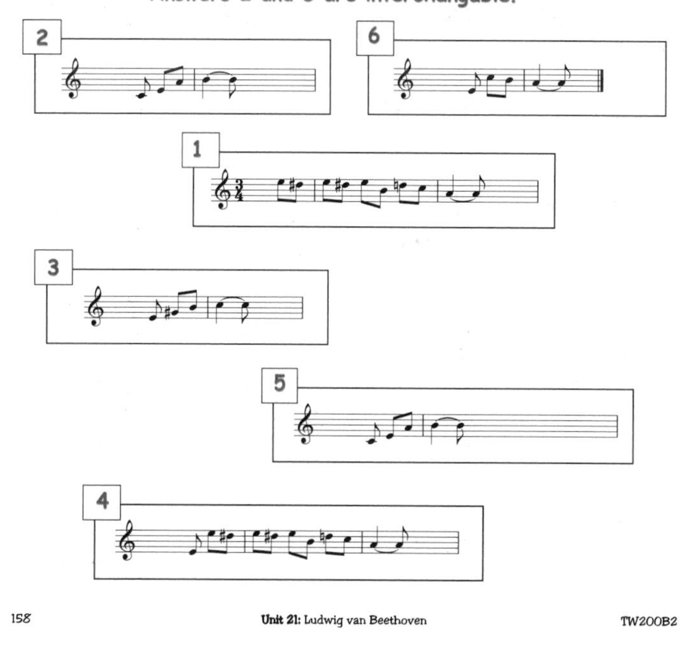

– Page 159 –

Beethoven's Fifth

Below is the first theme of Beethoven's Fifth Symphony. Find and circle the repetitions, then mark each with an "R." Find and circle the sequences, then mark each with an "S."

Exact= solid line Not exact but similar= dotted line

AUDIO CLIPS

The following listening examples (for use with corresponding pages of the student workbook) are also available online as audio clips at *www.kjos.com.* These recordings are professionally produced using a variety of music instrument sounds. They are valuable for independent student work wherever a student has access to the internet. To find these recordings, go to *www.kjos.com,* click on the Kjos Multimedia Library icon and then "Theory."

Spirito Listening Section Music Examples

Based on page numbers in Spirito theory book

Page 128: *Pitch: Same or Different*

1. *Ex. 1* *Ex. 2* **2.** *Ex. 1* *Ex. 2* **3.** *Ex. 1* *Ex. 2* **4.** *Ex. 1* *Ex. 2* **5.** *Ex. 1* *Ex. 2*

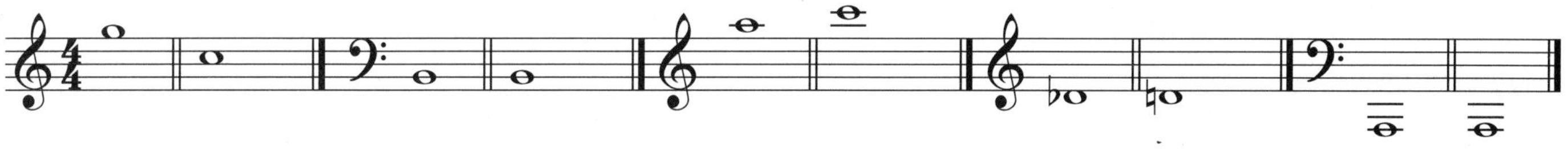

Page 128: *Melody: Same or Different*

1. *Melody 1* *Melody 2*

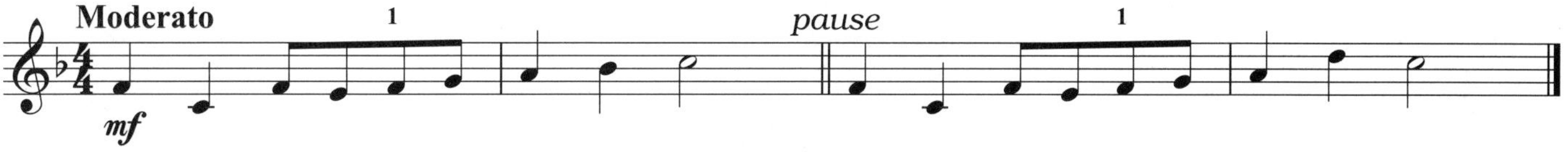

Moderato 1 *pause* 1

mf

2. *Melody 1* *Melody 2*

Allegretto *pause*

1 2 1 1 2 1

3. *Melody 1* *Melody 2*

Allegretto *pause*

mp

4. *Melody 1* *Melody 2*

Allegro *pause*

f

5. *Melody 1* *Melody 2*

Largo *pause*

ff 1 1

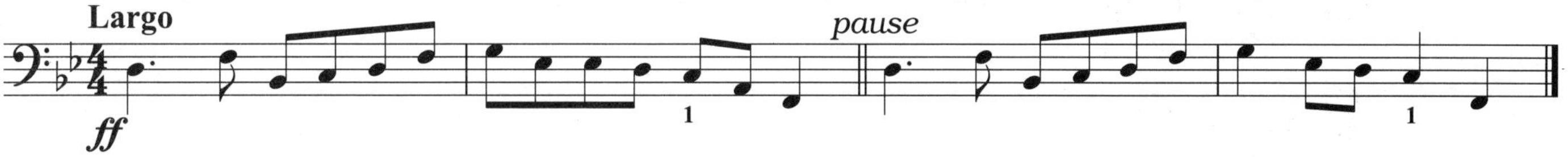

Page 129: *Major I Chord: Same or Different*

1. *Ex. 1* *Ex. 2* **2.** *Ex. 1* *Ex. 2* **3.** *Ex. 1* *Ex. 2* **4.** *Ex. 1* *Ex. 2* **5.** *Ex. 1* *Ex. 2*

Page 129: *Minor i Chord: Same or Different*

1. *Ex. 1* *Ex. 2* **2.** *Ex. 1* *Ex. 2* **3.** *Ex. 1* *Ex. 2* **4.** *Ex. 1* *Ex. 2* **5.** *Ex. 1* *Ex. 2*

Page 130: High or Low
Example 1
Lento
Example 2
Allegretto
Example 3
Allegro
Example 4
Andante
Page 130: Loud or Soft
Example 1
Moderato
Example 2
Moderato
Example 3
Maestoso
Example 4
Allegretto
Page 131: High or Low/Loud or Soft
Example 1
Andante
Example 2
March tempo
Example 3
Slow waltz
Example 4
Moderato
Example 5
Lento
Example 6
Maestoso
Page 132: Slow or Fast
Example 1
Adagio
Example 2
Allegretto

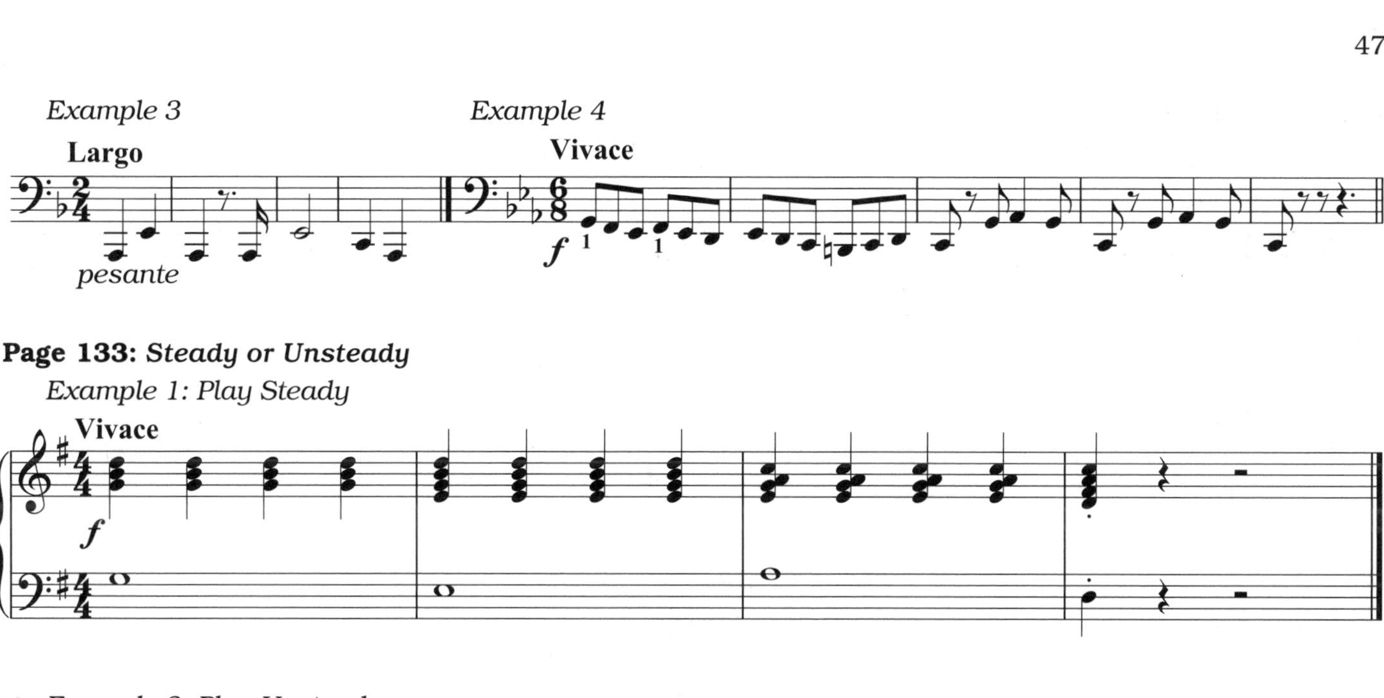

Example 2: Play Unsteady

Example 3: Play Unsteady

Example 4: Play Steady

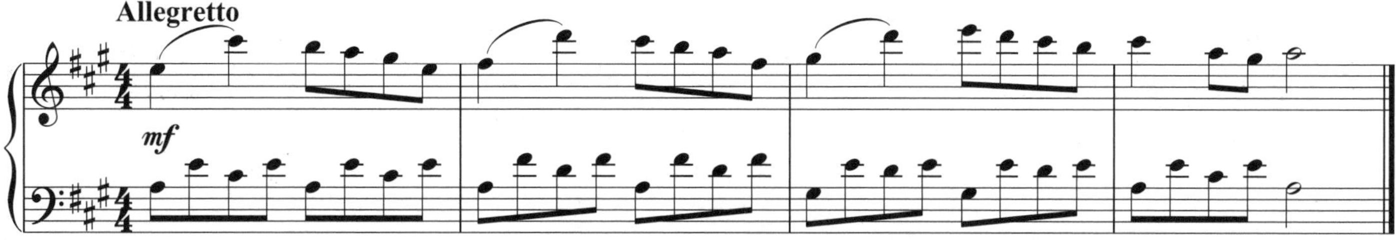

Page 134: ***Fast or Slow/ Steady or Unsteady***

Example 1: Play Steady

Page 134: ***Fast or Slow/ Steady or Unsteady (cont.)***

Example 2: Play Unsteady

Andante

Example 3: Play Steady

Largo

Example 4: Play Unsteady

Allegro

Page 135A: ***Crescendo or Decrescendo (Diminuendo)***

Example 1

Allegretto

f *p*

Example 2

Largo

p 3 *f* 5

Example 3

Andante

p *f* 2 3 3

Example 4

Lento

pp *f*

Page 135B: Ascending or Descending
Example 1
Vivace
mp
Example 2
Moderato
mf
Example 3
Allegretto
pp
Example 4
Adagio
mp
Page 136: Ascending or Descending/Crescendo or Decrescendo (Diminuendo)
Example 1
Vivace
mf
Example 2
Andante
f
Example 3
Allegro
mf
Example 4
Adagio
mp
f
Example 5
Allegretto
p
Example 6
Vivace
f
Page 137: Rhythm: Same or Different
1. First Rhythm
Second Rhythm
2. First Rhythm
Second Rhythm
3. First Rhythm
Second Rhythm
4. First Rhythm
Second Rhythm
5. First Rhythm
Second Rhythm
6. First Rhythm
Second Rhythm

Page 138: Rhythm: Which Do You Hear?
Example 1
Example 2
Example 3
Example 4
Example 5
Example 6
Page 139: Rhythm: Dictation
Example 1
Example 2
Example 3
Page 140: Rhythm: Dictation in $\frac{2}{4}$
Example 1
Example 2
Example 3
Example 4
Example 5
Example 6
Example 7
Example 8
Page 141: Rhythm: Dictation in $\frac{3}{4}$
Example 1
Example 2
Example 3
Example 4
Example 5
Example 6
Example 7
Example 8
Page 142: Rhythm: Dictation in $\frac{4}{4}$
Example 1
Example 2
Example 3
Example 4
Example 5
Example 6
Example 7
Example 8

Page 143: ***Five-Finger Patterns***

A. Major

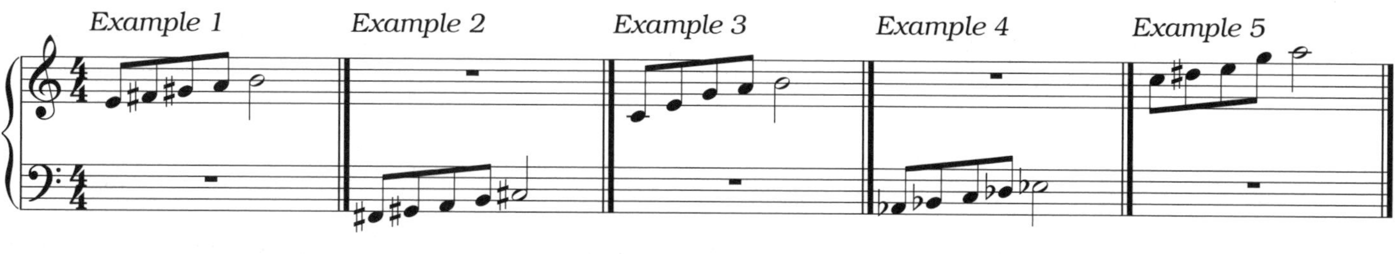

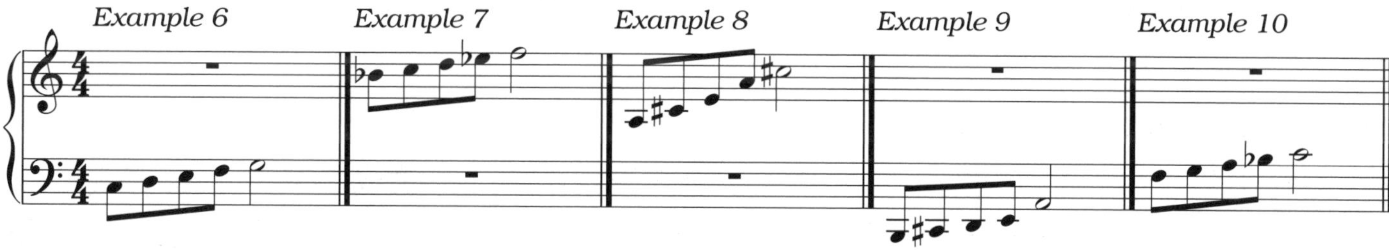

Page 143: ***Five-Finger Patterns***

B. Minor

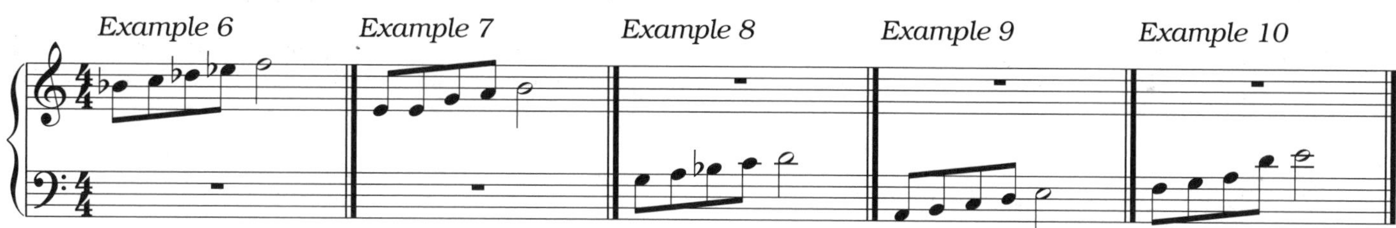

Page 143: ***Five-Finger Patterns***

C. Major or Minor

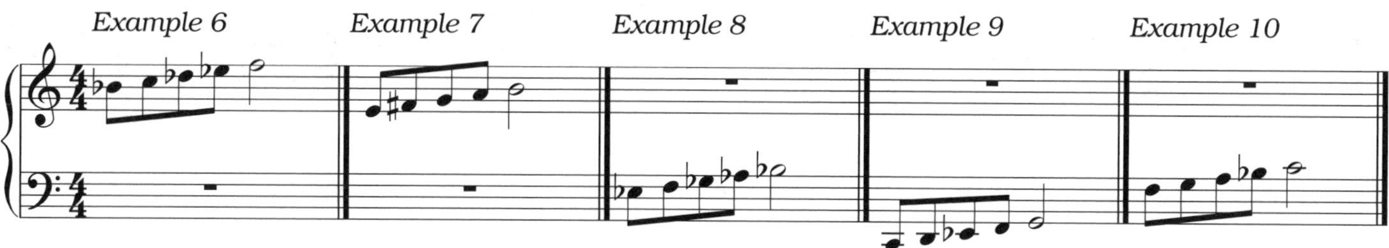

Page 144: ***Major and Minor I/i Chords***

A. Major

Page 144: ***Major and Minor I/i Chords***

B. Minor

Page 144: ***Major and Minor I/i Chords***

C. Major or Minor

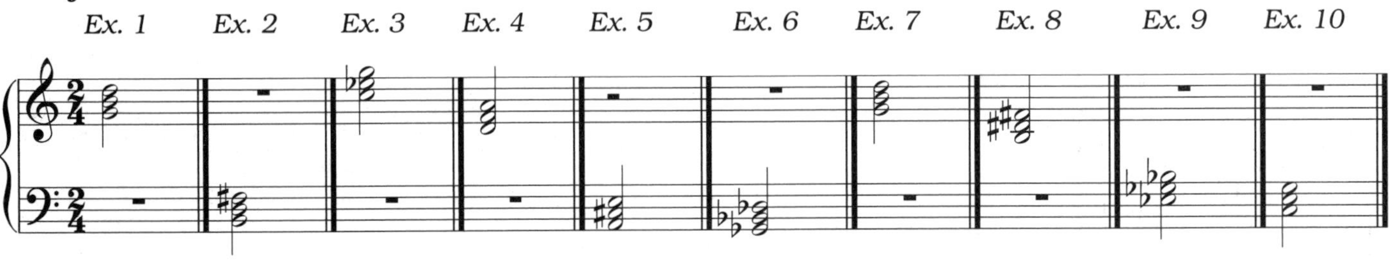

Page 146: ***Intervals: P1, M2, M3***

Page 147: ***Intervals: P1, P4, P5***

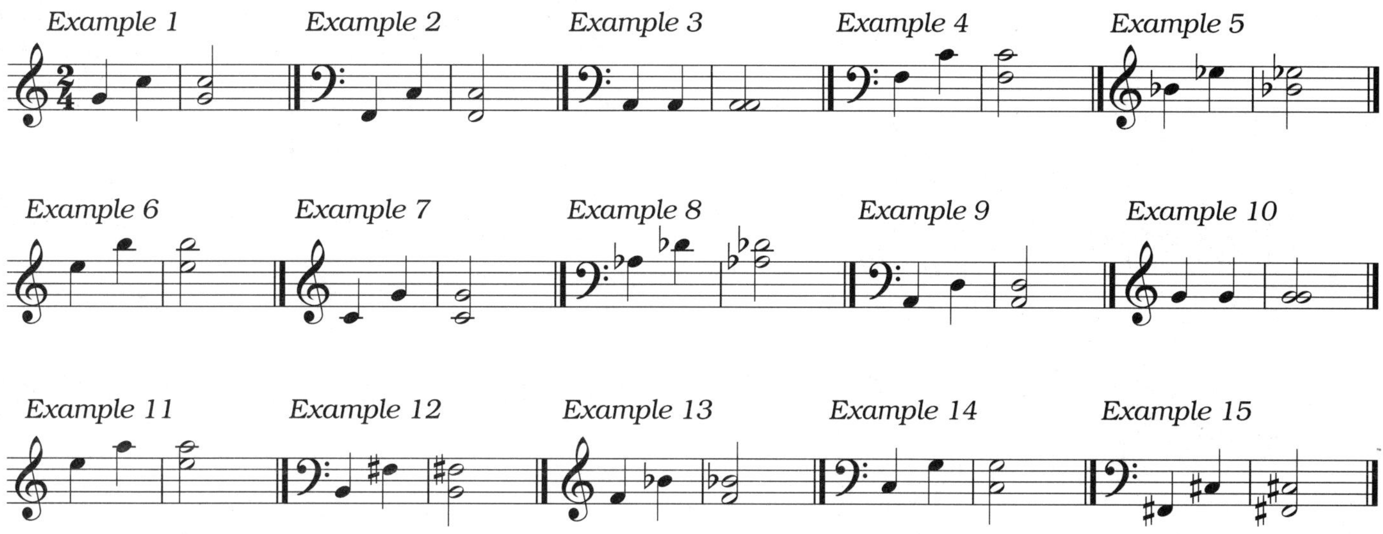

Page 148: ***Intervals: Top - P1, M2, M3, P4, P5***

Page 148: ***Intervals: Bottom - P1, M2, M3, P4, P5***

Page 149: ***Intervals in Any Major Five-Finger Pattern***

Page 150: ***Intervals in Any Major Five-Finger Pattern***

Page 153-B: ***Solfeggio: Melodic Dictation***

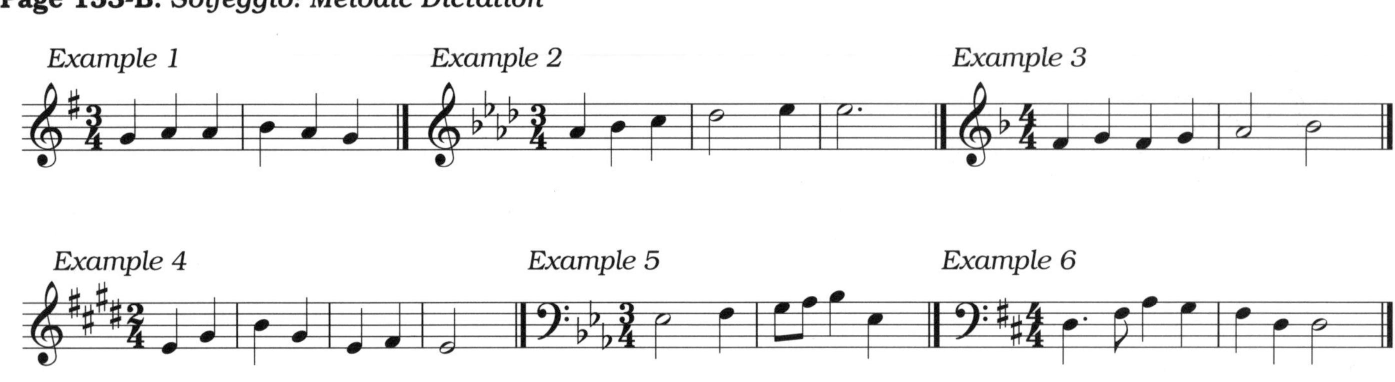

Keyboard Gymnastics®

Theory Test
Level B2
(Spirito)
Form A

Name______________________ **Date**__________ Score_____ /100

Points

1. Name the notes in the boxes provided. *15*

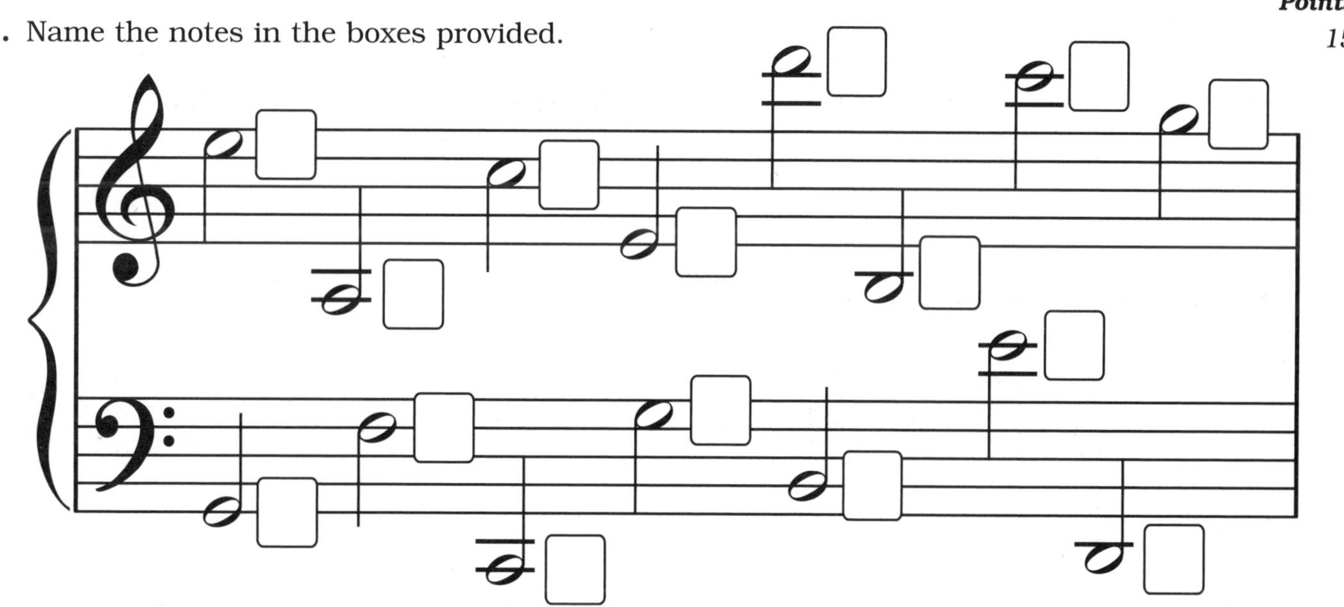

2. Write only one name for each of the shaded keys. (Enharmonic spellings are not necessary.) *8*

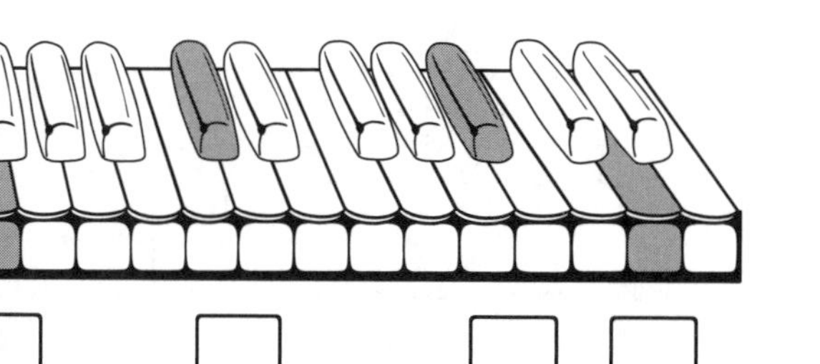

3. Circle the **dotted quarter note**. *2*

A.  B.  C.  D. 

4. Circle the **whole rest**. *2*

A.  B. C.  D.

5. The time signature $\frac{4}{4}$ means there are ☐ beats in every measure. *1*

6. Write the counts beneath each note and rest in the rhythm below. *4*

7. Mark the keys on the keyboard (with an X) to match the notes on the staff. Decide if the notes are a half step or whole step apart. **Circle your answer.** *6*

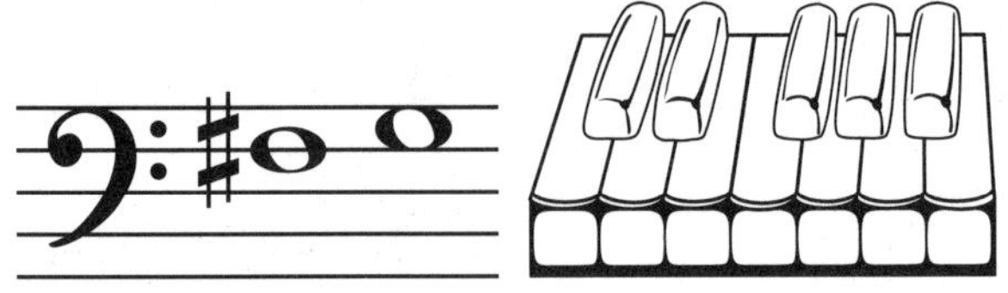

Half Step or Whole Step?

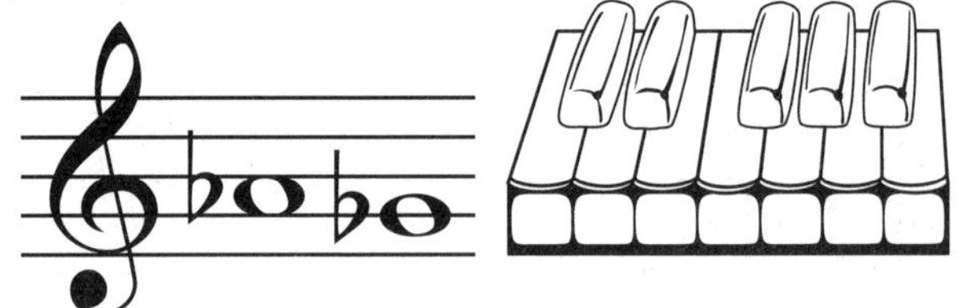

Half Step or Whole Step?

8. Mark the keys that belong to the **Major five-finger patterns** on the keyboards below. Using whole notes, draw the five-finger patterns and I chords on the staff. *12*

F Major
Five-Finger Pattern

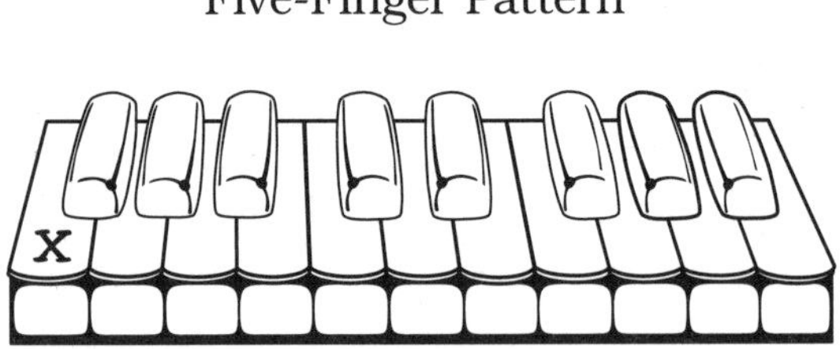

F Major
Five-Finger Pattern

FM
I Chord

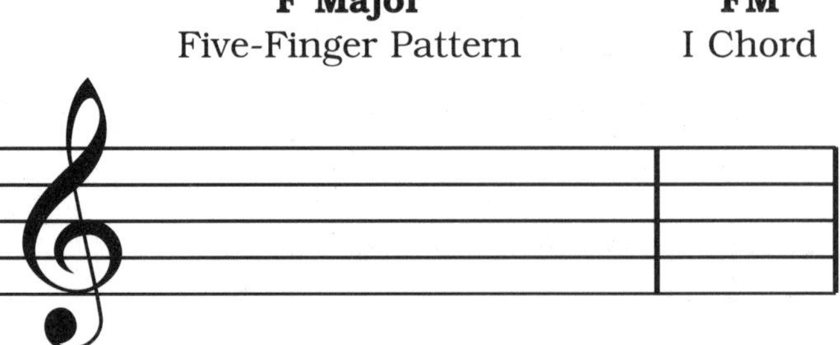

B Major
Five-Finger Pattern

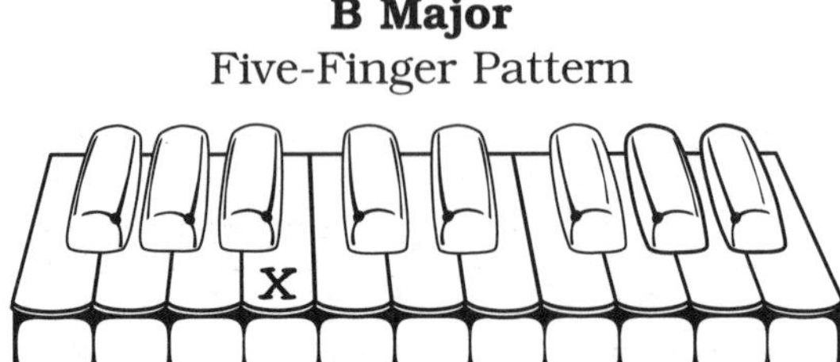

B Major
Five-Finger Pattern

BM
I Chord

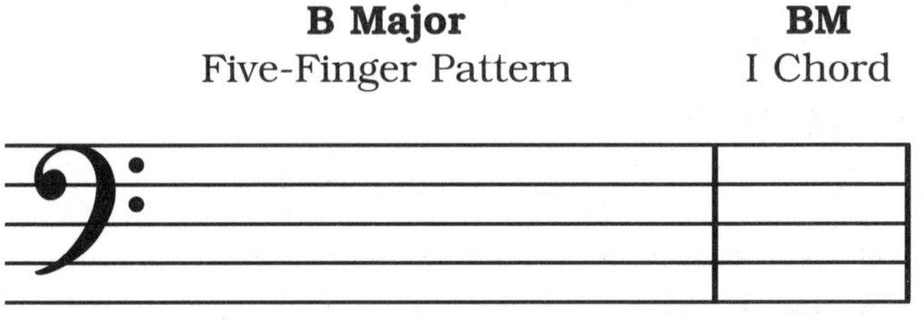

9. Mark the keys that belong to the **Major I chords** on the keyboards below. Using whole notes, draw the I chords on the staff. *5*

G Major
I Chord

G M
I Chord

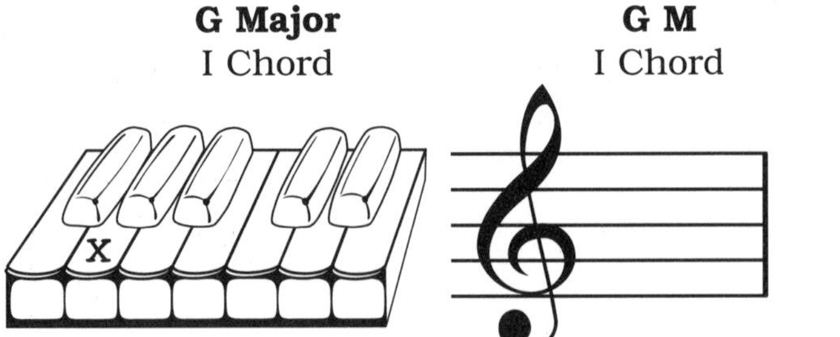

E♭ Major
I Chord

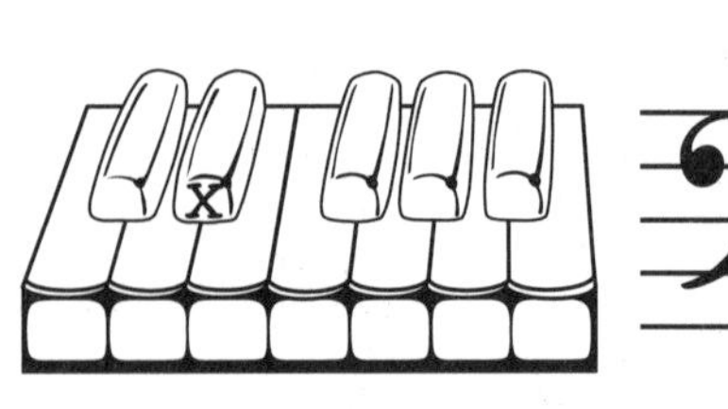

E♭M
I Chord

10. Mark the key that completes each interval with an X. *3*

F Major: M3

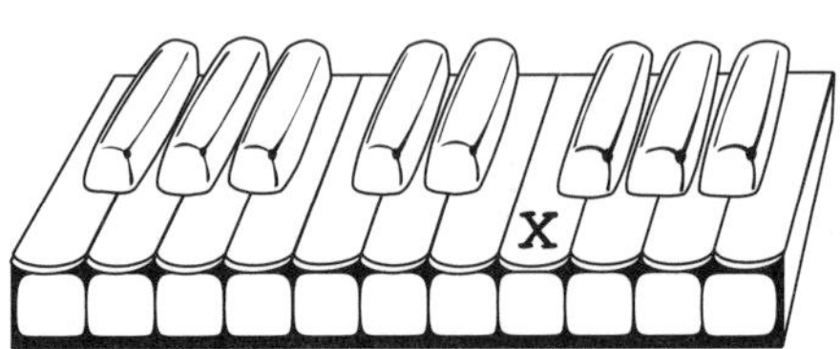

A Major: M2

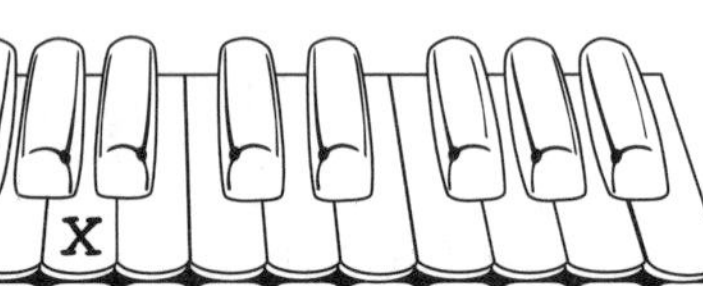

B♭Major: P4

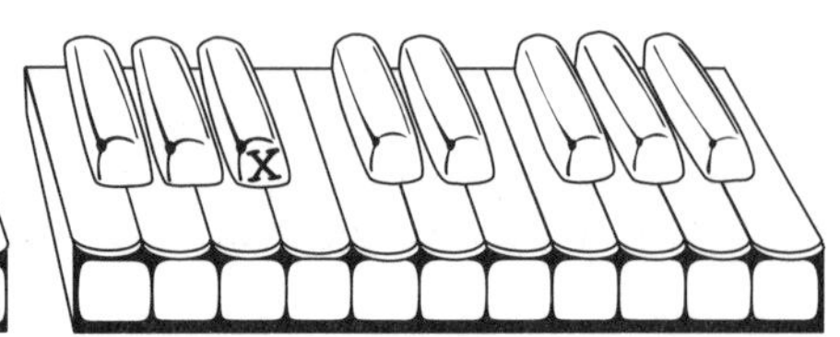

Points

11. Draw the note and accidental (if needed) to form the given interval. 3

F♯ Major: M3

C Major: P4

G Major: M2

12. Mark the keys that belong to the **minor five-finger patterns** on the keyboards below. Using whole notes, draw the five-finger patterns and I chords on the staff. 12

A minor
Five-Finger Pattern

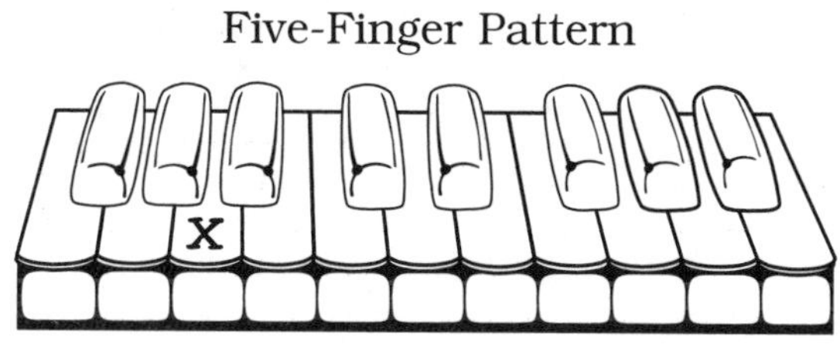

A minor
Five-Finger Pattern

Am
i Chord

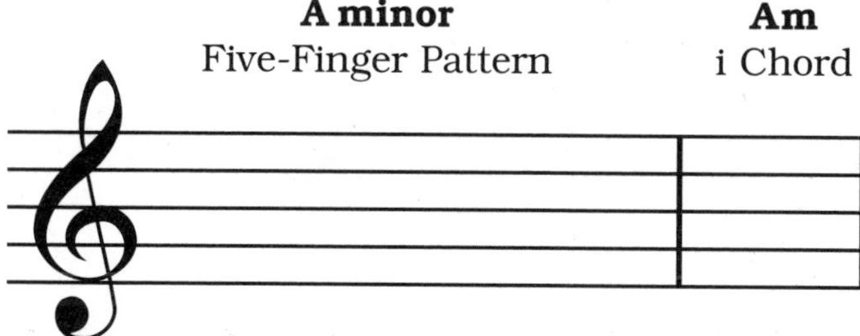

G minor
Five-Finger Pattern

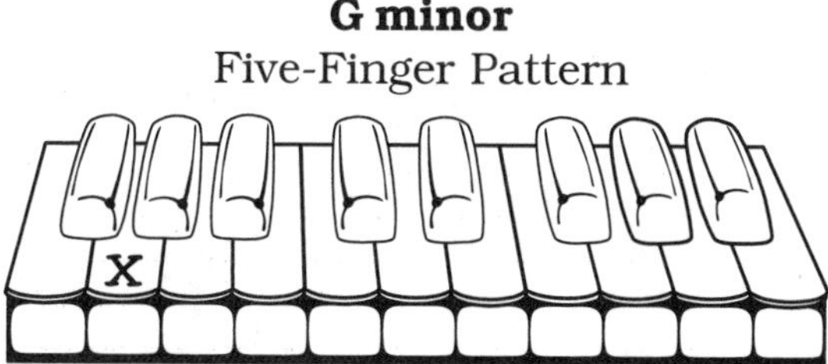

G minor
Five-Finger Pattern

Gm
i Chord

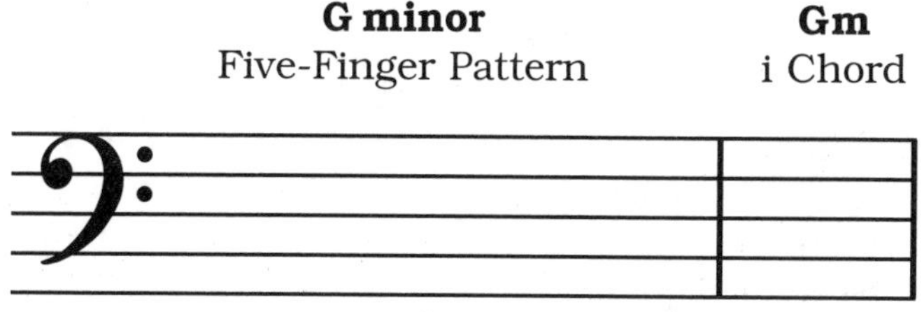

13. Mark the keys that belong to the **minor i chords** on the keyboards below. Using whole notes, draw the i chords on the staff. 5

F♯ minor
i Chord

F♯ minor
i Chord

D minor
i Chord

D minor
i Chord

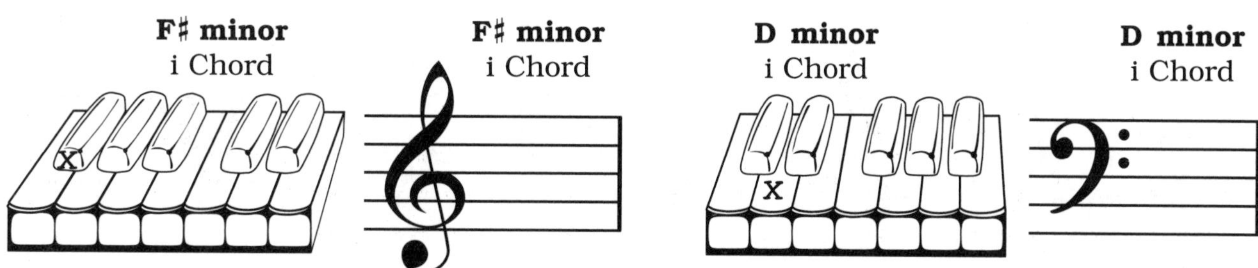

14. True or **False**. Beethoven gave public concerts to earn money.
He made the programs, sold tickets and cleaned the hall. 2

15. True or **False**. Beethoven was born in America. 2

I'm Done Workin' on the Railroad!

Points

16. There are many things circled in **I'm Done Workin' on the Railroad!** Find each sign and term listed below and write its number in the box provided. Write the number of the matching sign by the term in the box provided. *18*

Not all of the circled items will be matched below.

☐	Crescendo	☐	Accent	☐	Dynamic marking that means "loud"	☐	A whole step
☐	Staccato	☐	Brace	☐	Term meaning "slow down gradually"	☐	F Major I chord
☐	Treble clef	☐	Fermata	☐	P4 (Perfect fourth)	☐	Sequence
☐	Tie	☐	Decrescendo	☐	Term meaning "running tempo"	☐	Sharp
☐	Natural	☐	A dotted quarter note				

Keyboard Gymnastics®

Theory Test
Level B2
(Spirito)
Form A

Name KEY **Date** ______ Score ______ /100

Points

1. Name the notes in the boxes provided. *15*

E A C E D B C G
G F C G B E D

2. Write only one name for each of the shaded keys. (Enharmonic spellings are not necessary.) *8*

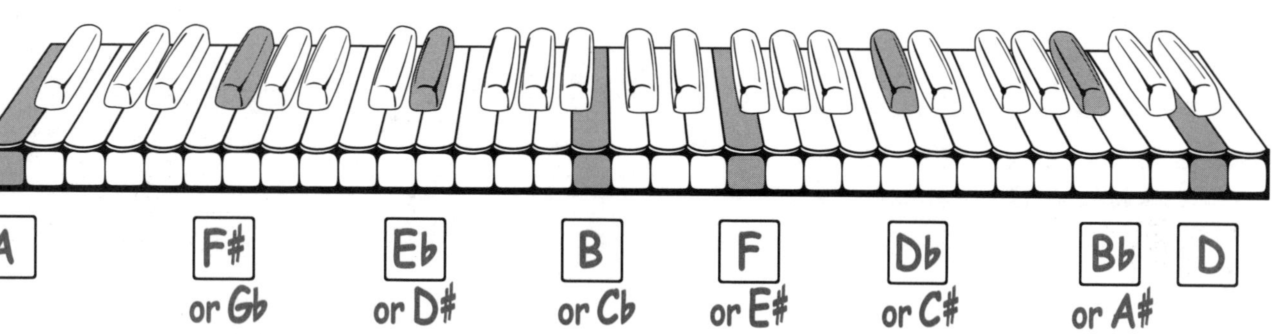

3. Circle the **dotted quarter note**. *2*

A.  B.  C. D. 

4. Circle the **whole rest**. *2*

A.  B.  C.  D. 

5. The time signature $\frac{4}{4}$ means there are 4 beats in every measure. *1*

6. Write the counts beneath each note and rest in the rhythm below. *4*

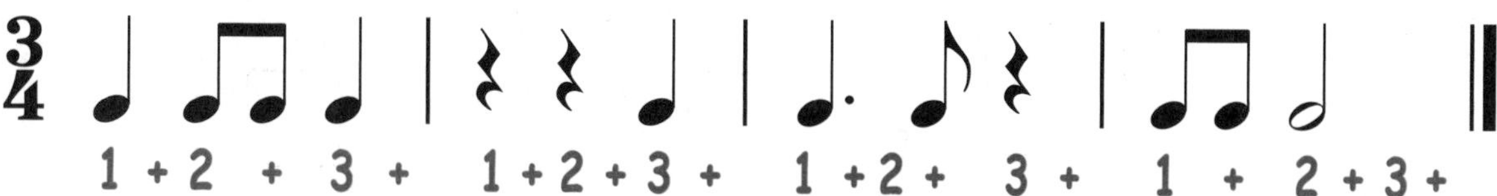

Points

7. Mark the keys on the keyboard (with an X) to match the notes on the staff. Decide if the notes are a half step or whole step apart. **Circle your answer.** *6*

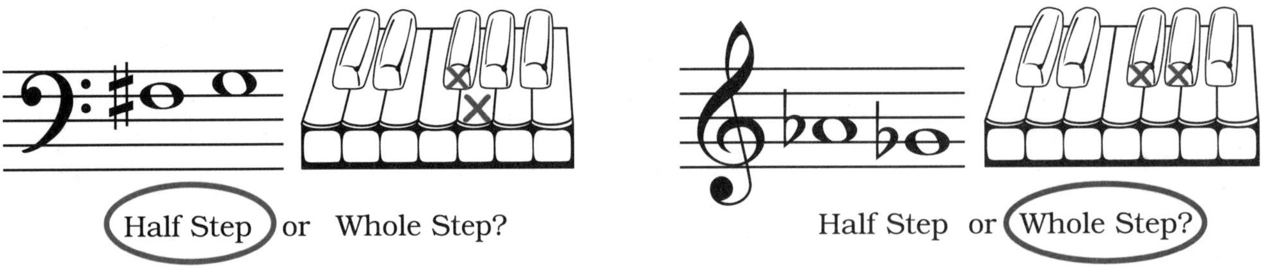

8. Mark the keys that belong to the **Major five-finger patterns** on the keyboards below. Using whole notes, draw the five-finger patterns and I chords on the staff. *12*

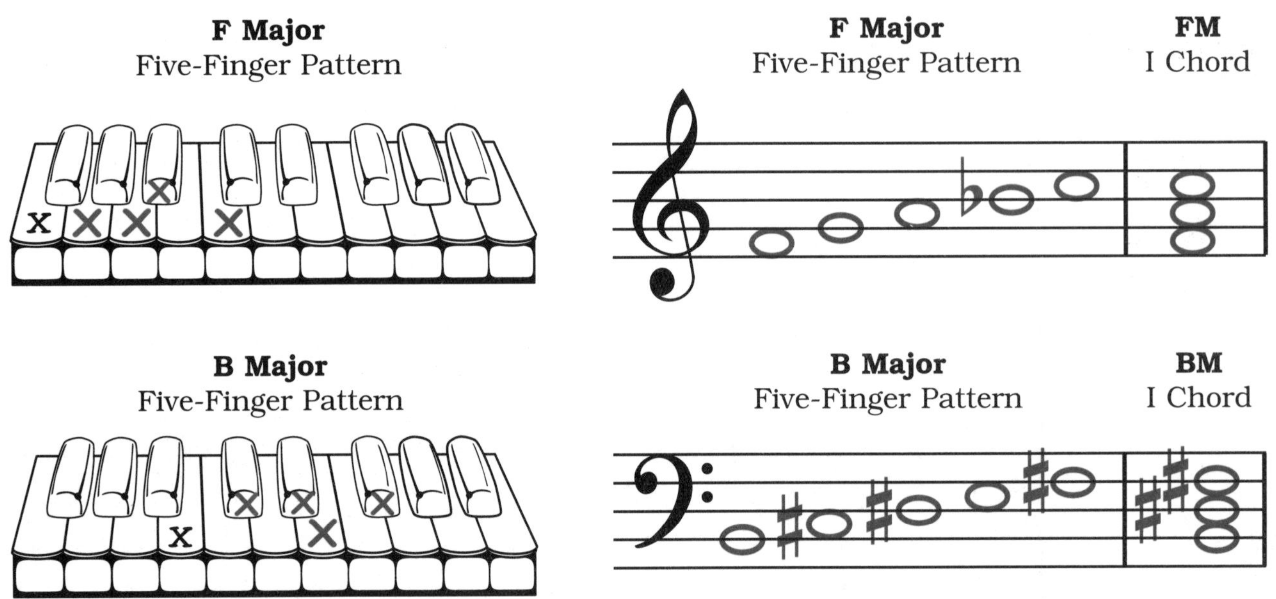

9. Mark the keys that belong to the **Major I chords** on the keyboards below. Using whole notes, draw the I chords on the staff. *5*

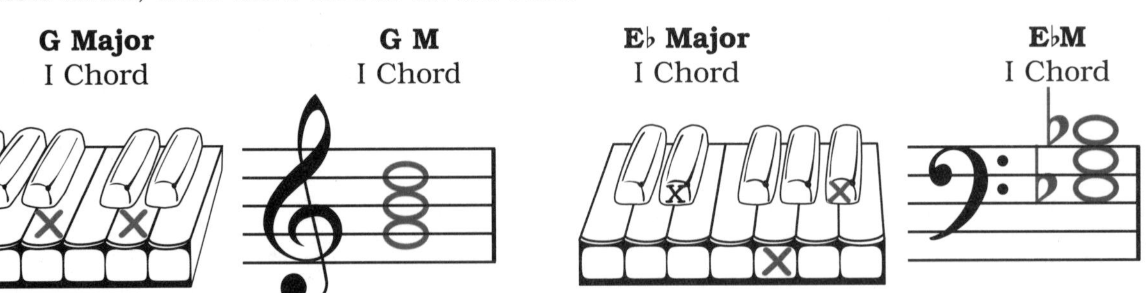

10. Mark the key that completes each interval with an X. *3*

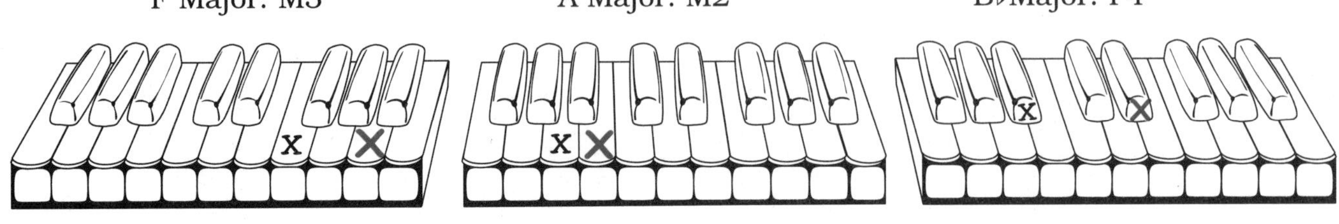

Points

11. Draw the note and accidental (if needed) to form the given interval. *3*

F♯ Major: M3

C Major: P4

G Major: M2

12. Mark the keys that belong to the **minor five-finger patterns** on the keyboards below. *12*
Using whole notes, draw the five-finger patterns and I chords on the staff.

A minor
Five-Finger Pattern

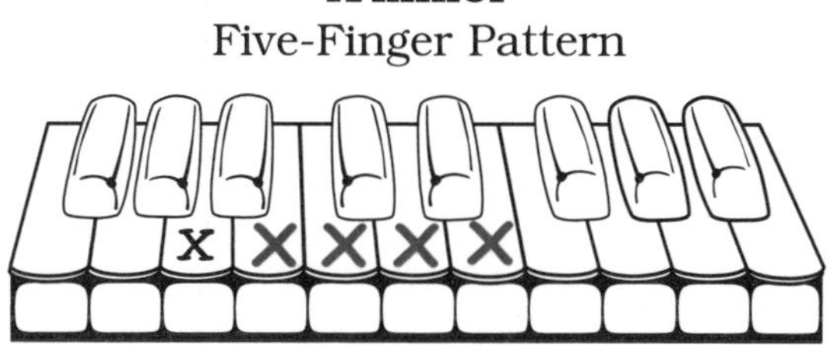

A minor
Five-Finger Pattern

Am
i Chord

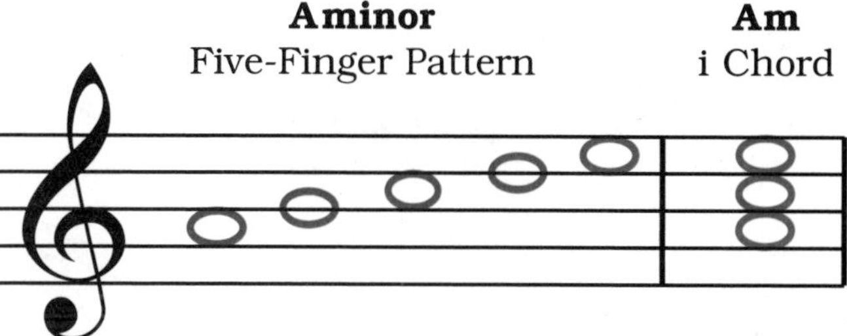

G minor
Five-Finger Pattern

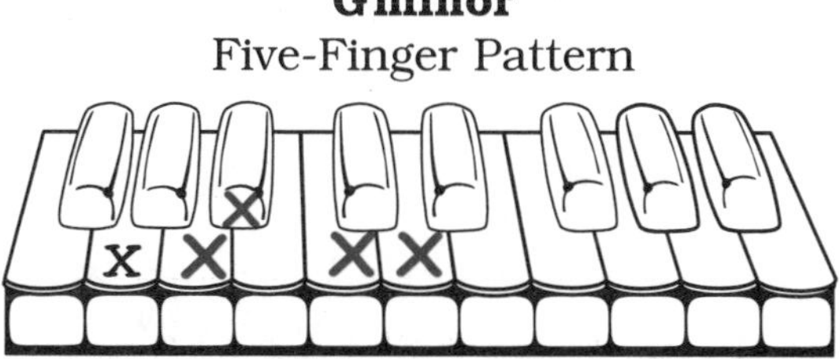

G minor
Five-Finger Pattern

Gm
i Chord

13. Mark the keys that belong to the **minor i chords** on the keyboards below. *5*
Using whole notes, draw the i chords on the staff.

F♯ minor
i Chord

F♯ minor
i Chord

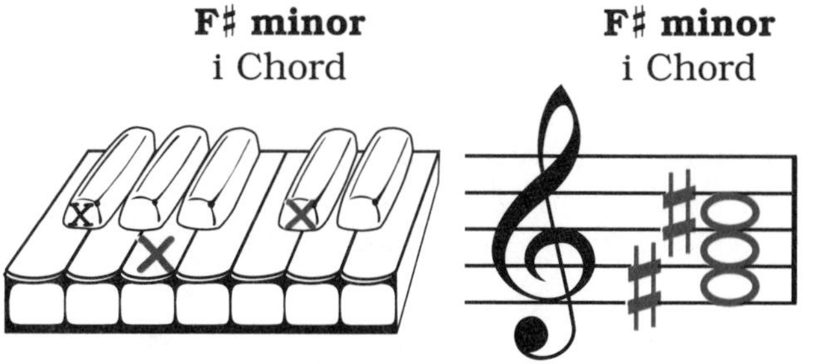

D minor
i Chord

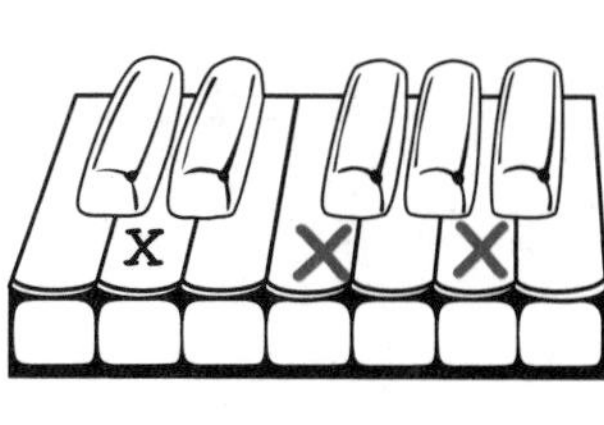

D minor
i Chord

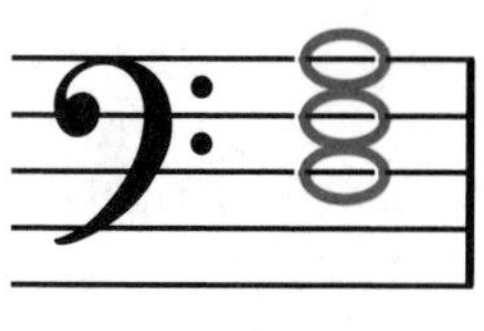

14. **True** or **False**. Beethoven gave public concerts to earn money. *2*
He made the programs, sold tickets and cleaned the hall.

15. **True** or **False**. Beethoven was born in America. *2*

I'm Done Workin' on the Railroad!

Points

16. There are many things circled in **I'm Done Workin' on the Railroad!** Find each sign and term listed below and write its number in the box provided. Write the number of the matching sign by the term in the box provided. *18*

Not all of the circled items will be matched below.

16	Crescendo	19	Accent	3	Dynamic marking that means "loud"	18	A whole step
17	Staccato	2	Brace	20	Term meaning "slow down gradually"	24	F Major I chord
8	Treble clef	23	Fermata				
9	Tie	22	Decrescendo	7	P4 (Perfect fourth)	10	Sequence
12	Natural	6	A dotted quarter note	1	Term meaning "running tempo"	13	Sharp

Keyboard Gymnastics®

Ear-Training Test
Level B2
(Spirito)
Form A

Name______________________________ **Date**____________ Score______ /100

Points

1. You will hear two pitches. If they sound the same, circle the small picture that matches the big picture. If they sound different, circle the small picture that looks different. *6*

A. 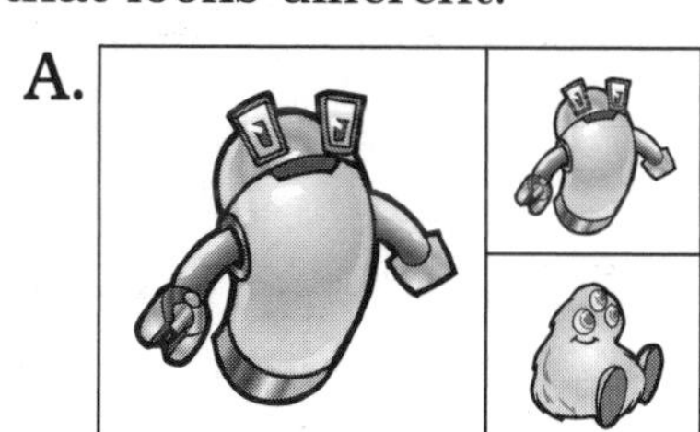

B. 

C. 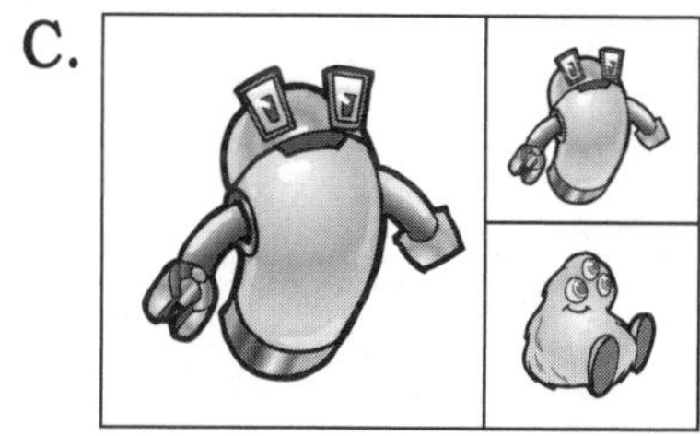

2. You will hear two melodies. If they sound the same, circle the small picture that matches the big picture. If they sound different, circle the small picture that looks different. *6*

A.

B. 

C. 

3. You will hear two I/i chords. If they sound the same, circle the small picture that matches the big picture. If they sound different, circle the small picture that looks different. *6*

A.

B. 

C. 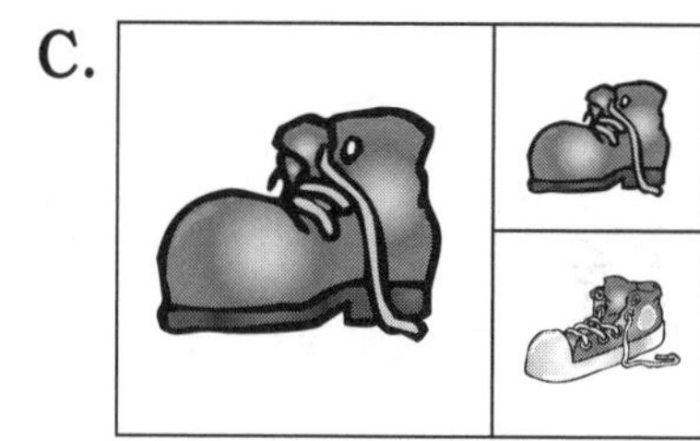

4. You will hear a combination of sounds that are either high or low and loud or soft. Circle **two** pictures that look like what you heard. *8*

A. 

B. 

5. You will hear a combination of sounds that are either fast or slow and steady or unsteady. Circle **two** pictures that look like what you heard. *12*

A. 

B. 

C. 

Points

6. In each example you will hear a combination of notes that are **ascending** or **descending** with a **crescendo** or **decrescendo**. Circle **two** pictures that look like what you heard. *12*

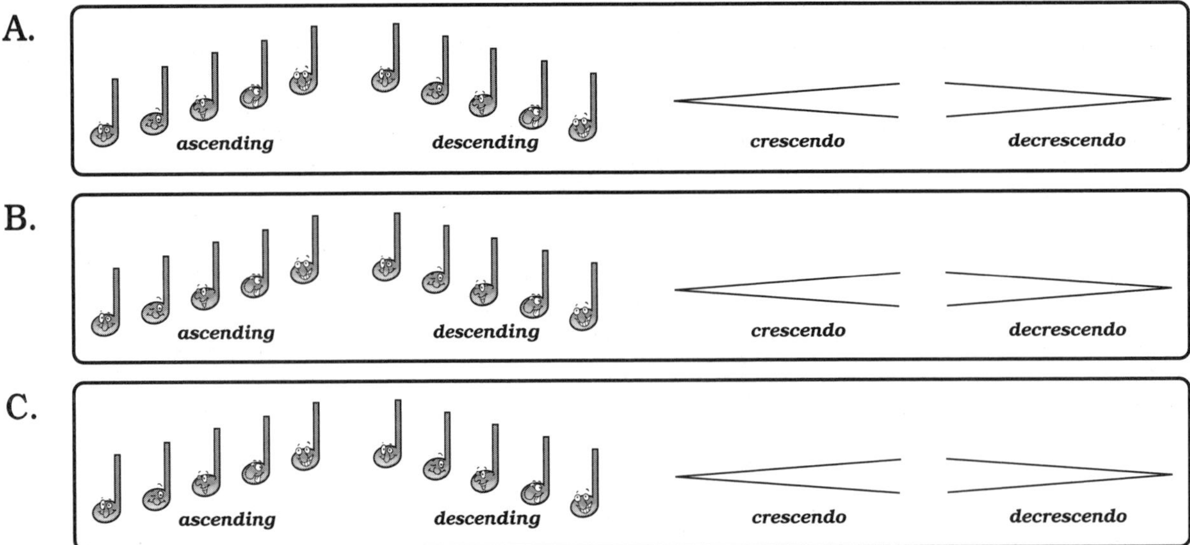

7. You will hear two rhythms. Is the second rhythm the same as the first, or is it different? Circle the second rhythm that you heard. 8

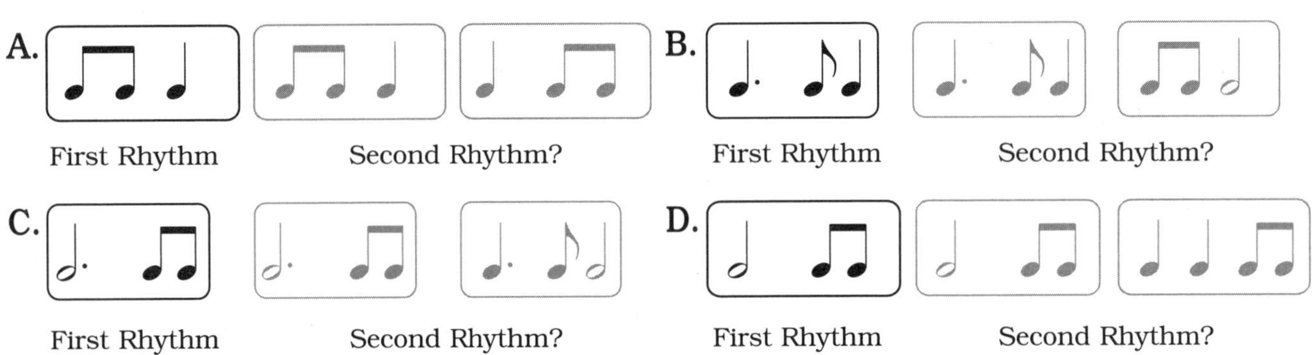

8. Circle the rhythm you hear. *8*

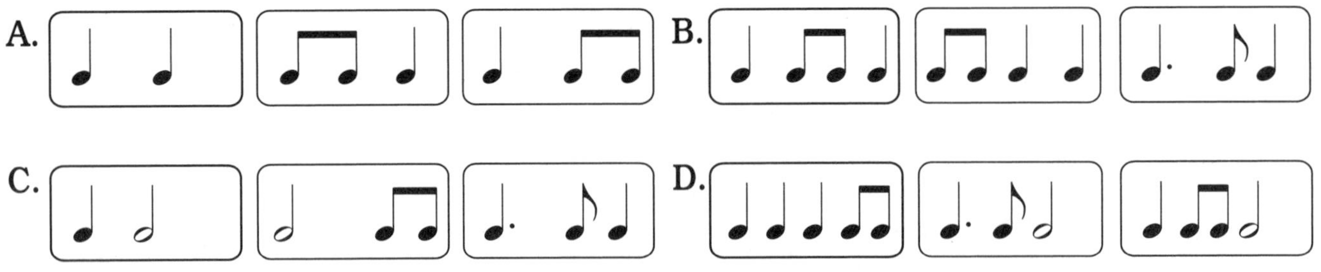

9. Identify the five-finger pattern you hear as **Major** or **minor**. Circle your answer. *9*

A. Major Minor **B.** Major Minor **C.** Major Minor

10. Identify the I/i chord you hear as **Major** or **minor**. Circle your answer. *9*

A. Major Minor **B.** Major Minor **C.** Major Minor

11. Identify the interval you hear by circling the box with the correct answer. *16*

A. P1 M2 M3 **B.** M2 M3 P5 **C.** M2 P4 P5 **D.** P1 M2 P5

E. P1 P4 P5 **F.** P1 M3 P4 **G.** M3 P4 P5 **H.** M2 M3 P4

Keyboard Gymnastics®

Ear-Training Test
Level B2
(Spirito)
Form A

Name____________________________ **Date**__________ Score_____ /100

Points

1. You will hear two pitches. If they sound the same, circle the small picture that matches the big picture. If they sound different, circle the small picture that looks different. *6*

A. 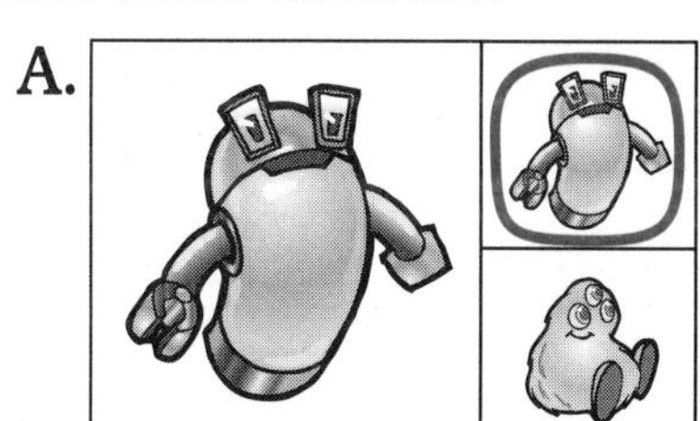
B. 
C. 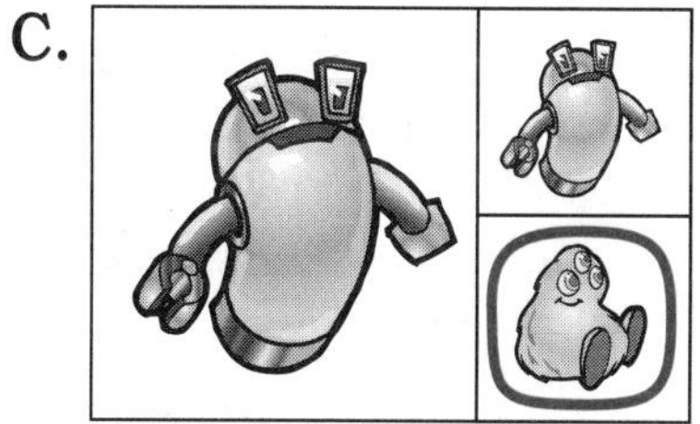

2. You will hear two melodies. If they sound the same, circle the small picture that matches the big picture. If they sound different, circle the small picture that looks different. *6*

A. 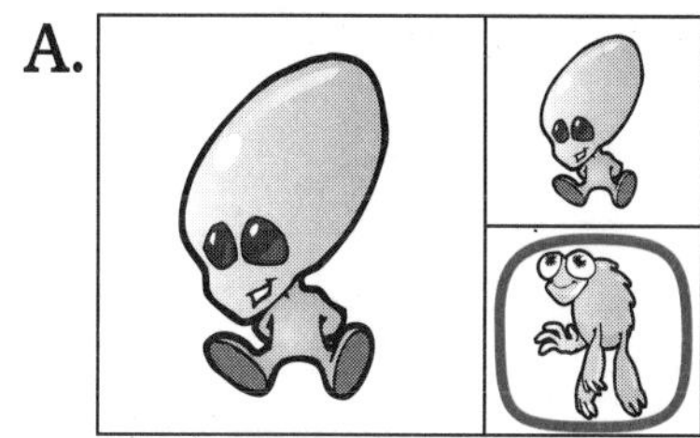
B. 
C. 

3. You will hear two I/i chords. If they sound the same, circle the small picture that matches the big picture. If they sound different, circle the small picture that looks different. *6*

A. 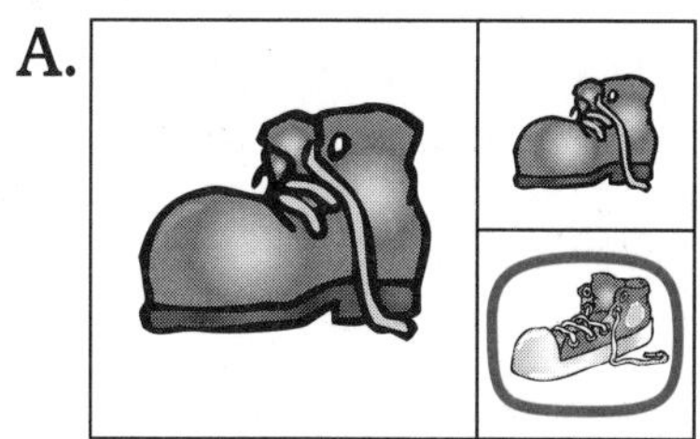
B. 
C. 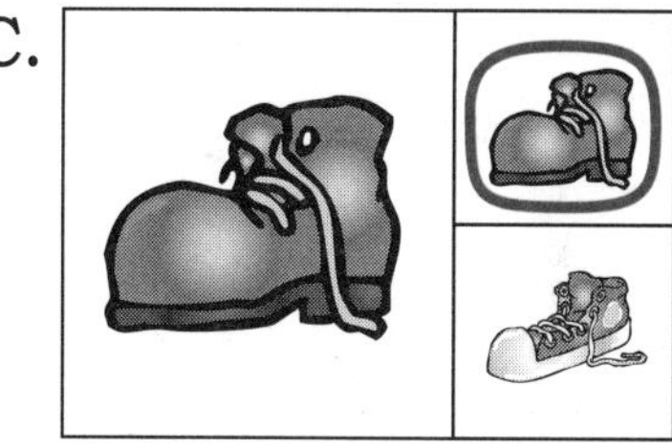

4. You will hear a combination of sounds that are either high or low and loud or soft. Circle **two** pictures that look like what you heard. *8*

A. 

B. 

5. You will hear a combination of sounds that are either fast or slow and steady or unsteady. Circle **two** pictures that look like what you heard. *12*

A. 

B. 

C. 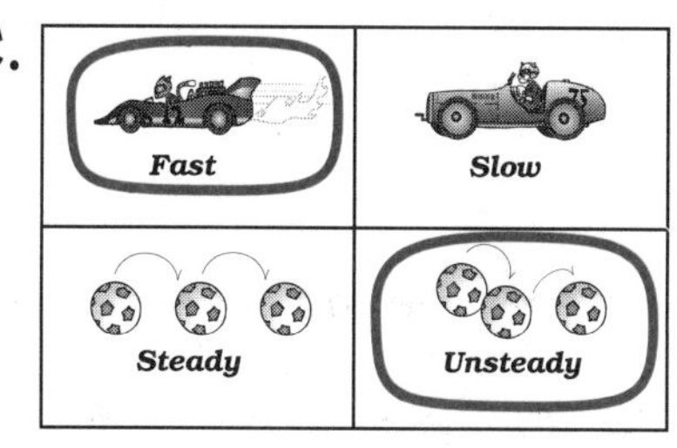

Points

6. In each example you will hear a combination of notes that are **ascending** or **descending** with a **crescendo** or **decrescendo**. Circle **two** pictures that look like what you heard. *12*

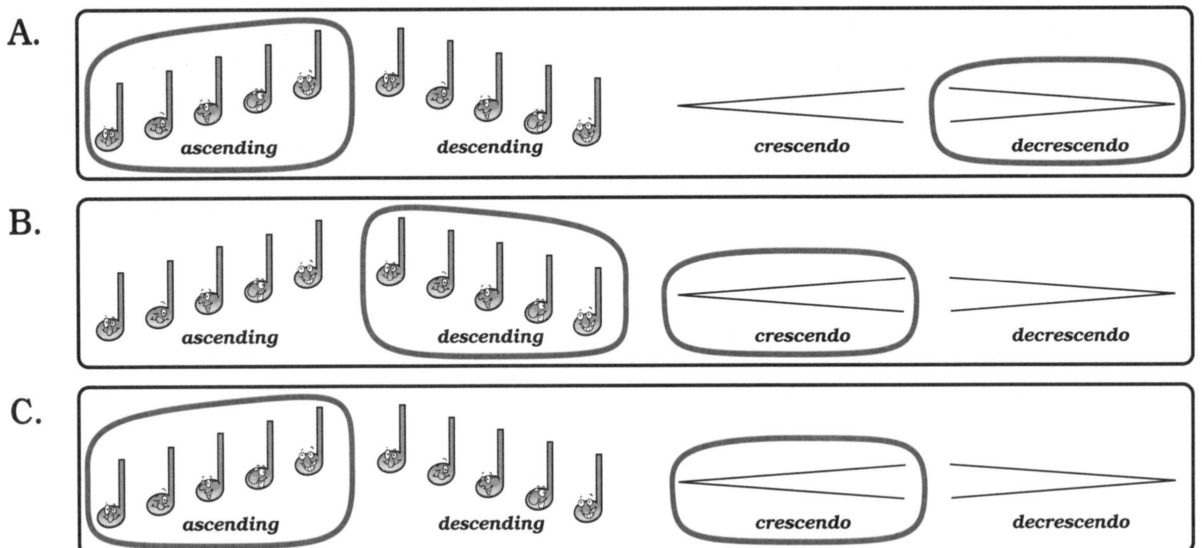

7. You will hear two rhythms. Is the second rhythm the same as the first, or is it different? Circle the second rhythm that you heard. 8

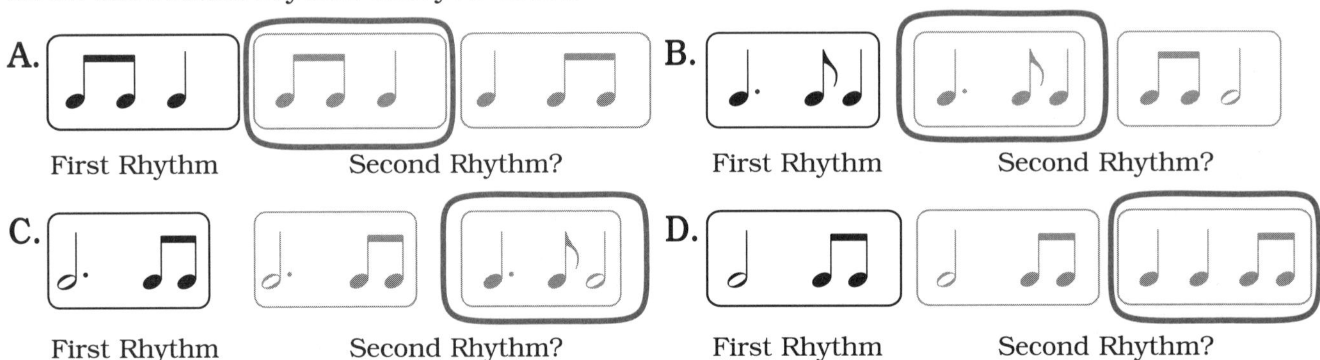

8. Circle the rhythm you hear. *8*

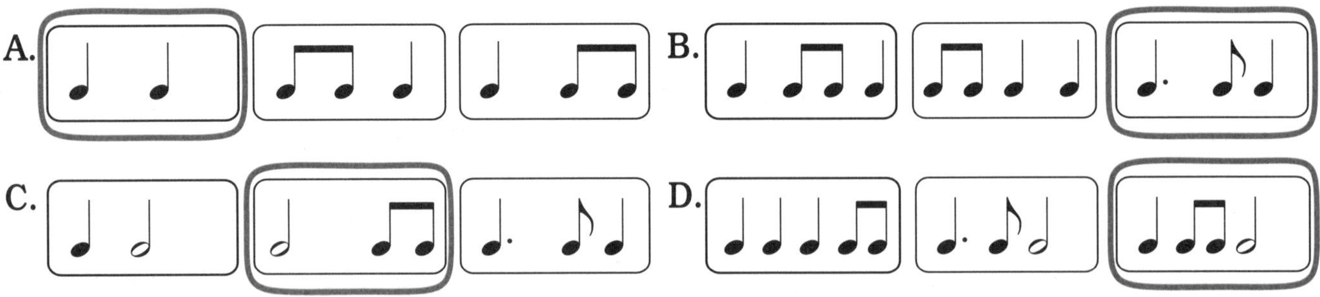

9. Identify the five-finger pattern you hear as **Major** or **minor**. Circle your answer. *9*

A. Major Minor **B.** Major Minor **C.** Major Minor

10. Identify the I/i chord you hear as **Major** or **minor**. Circle your answer. *9*

A. Major Minor **B.** Major Minor **C.** Major Minor

11. Identify the interval you hear by circling the box with the correct answer. *16*

A. **P1** **M2** **M3** **B.** **M2** **M3** **P5** **C.** **M2** **P4** **P5** **D.** **P1** **M2** **P5**

E. **P1** **P4** **P5** **F.** **P1** **M3** **P4** **G.** **M3** **P4** **P5** **H.** **M2** **M3** **P4**

Level B-2 Ear-Training Test Examples

FORM A

Points

1. You will hear two pitches. If they sound the same, circle the small picture that matches the big picture. If they sound different, circle the small picture that looks different. *6*

2. You will hear two melodies. If they sound the same, circle the small picture that matches the big picture. If they sound different, circle the small picture that looks different. 

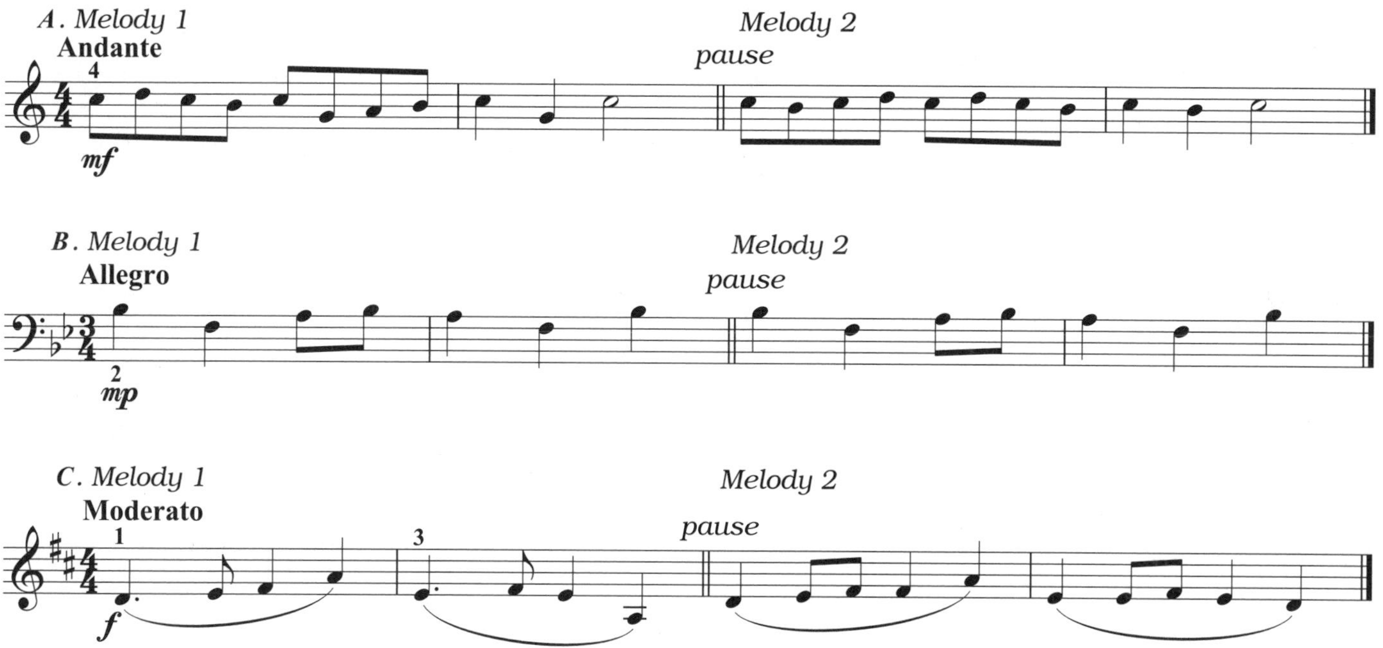

3. You will hear two I/i chords. If they sound the same, circle the small picture that matches the big picture. If they sound different, circle the small picture that looks different. *6*

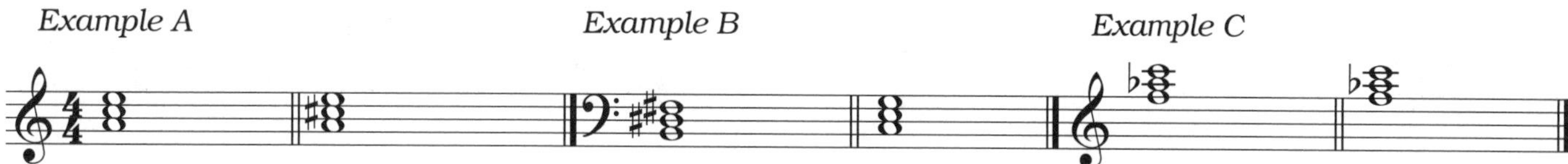

4. You will hear a combination of sounds that are either high or low and loud or soft. Circle two pictures that look like what you heard. *8*

Points

5. You will hear a combination of sounds that are either fast or slow and steady or unsteady. Circle **two** pictures that look like what you heard. 12

Example A: Play Steady

Example B: Play Steady

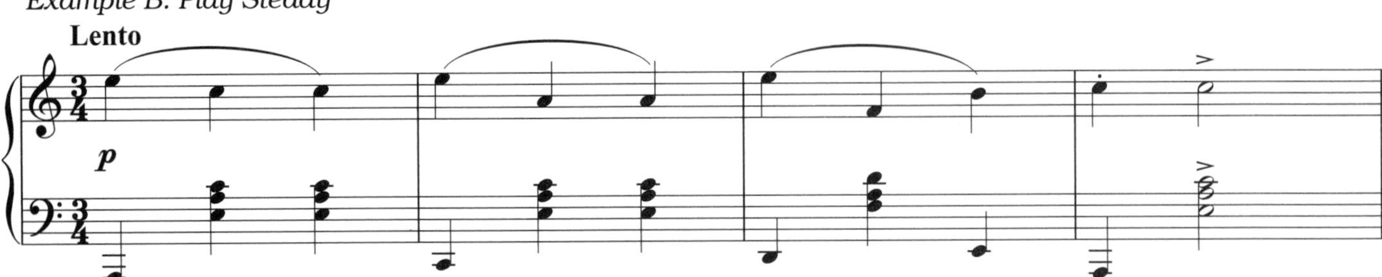

Example C: Play Unsteady

6. In each example you will hear a combination of notes that are **ascending** or **descending** with a **crescendo** or **decrescendo**. Circle **two** pictures that look like what you heard. 12

Points

7. You will hear two rhythms. Is the second rhythm the same as the first, or is it different? Circle the second rhythm that you heard. 8

8. Circle the rhythm you hear. *8*

9. Identify the five-finger pattern you hear as **Major** or **minor**. Circle your answer. *9*

10. Identify the I/i chord you hear as **Major** or **minor**. Circle your answer. *9*

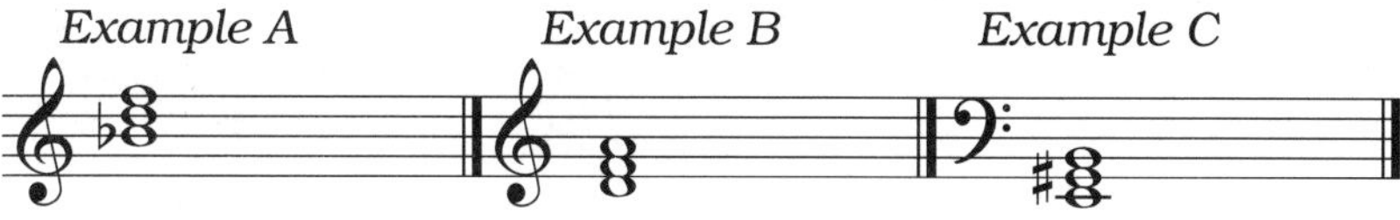

11. Identify the interval you hear by circling the box with the correct answer. *16*

This page is left blank intentionally.

Keyboard Gymnastics®

Theory Test
Level B2
(Spirito)
Form B

Name ______________________ **Date** __________ Score _____ /100

Points

1. Name the notes in the boxes provided. *15*

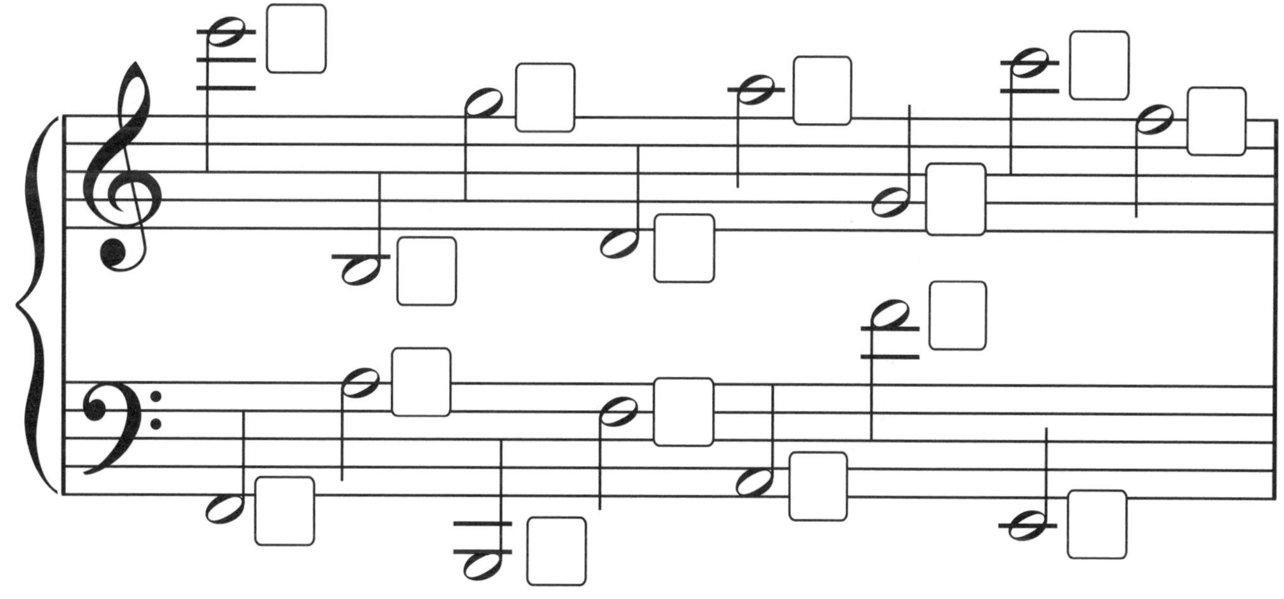

2. Write only one name for each of the shaded keys. (Enharmonic spellings are not necessary.) *8*

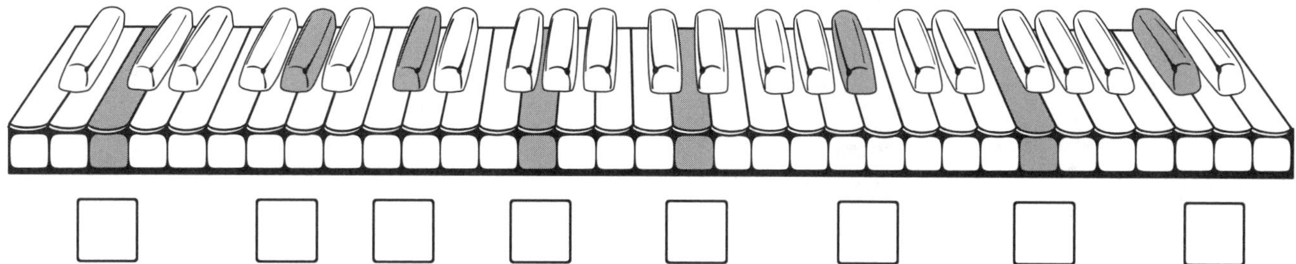

3. Circle the **dotted half note**. *2*

A. 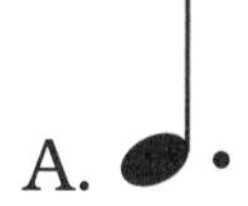 B.  C.  D. 

4. Circle the **half rest**. *2*

A.  B. C.  D.

5. The time signature $\frac{2}{4}$ means there are ☐ beats in every measure. *1*

6. Write the counts beneath each note and rest in the rhythm below. *4*

Points

7. Mark the keys on the keyboard (with an X) to match the notes on the staff. Decide if the notes are a half step or whole step apart. **Circle your answer.** *6*

Half Step or Whole Step?

Half Step or Whole Step?

8. Mark the keys that belong to the **Major five-finger patterns** on the keyboards below. Using whole notes, draw the five-finger patterns and I chords on the staff. *12*

D Major
Five-Finger Pattern

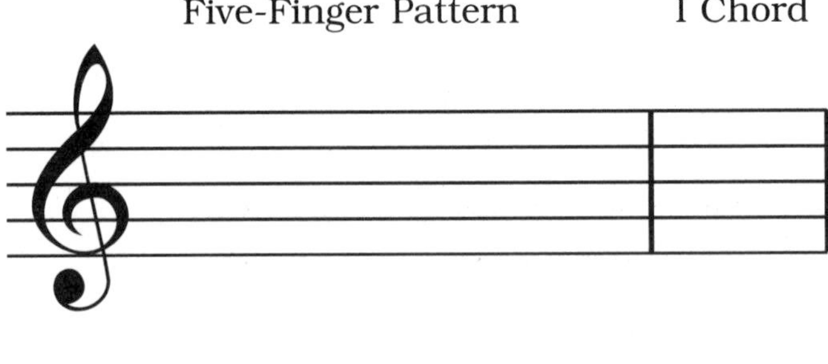

D Major
Five-Finger Pattern

DM
I Chord

B♭ Major
Five-Finger Pattern

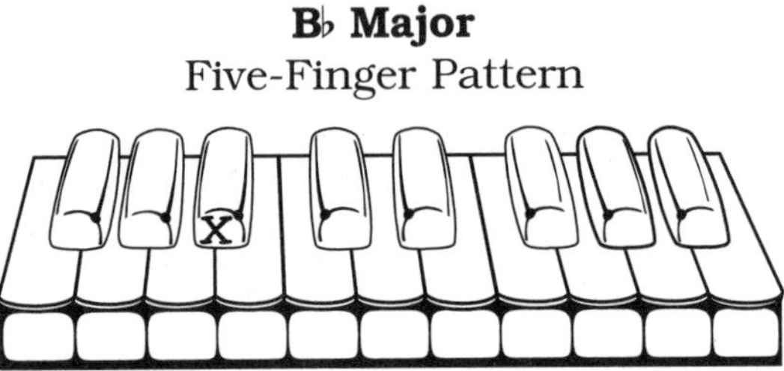

B♭ Major
Five-Finger Pattern

B♭M
I Chord

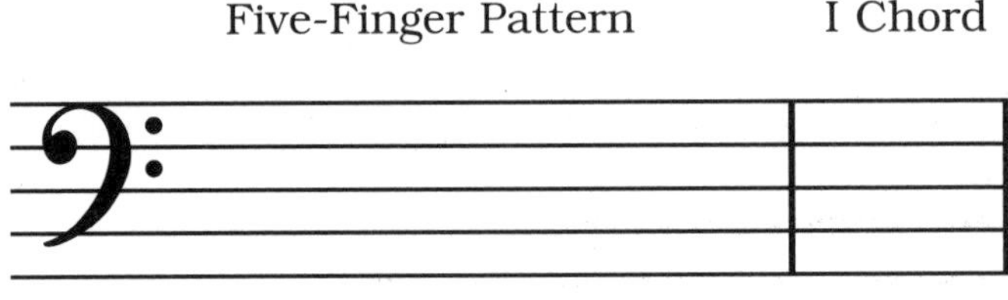

9. Mark the keys that belong to the **Major I chords** on the keyboards below. Using whole notes, draw the I chords on the staff. *5*

A♭ Major
I Chord

A♭ M
I Chord

F♯ Major
I Chord

F♯M
I Chord

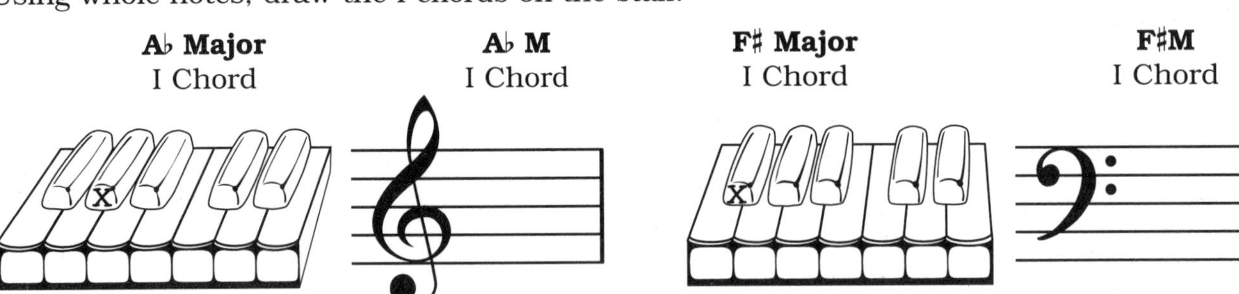

10. Mark the key that completes each interval with an X. *3*

D♭ Major: M2

E Major: P5

C Major: M3

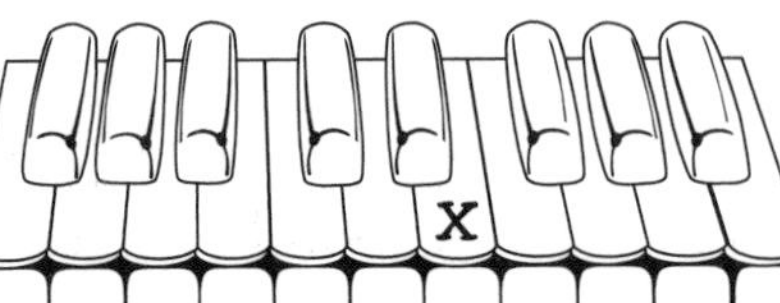

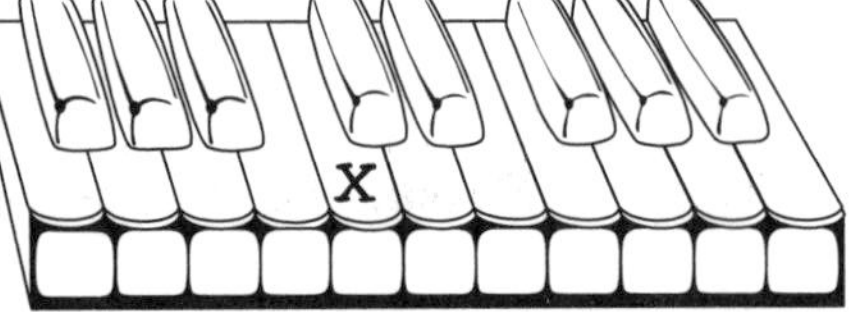

Points

11. Draw the note and accidental (if needed) to form the given interval. *3*

B Major: P5

G Major: M3

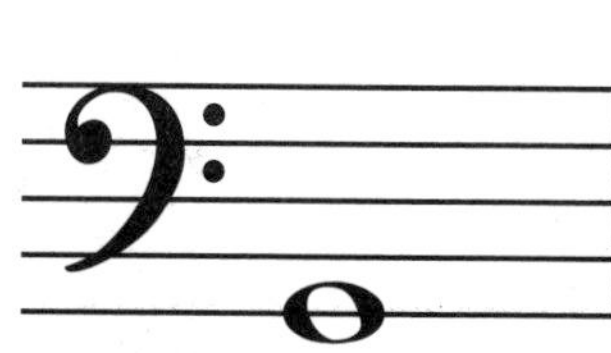

F Major: P4

12. Mark the keys that belong to the **minor five-finger patterns** on the keyboards below. Using whole notes, draw the five-finger patterns and I chords on the staff. *12*

E♭ minor
Five-Finger Pattern

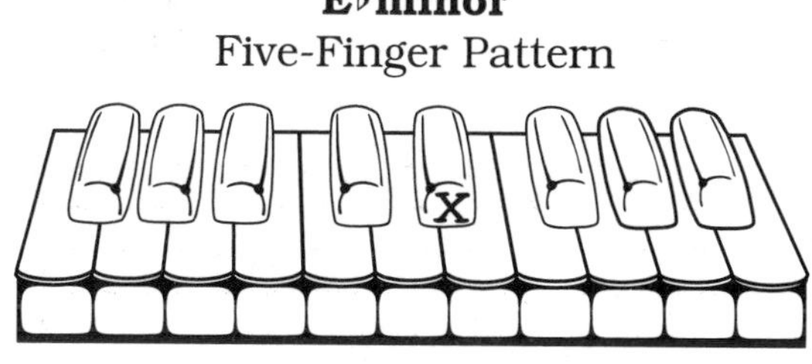

E♭ minor
Five-Finger Pattern

E♭m
i Chord

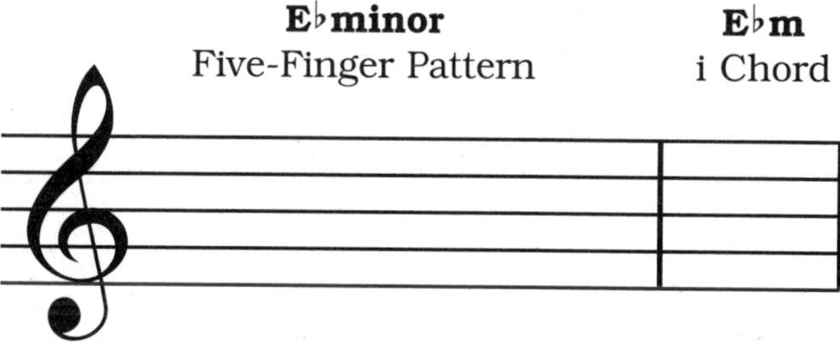

F minor
Five-Finger Pattern

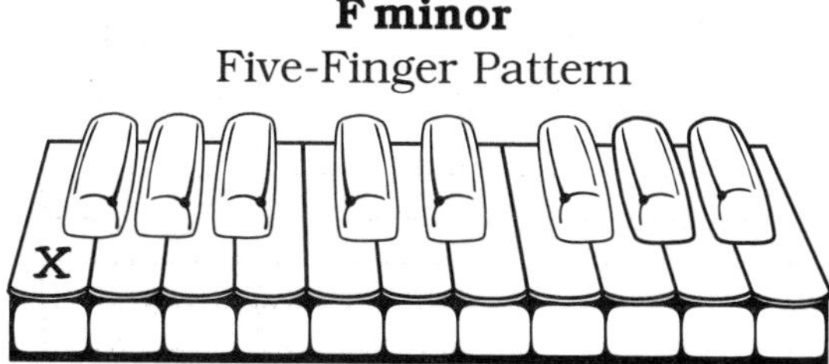

F minor
Five-Finger Pattern

Fm
i Chord

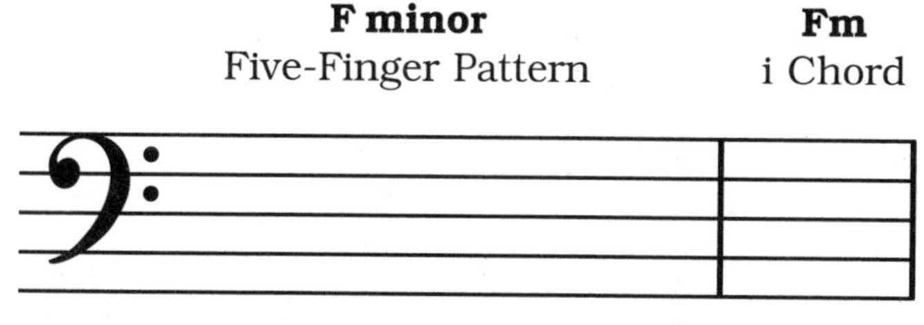

13. Mark the keys that belong to the **minor i chords** on the keyboards below. Using whole notes, draw the i chords on the staff. *5*

C♯ minor
i Chord

C♯ minor
i Chord

A minor
i Chord

A minor
i Chord

14. True or **False**. Beethoven could play the violin, viola, organ and piano. *2*

15. True or **False**. Beethoven's father was very kind to him. *2*

I'm Done Workin' on the Railroad!

Points

16. There are many things circled in **I'm Done Workin' on the Railroad!** Find each sign and term listed below and write its number in the box provided. Write the number of the matching sign by the term in the box provided. *18*

Not all of the circled items will be matched below.

☐	Crescendo	☐	B Natural	☐	Dynamic marking means "soft"	☐	A half step
☐	Staccato	☐	Double Bar	☐	Term meaning "slow down gradually"	☐	Descending B♭Major Five-Finger Pattern
☐	Bass clef	☐	Fermata	☐	M3 (Major third)	☐	Repetition
☐	Slur	☐	Decrescendo	☐	Term meaning "walking tempo"	☐	A Flat
☐	C Sharp	☐	A half note				

Keyboard Gymnastics®

Theory Test
Level B2
(Spirito)
Form B

Name KEY **Date**______ Score_____ /100

Points

1. Name the notes in the boxes provided. *15*

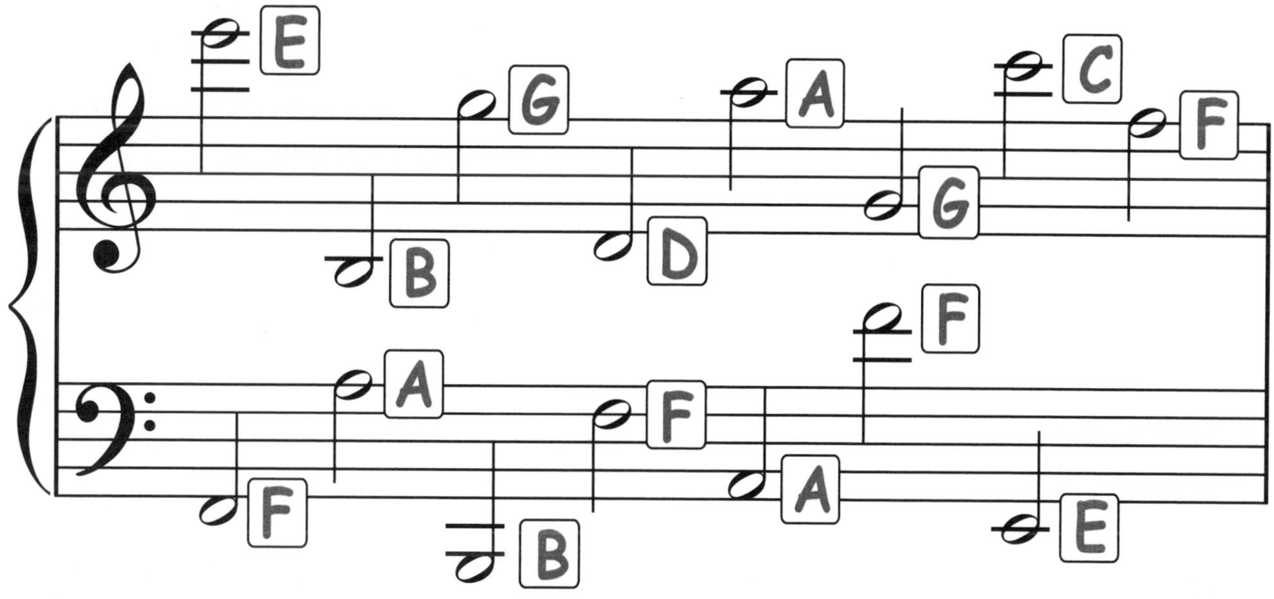

2. Write only one name for each of the shaded keys. (Enharmonic spellings are not necessary.) *8*

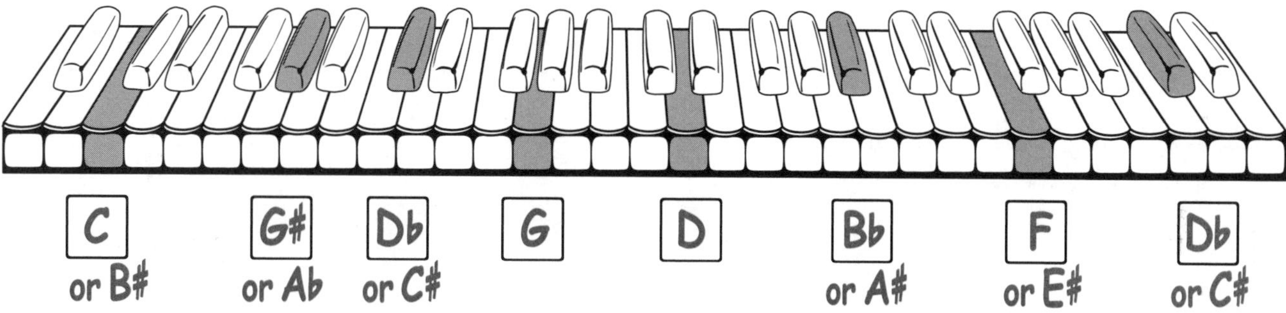

3. Circle the **dotted half note**. *2*

A.  B. 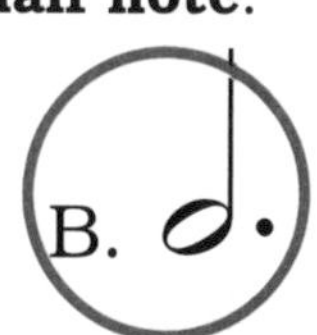 C.  D. 

4. Circle the **half rest**. *2*

A. 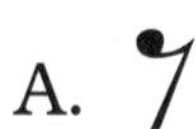 B. C.  D. 

5. The time signature $\frac{2}{4}$ means there are 2 beats in every measure. *1*

6. Write the counts beneath each note and rest in the rhythm below. *4*

Points

7. Mark the keys on the keyboard (with an X) to match the notes on the staff. Decide if the notes are a half step or whole step apart. **Circle your answer.** *6*

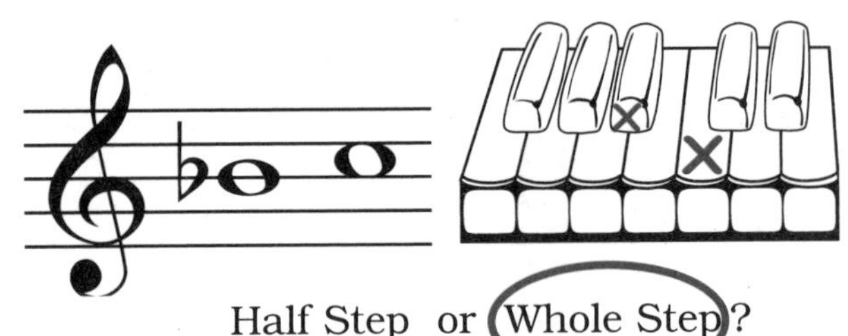

Half Step or Whole Step?

Half Step or Whole Step?

8. Mark the keys that belong to the **Major five-finger patterns** on the keyboards below. Using whole notes, draw the five-finger patterns and I chords on the staff. *12*

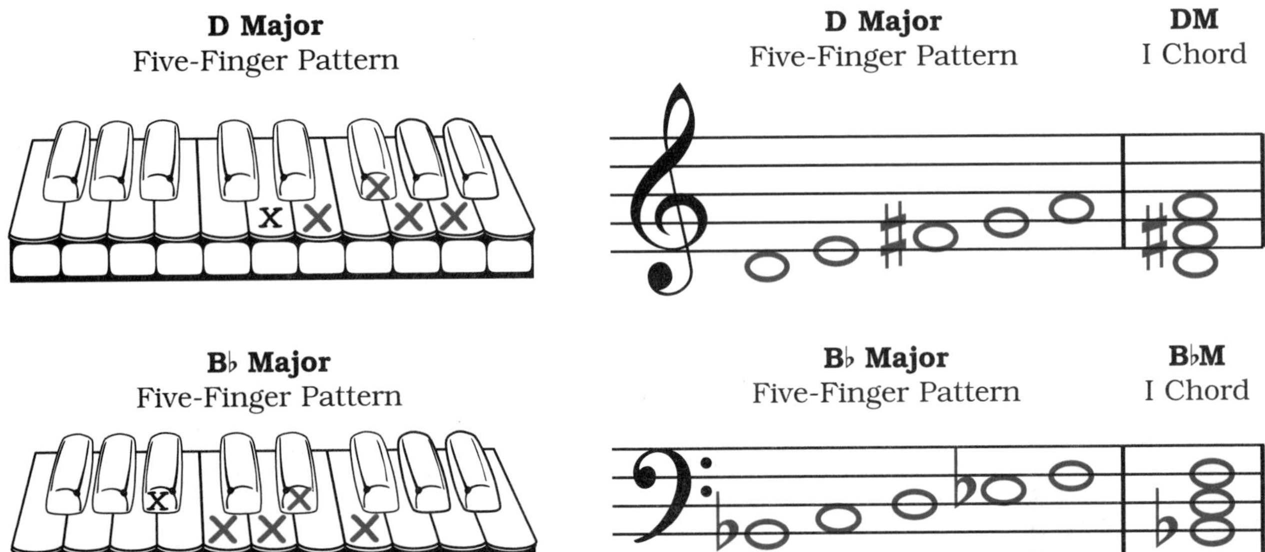

9. Mark the keys that belong to the **Major I chords** on the keyboards below. Using whole notes, draw the I chords on the staff. *5*

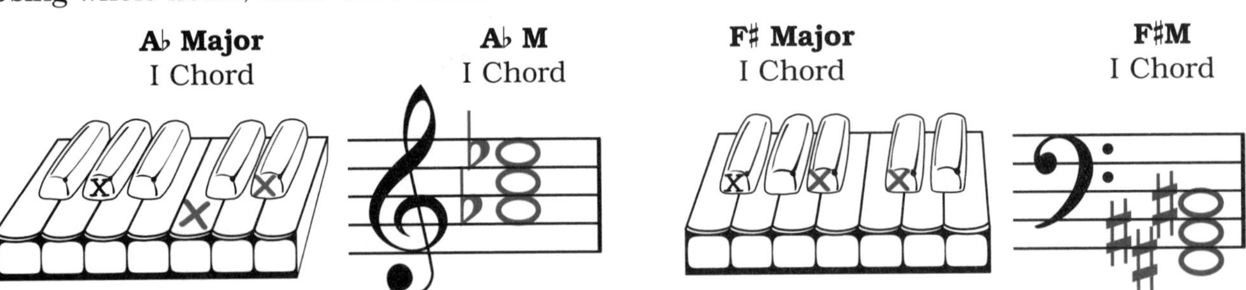

10. Mark the key that completes each interval with an X. *3*

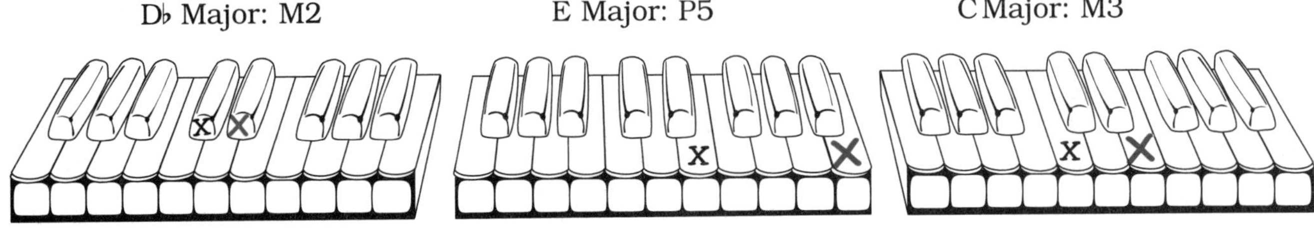

Points

11. Draw the note and accidental (if needed) to form the given interval. *3*

B Major: P5

G Major: M3

F Major: P4

12. Mark the keys that belong to the **minor five-finger patterns** on the keyboards below. Using whole notes, draw the five-finger patterns and I chords on the staff. *12*

E♭ minor
Five-Finger Pattern

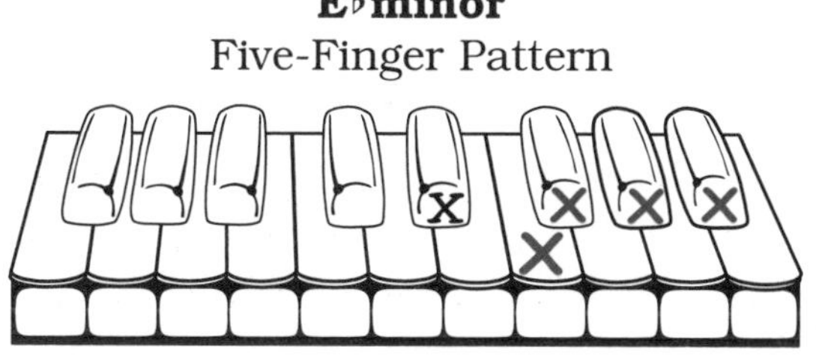

E♭ minor
Five-Finger Pattern

E♭m
i Chord

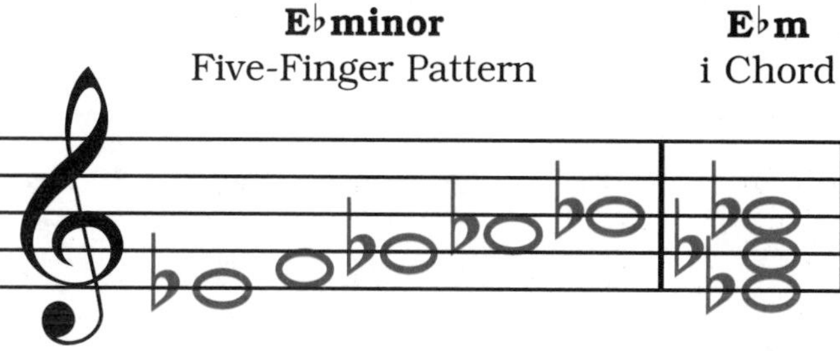

F minor
Five-Finger Pattern

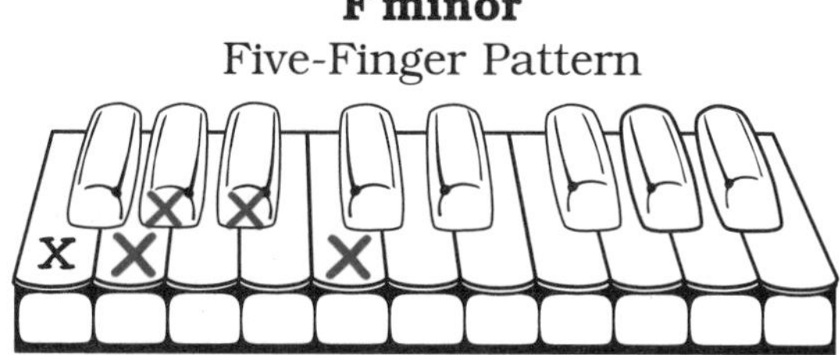

F minor
Five-Finger Pattern

Fm
i Chord

13. Mark the keys that belong to the **minor i chords** on the keyboards below. Using whole notes, draw the i chords on the staff. *5*

C♯ minor i Chord | **C♯ minor** i Chord | **A minor** i Chord | **A minor** i Chord

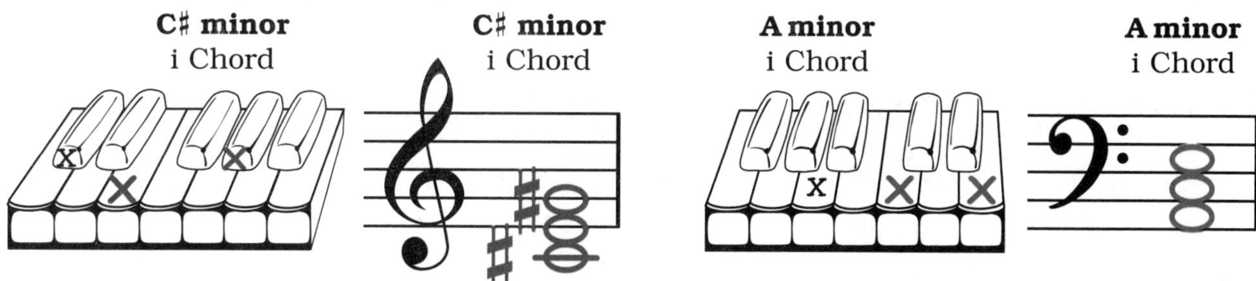

14. **True** or **False**. Beethoven could play the violin, viola, organ and piano. *2*

15. **True** or **False**. Beethoven's father was very kind to him. *2*

I'm Done Workin' on the Railroad!

Points

16. There are many things circled in **I'm Done Workin' on the Railroad!** *18*
Find each sign and term listed below and write its number in the box provided.
Write the number of the matching sign by the term in the box provided.

Not all of the circled items will be matched below.

19	Crescendo	12	B Natural	15	Dynamic marking means "soft"	13	A half step
17	Staccato	25	Double Bar	22	Term meaning "slow down gradually"	21	Descending B♭Major Five-Finger Pattern
6	Bass clef	24	Fermata	7	M3 (Major third)	16	Repetition
4	Slur	23	Decrescendo	1	Term meaning "walking tempo"	9	A Flat
18	C Sharp	14	A half note				

Keyboard Gymnastics®

Ear-Training Test
Level B2
(Spirito)
Form B

Name______________________________ **Date**____________ Score______ /100

Points

1. You will hear two pitches. If they sound the same, circle the small picture that matches the big picture. If they sound different, circle the small picture that looks different. *6*

A. 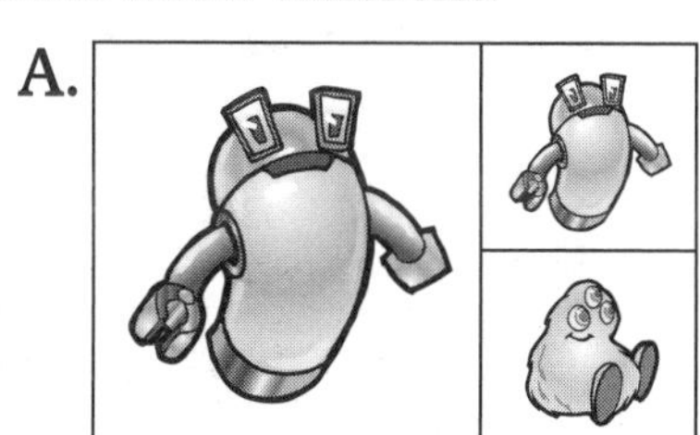

B. 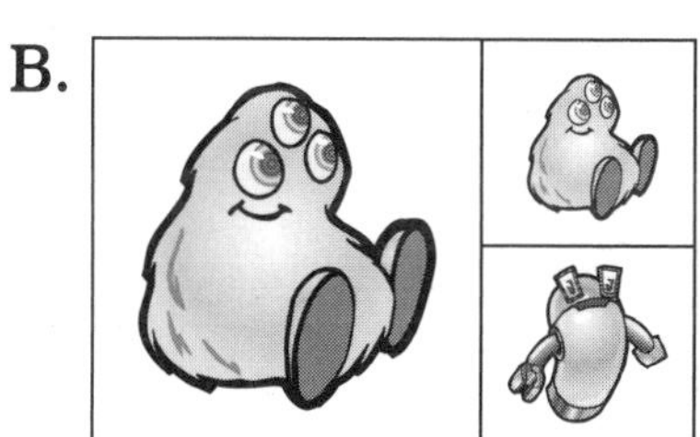

C. 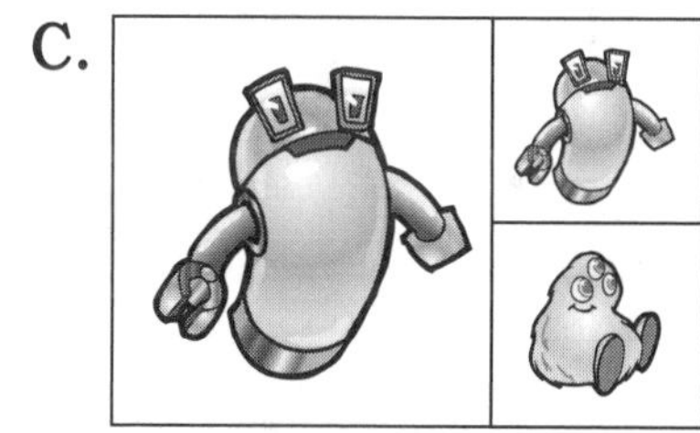

2. You will hear two melodies. If they sound the same, circle the small picture that matches the big picture. If they sound different, circle the small picture that looks different. *6*

A.

B. 

C. 

3. You will hear two I/i chords. If they sound the same, circle the small picture that matches the big picture. If they sound different, circle the small picture that looks different. *6*

A.

B. 

C. 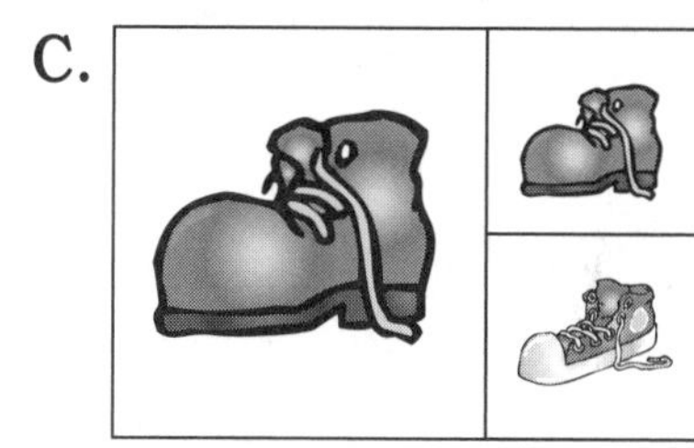

4. You will hear a combination of sounds that are either high or low and loud or soft. Circle **two** pictures that look like what you heard. *8*

A. 

B.

High Low Loud Soft

5. You will hear a combination of sounds that are either fast or slow and steady or unsteady. Circle **two** pictures that look like what you heard. *12*

A. 

B. 

C. 

Points

6. In each example you will hear a combination of notes that are **ascending** or **descending** with a **crescendo** or **decrescendo**. Circle **two** pictures that look like what you heard. *12*

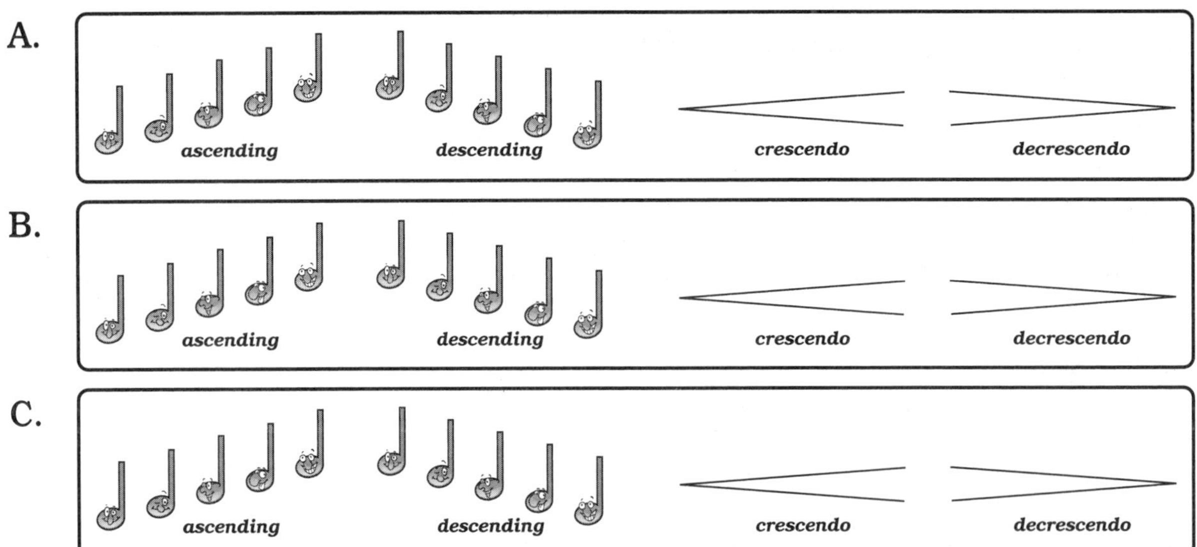

7. You will hear two rhythms. Is the second rhythm the same as the first, or is it different? Circle the second rhythm that you heard. 8

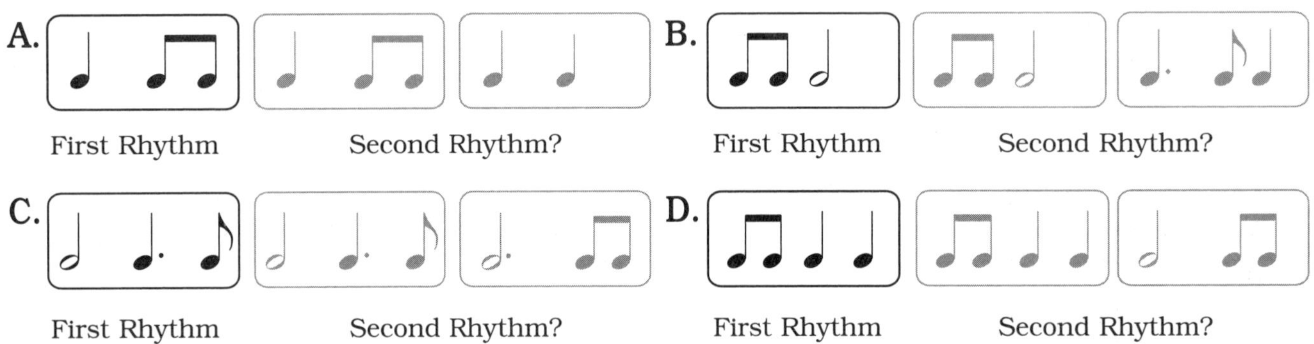

8. Circle the rhythm you hear. *8*

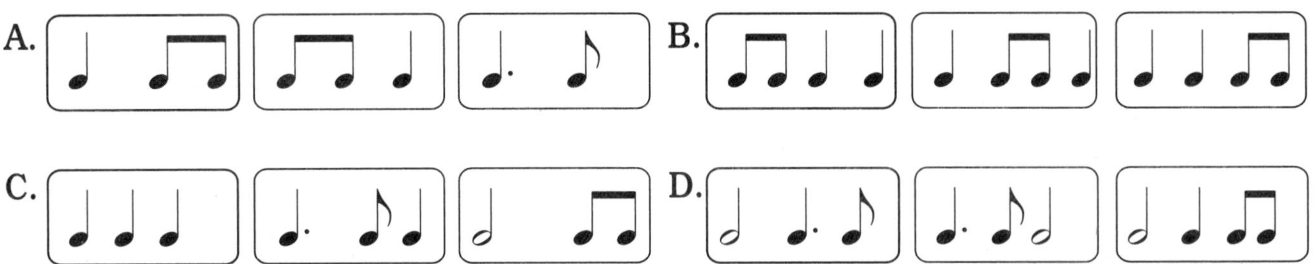

9. Identify the five-finger pattern you hear as **Major** or **minor**. Circle your answer. *9*

A. Major Minor **B.** Major Minor **C.** Major Minor

10. Identify the I/i chord you hear as **Major** or **minor**. Circle your answer. *9*

A. Major Minor **B.** Major Minor **C.** Major Minor

11. Identify the interval you hear by circling the box with the correct answer. *16*

A. P1 M2 M3 **B.** M2 M3 P5 **C.** M2 P4 P5 **D.** P1 M2 P5

E. P1 P4 P5 **F.** P1 M3 P4 **G.** M3 P4 P5 **H.** M2 M3 P4

Keyboard Gymnastics®

Ear-Training Test
Level B2
(Spirito)
Form B

Name________________________________ **Date**____________ Score______ /100

Points

1. You will hear two pitches. If they sound the same, circle the small picture that matches the big picture. If they sound different, circle the small picture that looks different. *6*

A. 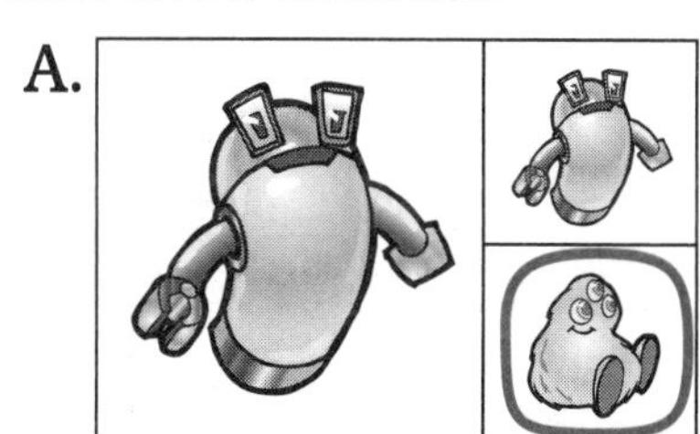

B. 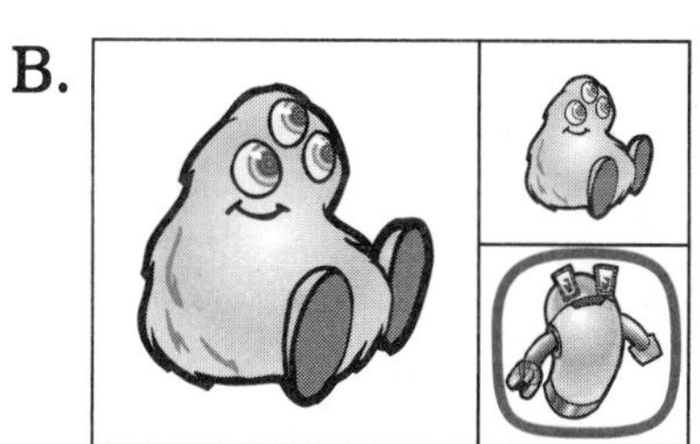

C. 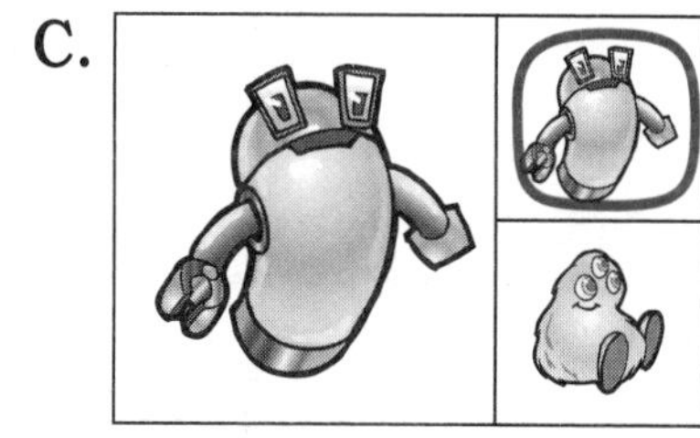

2. You will hear two melodies. If they sound the same, circle the small picture that matches the big picture. If they sound different, circle the small picture that looks different. *6*

A.

B. 

C. 

3. You will hear two I/i chords. If they sound the same, circle the small picture that matches the big picture. If they sound different, circle the small picture that looks different. *6*

A.

B. 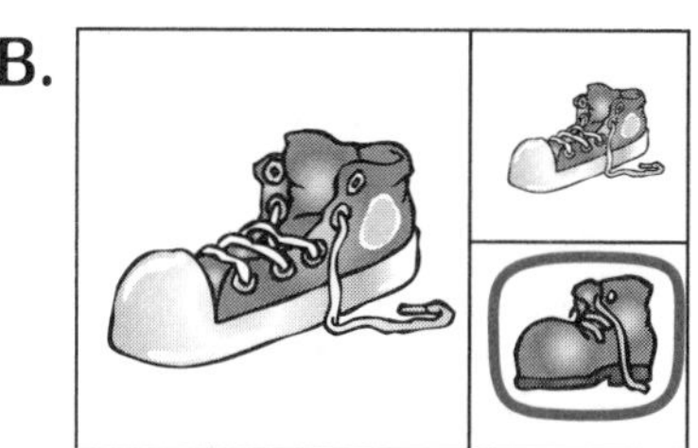

C. 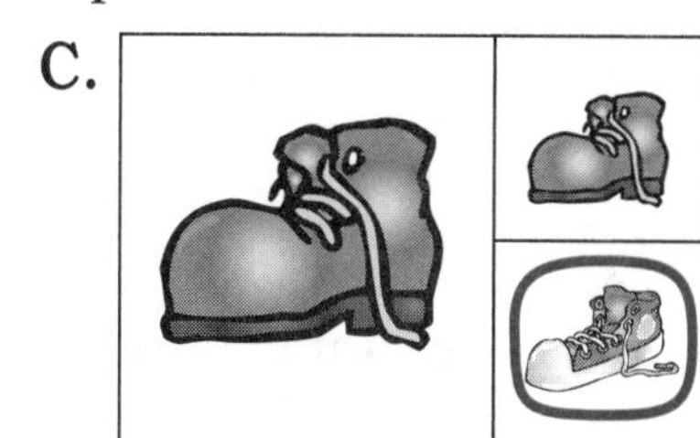

4. You will hear a combination of sounds that are either high or low and loud or soft. Circle **two** pictures that look like what you heard. *8*

A. 

B. High Low Loud Soft

5. You will hear a combination of sounds that are either fast or slow and steady or unsteady. Circle **two** pictures that look like what you heard. *12*

A. 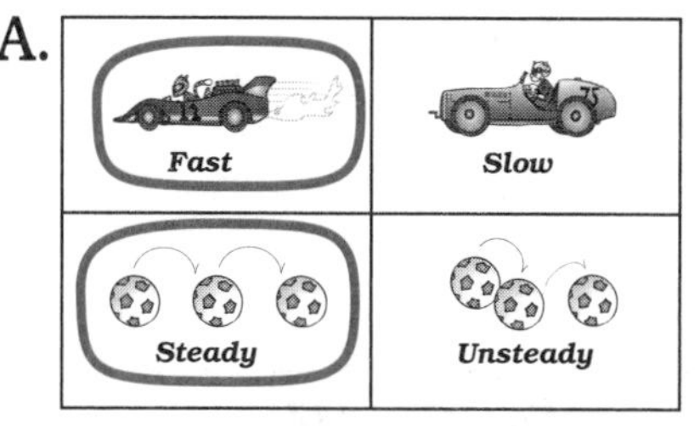

B. 

C. 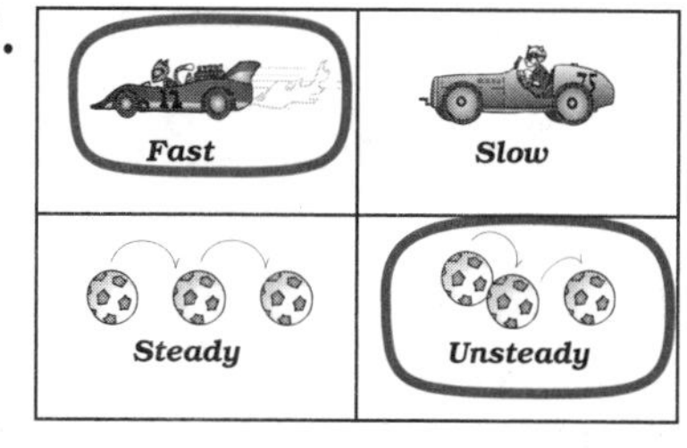

Points

6. In each example you will hear a combination of notes that are **ascending** or **descending** with a **crescendo** or **decrescendo**. Circle **two** pictures that look like what you heard. *12*

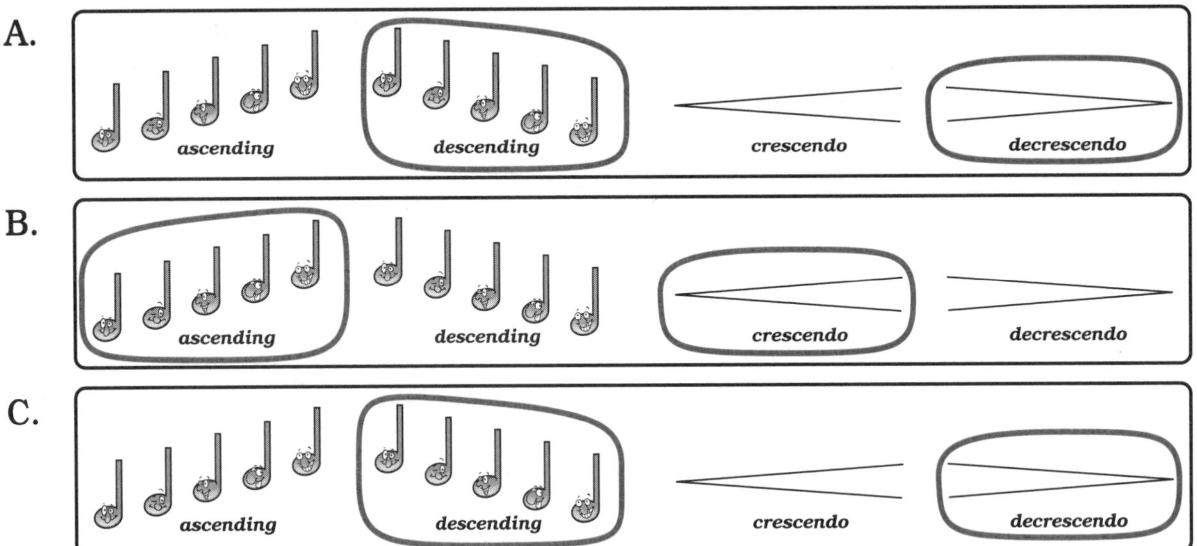

7. You will hear two rhythms. Is the second rhythm the same as the first, or is it different? Circle the second rhythm that you heard. 8

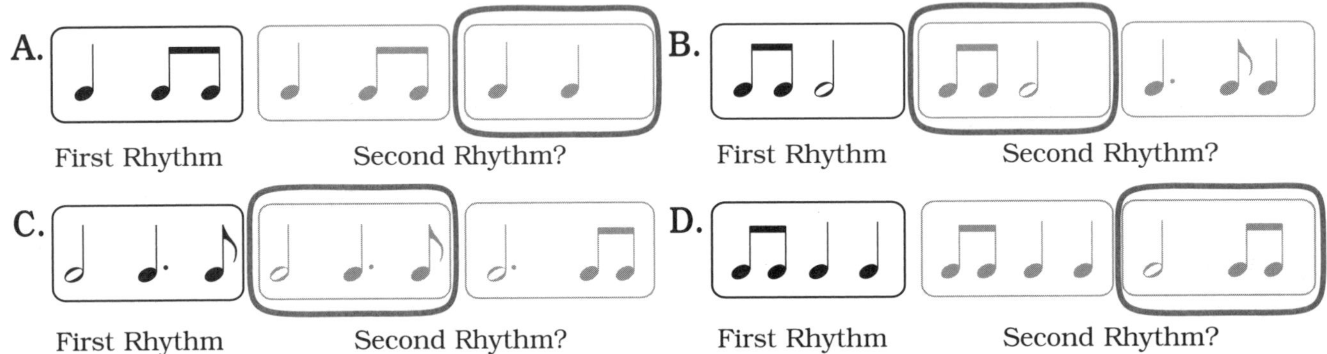

8. Circle the rhythm you hear. *8*

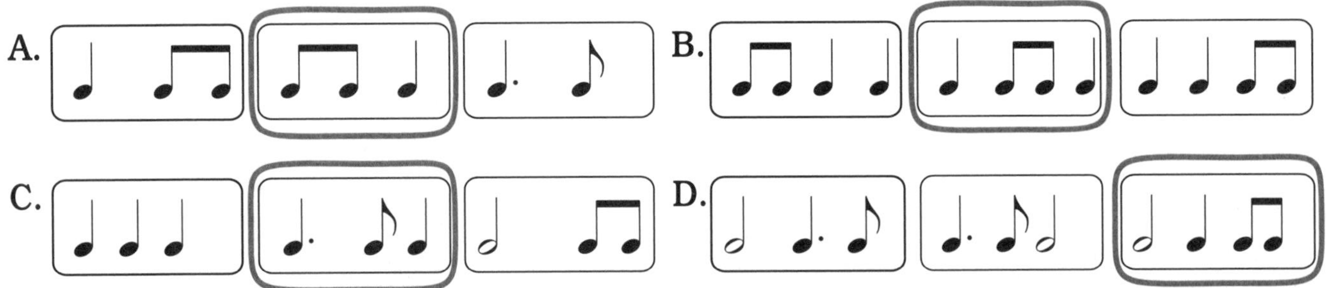

9. Identify the five-finger pattern you hear as **Major** or **minor**. Circle your answer. *9*

A. Major Minor **B.** Major Minor **C.** Major Minor

10. Identify the I/i chord you hear as **Major** or **minor**. Circle your answer. *9*

A. Major Minor **B.** Major Minor **C.** Major Minor

11. Identify the interval you hear by circling the box with the correct answer. *16*

A. P1 M2 M3 **B.** M2 M3 P5 **C.** M2 P4 P5 **D.** P1 M2 P5

E. P1 P4 P5 **F.** P1 M3 P4 **G.** M3 P4 P5 **H.** M2 M3 P4

Level B-2 Ear-Training Test Examples

FORM B

Points

1. You will hear two pitches. If they sound the same, circle the small picture that matches the big picture. If they sound different, circle the small picture that looks different. *6*

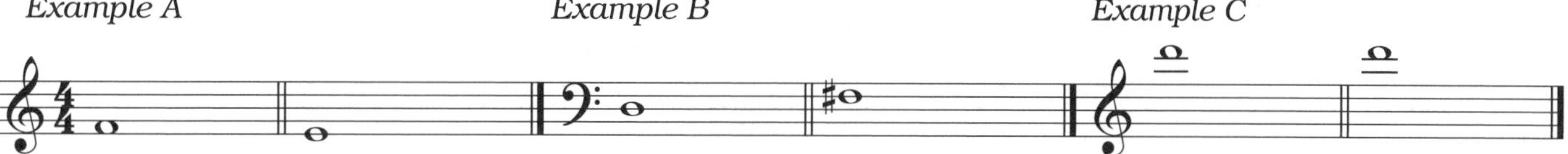

2. You will hear two melodies. If they sound the same, circle the small picture that matches the big picture. If they sound different, circle the small picture that looks different. *6*

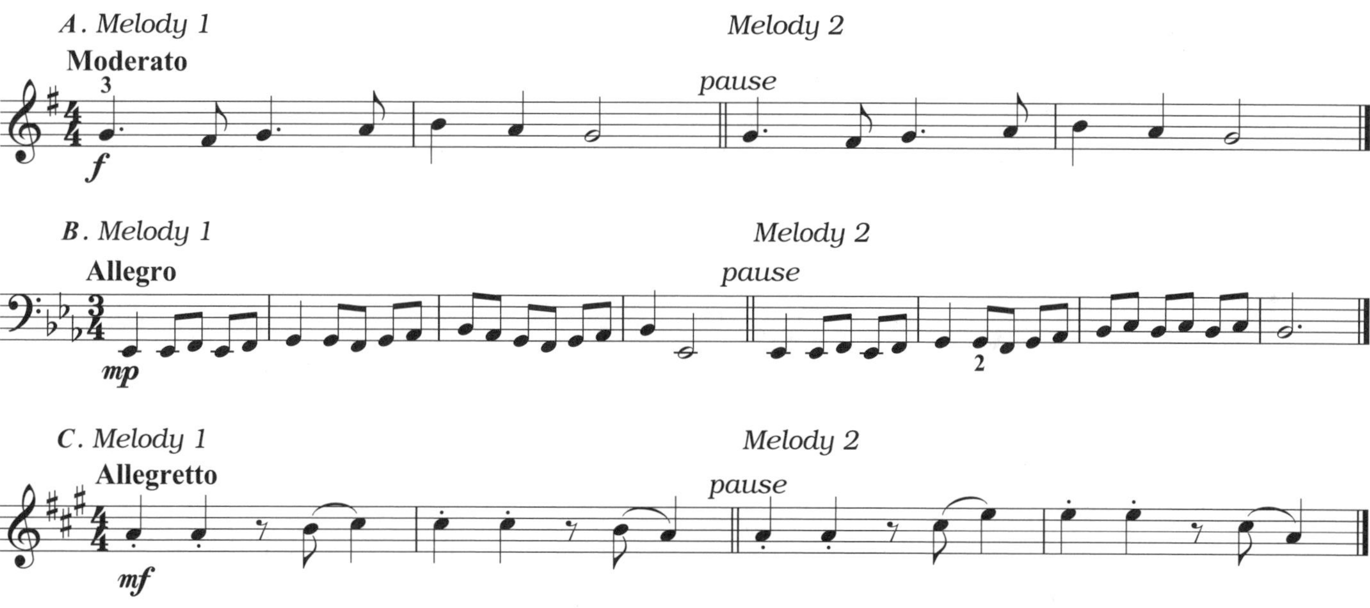

3. You will hear two I/i chords. If they sound the same, circle the small picture that matches the big picture. If they sound different, circle the small picture that looks different. *6*

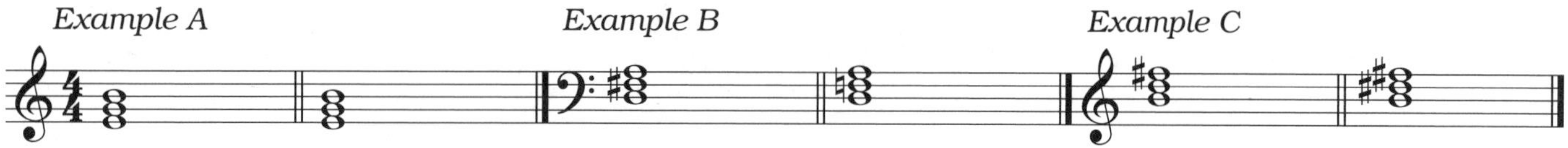

4. You will hear a combination of sounds that are either high or low and loud or soft. Circle **two** pictures that look like what you heard. *8*

Points

5. You will hear a combination of sounds that are either fast or slow and steady or unsteady. Circle **two** pictures that look like what you heard. *12*

Example A: Play Steady

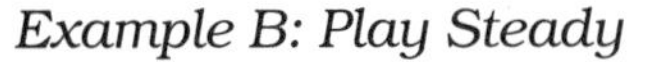

Example B: Play Steady

Example C: Play Unsteady

6. In each example you will hear a combination of notes that are **ascending** or **descending** with a **crescendo** or **decrescendo**. Circle **two** pictures that look like what you heard. *12*

Example A *Example B*

Example C

Points

7. You will hear two rhythms. Is the second rhythm the same as the first, or is it different? Circle the second rhythm that you heard. 8

8. Circle the rhythm you hear. *8*

9. Identify the five-finger pattern you hear as **Major** or **minor**. Circle your answer. *9*

10. Identify the I/i chord you hear as **Major** or **minor**. Circle your answer. *9*

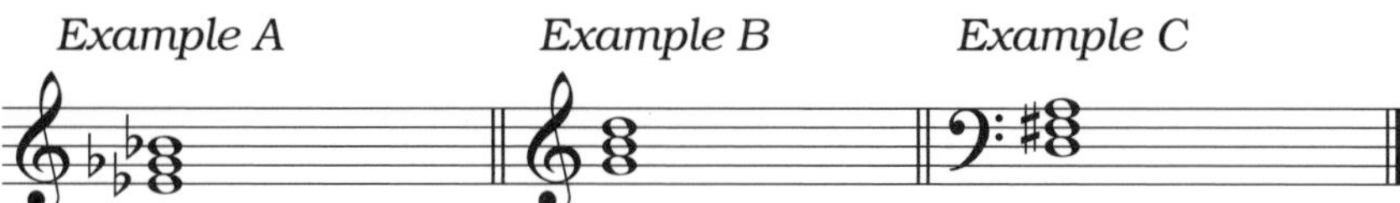

11. Identify the interval you hear by circling the box with the correct answer. *16*

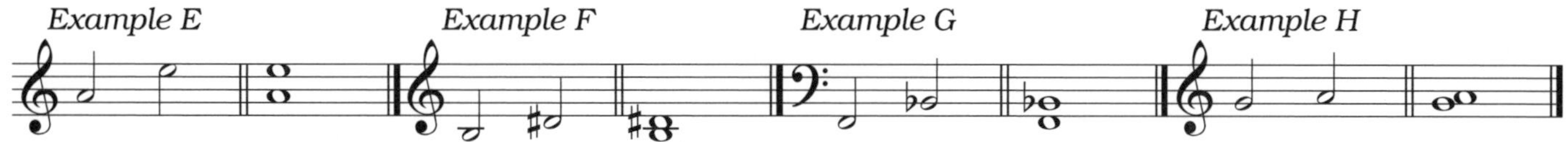